BACK TO HOME AND DUTY

Deirdre Beddoe is Professor of Women's History at the University of Glamorgan, Pontypridd. She has taught in secondary school and is an experienced lecturer in women's studies in adult, extra-mural and higher educ. She is involved in the propagation of w...... broadcasts and th........ film and television .... for All Time (Wale........ which traces the h........ movements. Her books include *Welsh Convict Women*, the story of women from Wales who sailed as convicts to the Australian penal colonies, and *Discovering Women's History* (Pandora 1983, 2nd edition 1993), a guide to the sources for anyone wishing to investigate local women's history. She is co-editor of *Parachutes and Petticoats: Welsh Women Writing on the Second World War*, (Honno, 1992).

BACK TO HOME AND DUTY

WOMEN BETWEEN THE WARS, 1918–1939

DEIRDRE BEDDOE

Pandora

An Imprint of HarperCollins*Publishers*

Pandora
An Imprint of HarperCollins*Publishers*
77–85 Fulham Palace Road,
Hammersmith, London W6 8JB
1160 Battery Street,
San Francisco, California 94111–1213

First published by Pandora 1989
3 5 7 9 10 8 6 4 2

© Deirdre Beddoe 1989

Deirdre Beddoe asserts the moral right to
be identified as the author of this work

A catalogue record for this book
is available from the British Library

ISBN 0 04 440515 4

Printed in Great Britain by
HarperCollinsManufacturing Glasgow

TO CHRIS AND KATIE WITH LOVE

CONTENTS

Preface   viii

Acknowledgements   ix

Introduction   1

1 DESIRABLE AND UNDESIRABLE IMAGES   8

2 EDUCATION   34

3 EMPLOYMENT   48

4 HOME AND HEALTH   89

5 LEISURE   114

6 POLITICS AND ISSUES   132

Notes   148

Bibliography   168

Index   176

PREFACE

I could not have written this book without the support and help of many people. Above all I want to thank Christine Lee and Katie Durbin for putting up with me whilst I researched and wrote it. I have frequently drawn on my friends for all manner of help and I wish to thank in particular Sheila Owen Jones, Judith Hewitt, Arrol Price, Martyn Howells and Rosalinda Hardiman.

Many people have given me very direct help and I am extremely grateful to them. David Doughan, Miriam Glucksmann, Anne Jones and Pauline Young have all read parts of this book and helped in many other ways too. I want to thank Amanda Farraday and Miriam Glucksmann for lending me their unpublished material. I thank Mary Stott for all her encouragement and my agent, Amanda Little, and my publisher, Karen Holden, for their help and enthusiasm. Nadine Michael deserves my thanks for typing out the manuscript.

I am indebted too to the staff of many libraries and archive offices. I owe particular thanks to Catherine Ireland and David Doughan of the Fawcett Library, to Dorothy Sheridan of the Mass Observation Archive at the University of Sussex and to the staff of the University of Glamorgan Library, the British Library, the National Library of Wales and the Trade Union Council Library, Glamorgan County Record Office and the City of Birmingham Record Office. I wish also to thank the Media Resources Unit of the University of Glamorgan.

Finally I wish to thank all the women, who lived through the inter-war years, and who were kind enough to share their memories with me.

Deirdre Beddoe
Penarth

ACKNOWLEDGEMENTS

The author and publishers would like to thank the following for permission to reproduce photographs in this book: Imperial War Museum for plate 1; British Library (Colindale) plates 2 and 3; Mary Evans Picture Library plates 5 and 6; Noya Brandt for plate 9; John Topham Picture Library plate 11; Labour Party Library plate 16; Humphrey Spender plate 17. Thanks are also due to the Department of Employment for permission to reprint statistical material from Catherine Hakim's, *Occupational Segregation*, Research Paper No. 9, (London, Department of Employment, 1979); the Manchester School for statistics from Edward James, 'Women and Work in Twentieth Century Britain', *Manchester School of Economics and Social Science* XXX (September 1962); Gilian Darcy for statistics on women in the professions and to Jennifer Hurstfield for statistics on the Anomalies Regulations.

INTRODUCTION

This book is the result of my curiosity about the lives of women in Britain in the inter-war years, 1918–39. I have been fascinated by this period for as long as I can remember and that fascination has been fed by so many things – by photographs in the family album, by old black and white feature films and documentaries, by the songs and dance music of the day, by novels, by older women talking of the hardship caused by unemployment and means-testing or sometimes of the fun they had had in the good old days. I was curious to find out more and I was motivated by far more than vague feelings of nostalgia. As an historian so many questions nagged at me. What had happened to the great mass suffrage movement of the years before the First World War? What happened to women workers who had proved so handsomely in the First War that they could do 'men's jobs'? What was it like to be a working-class girl in an elementary school in the 1920s or 1930s? How did unemployment hit women? Did women go to pubs? What films did they like? What did 'flapper' really mean? How did middle-class women spend their days? How did poor women manage to feed their families? Who were the new women Members of Parliament? What did shop girls read? Women got the vote, but how much did things really change?

I wanted answers to these and to many more questions. I found that whereas I and my students could turn to fascinating books, written in the new wave of feminist history, about the lives of women and the roles played by them in both the First World War, 1914–18, and in the Second World War, 1939–45, I was aware of no single book which presented an overview of women's lives for the interim period. Fortunately some very interesting research has recently been undertaken on specific aspects of women's lives in the inter-war years – on women as workers, on women's role as mothers, on women's health and on women's political involvement, and I am most grateful to be able to draw upon this. I was compelled, however, to cast the net much more widely for answers to all my questions, and I have drawn on a wide and diverse range of primary sources. These include women's magazines, films, government records (on – for example – national insurance, maternal mortality, centres for retraining the unemployed), novels, newspapers, oral interviews, school and college records, architectural plans, diaries and contemporary autobiographies.

What I have set out to do is to present a broad history of women in Britain in the inter-war years. It is a history which looks at women of all classes and which is as much concerned with women's private lives at home as with their public lives in the realms of work and politics.

There are many reasons why the inter-war period should be of interest to the present day reader. Firstly, there are clear parallels between that period and the present. Both the inter-war years and the present day follow on from eras when feminism had been a highly visible and vocal mass movement, ie the pre-World War I suffrage campaign and the women's movement of the 1970s. In the 1920s women were told that they had gained equality and achieved all they had set out to win; by the mid 20s mass feminism had fragmented into smaller, often single-issue groups and by the 1930s many feminists concentrated their efforts on the peace movement. It sounds familiar. In the 1980s women were told that they were liberated: the huge amorphous women's movement splintered into single-issue groups like the abortion campaign and the Three Hundred Group, and many feminists put their chief efforts into the anti-nuclear movement. In the 1990s we are told that we live in *post-feminist* times: had the expression been invented then, it would have been used in the 1930s. There are other parallels. Comparisons are often made between the state of the British economy today and that of the inter-war years. The similarities are striking. In the 1920s and 1930s two Britains existed, the North and the South, one under-privileged and depressed and the other affluent and buoyant. During the 1980s the same two Britains were again clearly evident, although the impact of recession in the early 1990s upon the South has blurred the sharp distinction between the two. It has long been the practice to compare present day unemployment statistics with those of the 30s. Then, as now, concern focused on the loss of male jobs. But unemployment hit women too in the 1920s and 1930s though historical accounts present us only with its impact upon them as wives and mothers and not as workers. Governments, then as now, were adroit at keeping women off the unemployment registers and devised measures specifically to do so.

Many other parallels will strike the reader, but there are other reasons too for looking closely at the history of women in inter-war Britain. At a first and superficial glance it is tempting to over-emphasise the common ground between women living then and now. It is an easy trap to fall into and so much of the period, which is not remote in time from us, looks familiar. In the 1920s and 1930s Britain came to look very much as it does today with council estates, suburbs full of semi-detached houses, arterial roads and motor-cars. We are familiar with how people looked through films of the period, and since at least the young women wore short hair and short skirts they do not look as different from us as say Victorian women. Women had the vote, they entered careers and many led independent lives. But in many other ways these women lived in a totally different world from us. Theirs was a world in which there was no National Health Service; in which childbirth (for most of the period) became more not less dangerous; in which the majority of girls received no secondary education; in which women teachers, clerks and shop assistants received far less remuneration than their male colleagues, who did exactly the same job; in which a police-woman was an extremely rare sight and in which many working-class girls had no option but to become domestic servants. Finally any reader who looks to women's history to offer explanations as to how women have reached their present position, will find this a key period which cannot be omitted. There were important legislative gains with regard to the suffrage, admission to the professions, divorce, child custody and pensions. Other struggles of these years brought future success in, for example, education, equal pay, family allowances and even in being allowed to eat in a restaurant at night without a male companion. Whilst it is important to acknowledge a debt to the women and men who brought about advances, it would be quite wrong to regard the inter-war period as a whole as an era of progress. A brief review of some of my findings will confirm the anti-progressive and reactionary character of this era in British women's history.

The single most arresting feature of the inter-war years was the strength of the notion that women's place is in the home. When the First World War ended, women who had contributed so much to the war effort in engineering, on the buses, trams and railways, in the services and in government offices were dismissed in vast numbers and expected to return to the home to fulfil their natural roles as wives, mothers, daughters and sisters. How quickly praise for our gallant wartime girls gave way to attacks on women who persisted in working or tried to claim dole money! They were dubbed as hussies, pin-money girls, dole scroungers and women who stole men's jobs; by 1920 it was considered wilful and perverse of a woman to wish to earn her own living. But it was more than verbal abuse which pushed women back to the home: the workings of the national insurance acts and of the dole offices coaxed many women out of the workforce altogether, and marriage bars in the professions made sure that only single women could engage in them. Working-class girls received an education heavily weighted towards domestic skills, so that they could put these into practice in their own home as wives and mothers or in somebody else's as servants. Media images, most notably in the rash of new domestically-orientated women's magazines, put before women the shining ideal of the stay-at-home housewife: 'a husband, a cosy home and kiddies: what more can any woman have to make her happy?' asked one magazine. Women were needed as mothers to bear and raise children in a generation tragically depleted by the First World War. Throughout the inter-war period women in Britain received the message that their place was in the home almost as loudly and clearly as the womenfolk of Germany under Nazi rule. In short, what happened to women in Britain at the end of the First World War is the same as what happened to women in America at the end of the Second World War, when Rosie the Riveter (of the film of that name) was compelled to lay down her tools and pick up her cookery books.

It would not be going too far to say that the climate in inter-war Britain was anti-feminist. There were hysterical advocates of anti-feminism like Anthony Ludovici, but if few people would go as far as him in labelling single women as 'morbid' there was a general tendency to ridicule or at best to pity single women. A distinct phobia of lesbians emerged, and single women lived in fear of being labelled sexually deviant; it was a new device to make independent women keep their place. The only image projected by the various media agencies for women to emulate was that of the housewife and mother. Hollywood films may appear to have celebrated career women, but such films normally end with wedding bells.

I think that the media portrayal of the housewife as the only desirable image a woman should adopt is of great significance. In fact, I consider this manipulation of women to be so important and so central to an understanding of women's lives in these years, that this book begins with an examination of the desirable and undesirable images of women as shown by the contemporary media.

The climate of opinion emerges as distinctly hostile to the employment of women, a factor which operated in tandem with the clearly stated notion that a woman's place is in the home. Female participation rates in the workforce were lower in 1921 and 1931 than they had been in 1911. Women were regarded as a reserve army of labour to be brought in and out of the workforce to suit the changing needs of the economy. But this analysis does not explain everything. The number of insured women workers rose more quickly than that of men and there was, to the consternation of some contemporaries, an increase in the number of young married women in paid employment. At least one more concept needs to be brought into play to explain some of this. Manual dexterity, or in the jargon of the day 'tiny fingers', was used to justify the employment of women in the new industries which made washing machines, radios and vacuum sweepers; in reality women were taken on in these new jobs because they could be paid far less than men. These developments are discussed in chapter three, which looks at women both in the old industries, particularly textiles which were hard hit in those years, and the new – but concentrates upon the single largest group of women workers, domestic servants. One of the most shocking conclusions of this book is that there really was a government policy of enforced domestic service for working-class women and that this was enforced by employment exchanges: to refuse a job as a domestic meant loss of benefit. The number of women in office work rose, when compared to those so employed before the First War. This rise is seen in both the private sector and in the lower ranks of the Civil Service, but the fact that women were taking over work formerly done by men meant a lowering of status for the job and lower wages. I would like to stress that these years saw the implementation of marriage bars for women who were teachers, doctors and civil servants. Women had to give up work on marriage and those who wished to carry on with careers had virtually to take the veil.

At no point in this study can one escape class and class divisions. It is obvious in every area of women's lives. Whereas working-class Mrs N. of Derby who lived in two tiny squalid rooms in 1939 had only 14s 3d a week for food for five people, the middle-class *Good Housekeeping* thought a sum of between 12s 6d and £1 would adequately feed *one* person for a week, and that figure represents an enforced economy in the hard times of 1931. Housing, education, health, clothing and attitudes were conditioned by class. Perhaps nowhere were class differences more evident than in the section of this book dealing with leisure. The word had a completely different meaning for women of varying social classes. To an upper-class woman it might mean spending the mimosa month on the Riviera, whilst to a working-class mother it meant sitting down at night, after a sixteen hour day, to darn socks.

Important issues are raised in the section dealing with health. The state, concerned about falling birth rates, limited its interest in women's health to their role as mothers. 1918 saw the passage of the Maternal and Child Welfare Act, but even so maternal mortality rates rose for most of our period. On the other hand these years form a key period in the history of the struggle to provide birth-control knowledge. Marie Stopes' is the most famous name associated with this, but many other women and men campaigned to secure the establishment of birth-control clinics. Theirs was a major victory, but nevertheless birth-control provision remained inadequate in inter-war Britain and many women continued to use abortion as a means of birth control without even realising it was illegal. Perhaps one of the most surprising things to the present-day reader looking at women's health then, is the generally low level of health tolerated by working-class women. The Women's Health Enquiry of 1939 paints an achingly depressing picture of women's lives made wretched by ailments they could not afford to have treated.

The history of women's political involvement in both women's own politics and in national and international affairs has been amazingly neglected; the story of these years deserves to be far more widely known. The final chapter of this book examines the partial suffrage victory of 1918 when some women over the age of thirty gained the vote, and traces the continuing campaign for the enfranchisement of women 'on the same terms' as men down to 1928. Fascinating issues arise. If women were 'given' the vote in gratitude for their contribution to the war effort, why were the very women who had done most – young women – left out? There were important developments within feminism. Not only did the mass movement of pre-war days fragment into single-issue groups, but there was a more fundamental split along the lines of 'old' and 'new' feminists. Old feminists kept to the path of equal rights with men, whereas new feminists were primarily concerned with the welfare of women as wives and mothers. Central to new feminism was the campaign for family allowances of which Eleanor Rathbone was the chief advocate. New feminism won the day and that fact influenced the course of British feminism up to the late 1960s.

In looking at inter-war feminism, it is important to distinguish between the 1920s and the 1930s: feminism in the 1920s, though diminished from its mass suffrage campaign days, was still alive and kicking: by the 1930s it is hard to find traces of it. Throughout the whole period however women took up a broad range of women's issues from housing to birth control to securing women police. Women entered for the first time the hallowed territory of parliament, at least the House of Commons. The Lords did not admit Lady Rhondda despite her efforts. The number of women MPs was never particularly large but their election had a tremendous effect on women who thought that they would never see the day when women would come to sit in parliament. There were outstanding women such as Lady Astor, Ellen Wilkinson and Eleanor Rathbone, and there is evidence that women were on occasions prepared to stick together across party lines. On the other hand the patriarchal political parties frequently clashed with women's interests: for example, women in the Labour party clashed with the party on the issue of birth control. The women MPs and many other active women did not concern themselves solely with issues concerning their own sex. It is an important part of this book to acknowledge the role played by them in many other struggles: British women marched against unemployment at home, helped refugees from Spain and worked for peace in Europe. We should not ignore or forget their role.

To sum up this period as a whole, I would say that women had won the vote, entry to parliament and to the professions and some legislative improvements. But winning the vote had not changed the world or heralded in a brave new era of sex equality in which women's moral values prevailed. The optimism of 1918 was replaced by a more cautious and tentative approach by the late 1930s. The number of women MPs was small and women's advance in the profession was disappointing: women came to realise that nothing had changed fundamentally. The reality is that socially and economically the lives of the vast majority of women remained much the same as before the First War. A woman's place was in the home and if she went out to work it was as a low paid worker.

1

DESIRABLE AND UNDESIRABLE IMAGES

I have chosen to begin this book on the lives of women in Britain in the years between the two world wars by looking at media images of women. I have done so because I believe that media stereotypes, as portrayed in magazines, advertisements and films, played a powerful part in shaping women's lives. Nowadays there is widespread realisation and much discussion about the power of images.[1] We know that images tell us what to be, how to look and how to behave. Likewise they tell us what not to be, how not to look and how not to behave. We are made to feel uncomfortable and excluded if we do not conform to what are held up to be desirable images and we are taught to scorn what are deemed undesirable images. Images operated in exactly the same way then, but there was only very limited awareness of their persuasive powers.

In the inter-war years only one desirable image was held up to women by all the mainstream media agencies – that of the housewife and mother. This single role model was presented to women to follow and all other alternative roles were presented as wholly undesirable. Realising this central fact is the key to understanding every other aspect of women's lives in Britain in the 1920s and 1930s.

Images however do not work alone. Alongside the media stereotypes even more powerful factors were at work, which coerced women into adopting the single desirable role model. Women were forced into the role of wife and mother by the workings of labour exchanges and the National Insurance Acts, by unequal pay, by marriage bars and by an outcry against women taking 'men's jobs'. Nor do images stand still: they change over time to suit the changing needs of the nation and society. (When the words 'nation' and 'society' are used in this way, they appear not to include women.) At various times the nation and society may have need of women as workers and at these times the imagery of what is desirable changes. There is no fixed definition of femininity and of the female role: such definitions are shaped and moulded by the times, and whatever is deemed to be the most desirable definition of the female role will have a profound effect upon the lives of contemporary women.

This chapter has a very important function. It shows how women were manipulated to embrace the role of housewife and mother and to scorn other role models: flappers, career women, spinsters and lesbians were all portrayed as highly undesirable stereotypes, to be rejected at all costs. Only feminist magazines advocated the role of career women, and although such small publications celebrated women's achievements and triumphed at each new step forward, it was as though they were whistling in the wind and their thin voice drowned out by the roar that 'women's place is in the home'. Echoes of this notion are to be found in every chapter of this book, whatever subject it deals with, and images of women in any age should be seen as a central and not a side issue. Not only does this chapter provide the dominant theme of the inter-war years and act as the springboard to understanding, for example, the employment of women or the education of girls, it has another key role to play. It provides us with the idealised image of the housewife or the young single girl who will become a housewife. It presents us with the fantasy version. The rest of this book deals with the reality of women's lives. The reader is invited to refer back to the glossy images of the magazines and films when reading about the real-life experiences of working-class wives in poor housing and girls in dingy offices and to remember the damnable stereotypes when reading about the lives of single women and women who earned their own livings.

In order to fully understand some features of the inter-war images and in order to set these in the context of what had gone immediately before, we need to look back at some earlier stereotypes.

Images of women are not static.[2] The nineteenth century produced two distinct images of British womanhood, the one approving and the other disapproving, the Perfect Lady and the New Woman. Both are historical phenomena which can be located precisely in time and are linked to particular circumstances. The Perfect Lady, the delicate, angelic wife and mother was firmly based in the home: she was isolated from the outside world of industry and squalor and represented the warmth and refuge of the hearth. She had been created as an image trumpeted from pulpit, tract, magazine and domestic manual in an attempt to stabilise British society in the troubled times of the early nineteenth century, when disorder threatened from without, from revolutionary France, and from within, with the rapid and unsettling process of industrialisation.[3] She enjoyed her heyday in the mid nineteenth century, but nevertheless echoes of the Perfect Lady reverberate in the twentieth-century image of the housewife.

As the nineteenth century wore on many women began to oppose this tightly circumscribed role and sought access to the public world of men. The burgeoning women's movement with its demands for education, entry into careers and a political voice gave rise to a new media image – the New Woman. The New Woman, again an image not of women's making, denotes disapproval and ridicule: it is a hostile and mocking parody. The New Woman is depicted usually as an ugly 'blue stocking', wearing a high collared blouse and tie, smoking and adopting overtly masculine poses.[4] The barb central to the image of the New Woman is that she is somehow not a woman at all. This particular image continued well into the interwar years but two interesting developments took place within it. Firstly, the image of the flapper is partly an elaboration of the New Woman theme, but she is the New Woman stripped of her serious side and hell-bent on having a good time. Secondly, the New Woman herself became associated with lesbianism: to be a New Woman in the later 1920s or in the 1930s was to invite the suspicion of being lesbian.

No change of image was to be as abrupt as that brought about by the advent of the First World War in 1914. In fact the change of image was far more abrupt than the change in reality since women had in fact long worked in industry. At first the government had even shown a reluctance to accept women's offers to help the war effort but such hesitation gave way in the face of a demand for munitions and a shortage of labour created by the conscription of men in 1916.[5]

The emergency conditions born of the First World War (1914–18) caused 'society' to transform its notions of women's role and consequently drastically to remodel its images of women. During the course of the war women were called on to do men's jobs in industry, commerce and on the land.[6] They worked on buses and trams, on the railways, in munitions and in engineering; they became bank tellers and civil service clerks; they walked behind the plough and mucked out animals in Lloyd George's land army. They went to France, too, as nurses in Queen Mary's Army Auxiliary Corp (QMAC) or in Voluntary Aid Detachments (VADs): they drove ambulances as members of the First Aid Nursing Yeomanry (FANY) or they joined the various branches of the women's auxiliary service – WRAC, WRNS and WRAF. In short, the demand upon women of all social classes altered: the working-class girl, who might well have been in service, was required as the munitionette, and Lady Diana Cooper, the socialite daughter of the Duke of Rutland and known as 'the most beautiful woman in England', became a VAD. Lady Diana left her home at Belvoir castle to work ten-hour shifts at Guy's Hospital in Southwark, which she described as 'a stinking bolting hutch of beastliness'.[7] The dominant media images of women shifted to accommodate their new and necessary roles. Baden Powell's poster of 1915 showed women and men contributing to the war effort – the women represented as a nurse and a munitions worker – and asked, 'Are YOU in This?'[8] In a recruitment poster for QMAC, a cheery young woman beckons others to become, like her, 'The Girl behind the Man behind the Gun'.[9] Uniformed women urged other women to join all the auxiliary services and photographs and paintings recorded and celebrated women's war work in industry and agriculture. Other wartime posters continued to give prominence to the image of the mother. This time the perfect mother is willing to sacrifice her son in the interest of the Empire. A grey haired but spritely old mother, in the words of one wartime poster in the Imperial War Museum's collection, tells her son, 'Go! It's Your Duty Lad. Join Today'. Similarly in advertisements elderly mothers feature prominently.

Magazines and newspapers extolled the part played by women in wartime industries. The *Illustrated Sunday Herald* emphasised the dainty femininity of women war workers,

> I could not help contrasting the dainty little khaki-class miss, curls peeping from underneath her spongeback hat, with the setting. She might have stepped out of a West End Revue. Actually she was a checker, fulfilling her important and appointed task amidst the scream and noise and steam, the clanging of a thousand hammers.[10]

The *Daily Chronicle* in August 1918 under the heading 'Our Amazons' stated: 'The Spirit in which these women have come forward is beyond praise'; it went on to praise their moderating influence in trade disputes; their bravery in danger; their physical endurance and their morality.[11] There are many similar items which express amazement that women could do such work and at the same time glamorised the jobs, underrated the dangers and overrated the wages.

Punch cartoons which had ridiculed New Women before the war, changed their tune during it. In a cartoon of 1915 an eminent woman surgeon who is also a suffragette tends a large wounded guardsman. She leans over him and says, 'Do you know your face is singularly familiar to me. I've been trying to remember where we met before.' The prostrate guardsman replies sheepishly, 'Well, Mum, Bygones be bygones. I was a police constable.'[12]

Pre-war enemies, the suffragette and the policeman are united in the war effort. Popular songs condoned women's new roles. Lee White's song 'Goodbye Madam Fashion, Come Again Some Day', maintained,

> Dainty skirts and delicate blouses
> Aren't much use for pigs and cowses.[13]

Instead the land girl opted for 'overalls and trousiz'. The nurse in France is immortalised as 'The Rose That Grows in No-Man's Land':

> It is the one red rose
> The soldier knows
> It's the work of the Master's hand
> In the war's great curse
> Stood the Red Cross Nurse
> She's the rose in no-man's land.

Advertisements have increasingly in our day come to be regarded as an accurate reflection of media views of women's roles. Wartime advertisements frequently featured illustrations of women war workers or nurses, but in the months following the end of the war advertisements rapidly changed their images of women from workers to stay-at-home wives and mothers. We can see this transition by tracing the changing image in seven Rowntree's cocoa advertisements which ran from January to April 1919, a time when women war workers were being laid off and the troops were returning home. The advertisement published in the magazine *Everywoman's* on 25 January 1919 portrays a woman factory worker, Nell, happily operating a drill; it carries the caption 'Breakfast was a bit short: with neither butter nor eggs, Nell had hit on the bright idea of having two cups of cocoa. Mother smiled and brought out the biggest cup she could find. "I shan't worry about you now, Nell," she said, and I went off to the factory as fit as I could be'.[14] The Rowntree's advertisement of 1 February 1919 appearing in *Everywoman's* shows a woman worker emptying a wheelbarrow full of small coal into a container. The scene is an outdoor one, on the banks of a canal: the caption reads 'I didn't believe it' and refers to the fact that the girl in the advertisement did not believe it when 'I heard Mary telling some of the girls that she didn't feel cold at all. I didn't believe it. But then she said she had Rowntree's cocoa for breakfast'.[15] The advertisement of 8 February had the heroine, wearing trousers, lifting heavy planks in a timber yard;[16] that of 15 February showed a land girl loading turnips onto a cart; the legend on the latter read, 'I get up in the dark'.[17] By March 1919, however, a change appears: in an advertisement of 8 March the heroine is dressing herself in heavy waterproofs to brave the weather. She is apparently setting out for work and reminds mother that she must buy a tin of Rowntree's cocoa because Jack is coming home from the front and 'None but the best is good enough for Jack'.[18] The advertisement appearing two weeks later shows mother and son drinking cocoa together before the fire: there is no young woman in this advertisement at all, only the elderly mother.[19] By the next week the transformation was complete and Rowntree's cocoa is a drink prepared by a loving wife, who explains to her husband just returned from the war how Rowntree's cocoa kept her and their son fit in the years of war shortages.[20]

Other advertisements changed equally abruptly from depicting war workers to housewives. In April 1919 'Glitto', which removes grease, oil and dirt from the hands, was portrayed as a gift to the munition worker;[21] in May we are told it makes the kitchen glitter.[22] Oatine Face Cream advertisement copywriters were even quicker off the mark. In February 1919 they depicted two pretty women at home who apply Oatine Face Cream to their faces; the bold legend underneath reads, 'Back Again to Home and Duty'. This advertisement advised readers,

Now the war is won, many women and girls are leaving work, their war job finished. They are naturally desirous of regaining their good complexions and soft white hands freely sacrificed to the National need. Oatine is invaluable for this purpose.[23]

The media had praised our gallant girls during the war, but when the war ended it quickly changed its tune. As the feminist historian of the suffrage movement, Ray Strachey, recorded,

If women went on working it was from a sort of deliberate wickedness. The tone of the press swung all in a moment from extravagant praise to the opposite extreme, and the very same people who had been heroines and the saviours of their country were now parasites, blacklegs and limpets. Employers were implored to turn them out as passionately as they had been implored to employ them.[24]

The blunt fact was that when the war ended women were turfed out of the workforce: within a year of the Armistice three-quarter million were dismissed (see chapter 3). Some feminists, who had worked so hard for the vote, for better education and careers for women, remained optimistic in 1919 that their hopes for women's emancipation were about to bear fruit: they genuinely believed that the war had revolutionised men's minds about their conception of the sort of work of which ordinary everyday women were capable. Among the optimists were Millicent Garrett Fawcett, the moderate feminist leader; Mary MacArthur, a leading trade unionist; and Adelaide Anderson, a factory inspector. Other women, including many industrial women, were more astute. The socialist feminist Stella Browne correctly predicted in 1917 that after the war there would be an adverse reaction to the advances made by women, and that this would show itself in 'a specialized education for girls concentrating on the sentimental and the domestic, and a fevered propaganda in favour of what some would call the normal family'.[25]

A wide range of media agencies projected the new idealised image of the housewife and mother and for the most part rejected alternative images. Despite economic recessions, the communication industry boomed. The popular press expanded rapidly and by the end of the 1930s there were circulation wars. Newspapers were aware of the vast women's readership, and shrewd newspaper proprietors – such as Lord Northcliffe of the *Daily Mail* – advised his editors always to have a 'woman's story' in the headlines.[26] By 1930 a typical issue of the *Daily Express* contained not only 'news' but a woman's page and many feature articles by experts such as 'Woman Doctor', 'Psychologist', 'Nursery Expert' and 'Masseur'.[27]

Women's magazines proliferated too in the inter-war period. Some sixty new ones were launched between 1920 and 1945.[28] A glance at the list of new titles shows at once the domestic bias: among the new titles were *My Little Home, Mother, Woman and Home* and *Good Housekeeping*. The range of magazines was extensive. At the top end of the market were such titles as *The Lady* and *The Queen*, which catered for the aristocracy and gentry but were read by many women who merely aspired to such ranks. Many well-to-do women suffered from a redistribution of incomes after the First War and given the further difficulty of finding domestic servants after the war, such magazines became increasingly domestic, giving advice on how to do jobs about the home. A new range of women's magazines aimed at the affluent middle class came into being. These were quite expensive monthlies such as *Good Housekeeping* (1922), *Woman and Home* (1926), *My Home* and *Modern Home* (1928): the emphasis of many of these was on informing middle-class women how to run a home without domestic help. Better known to us are the new weeklies which aimed at the lower middle class. The best known of these are *Woman's Own* (1932) and *Woman* (1937). These magazines were fully illustrated in sepia and white. *Woman's Own* was launched in October 1932 and introduced itself as follows:

How Do You Do?
We introduce ourselves and our new weekly for the modern young wife who loves her home.
Woman's Own will be a paper with a purpose – a paper thoroughly alive to the altered conditions of the present day. The home paper that makes any girl worth her salt want to be the best housewife ever – and then some.[29]

The first issue, which came with a free gift of a skein of wool, set the pattern for future numbers. It contained the first episode of a romantic serial by Ruby M. Ayres entitled, 'From this Day Forward'. Features included 'The right sort of frocks' (easily-made fashions for wear in the house), an article on knitting ('Make this beret and bag from our gift wool'), another piece on embroidery, a pseudo-medical piece ('A baby is coming to town' by Mumsie, the wife of a famous children's doctor), household tips, a life of the Prince of Wales and – since this was issue number one – a letterless problem page.

Woman, particularly under the editorship of Mary Grieve, provided a similar mix. Mary Grieve wrote that she was conscious that she could make no reference to daily baths, telephones or holidays abroad. Class differences, she believed, held back the major boom in women's magazines until after the Second World War: in the inter-war years, 'habits of cooking and entertainment, uses of leisure, aesthetic preferences, standards of home-making, vocabulary and hygiene all had so many shades of acceptance' and consequently limited the class range to which any single magazine might appeal.[30] Nevertheless the circulation of *Woman* reached two million by 1940 and its actual readership was around four million. Mary Grieve believed that it was important that readers should be able to identify with the women portrayed in the magazines, and that the images should not be of richer, luckier women than the readers. *Woman* and *Woman's Own* were service magazines for lower middle-class housewives. *Woman's Friend* and *Woman's Companion* performed similar services for working-class women. In addition to these there was a great range of specialist skill magazines devoted to knitting and sewing.

Other non-domestically orientated women's magazines had readerships drawn from the very wealthy to the very poor. *Vogue's* ritzy pages kept its affluent readers up to date on the social and fashion scene of New York, Paris, London and the Riviera. At the lowest end of the scale were weekly pulp-fiction magazines or 'books', as working-class girls called them. *Peg's Paper* (1919) was the first of this new group of fiction weeklies. Others followed – namely *Red Star* (1929), *Secrets* (1932), *Oracle* (1933), *Glamour* (1938) and many others.[31] Printed on the cheapest paper and melodramatically, if smudgily, illustrated, they contained lurid tales of love, crime and adventure. The word 'revenge' figures frequently in the titles of stories in *Peg's Paper* as do 'passion' and 'jealousy'. Readers of that paper could read 'A rich girl's revenge', 'Her mad jealousy', 'In passion's coils'. Graphologists and palmists were given a great deal of space and the many free gifts included lucky charms: the New Year gift for 1925 was a twisted little base metal swastika love charm. The advertisements read like jokes – 'All ugly noses improved in a few weeks by using Our Improved Nose Machine'; 'Are You Fat? Thinzu tablets work in a few weeks'; 'How to Grow Taller'; 'Blushing – Complete Cure'. Among the foolish advertisements are the poignant ones – 'Drunkards Cured Cheaply'; 'Rankins Head Ointment kills all nits and vermin'; 'Fits Cured'; 'Dr Cassell's Tablets for Rickets and Wasting'; 'Bad Legs? visit The National Infirmary for Bad Legs'; 'Poplets do actually cure *all* ladies' ailments'. There were many advertisements for abortifacients and venereal disease clinics. But neither *Vogue* nor the pulp papers contribute significantly to the media hype of the housewife; reading the latter however formed an important part of the leisure of working-class girls and women's leisure. (See chapter 5).

Last but not least there were the feminist magazines. Lady Rhondda and her board of women directors launched *Time and Tide* in 1920: it addressed itself to the major issues of the day as they concerned women. There were two other important feminist weeklies published in the 1920s – *Woman's Leader* and *The Vote*: both evolved out of previous suffrage publications and represented the National Union of Women's Suffrage Societies and the Women's Freedom League respectively.[32] They make lively and informative reading but as a store of images they were out of step with the mainstream: only the feminist magazines projected an image of the career woman and the adventurous woman as positive and desirable. In fact they raised these to the status of heroines.

Of course women read novels too. This meant anything from pulp-fiction (longer versions of *Peg's Paper* and *The Oracle*'s brand of lurid story telling) and light romances, such as flowed from the pens of Ethel M. Dell or Baroness Orczy, to that superb collection of 'women's novels' written by such writers as Elizabeth Bowen, Rose Macaulay, E. M. Delafield, Winifred Holtby, Storm Jameson, Rosamond Lehmann, F. M. Mayor, Dorothy Richardson, Rebecca West or Virginia Woolf. Women writers dominated the scene. Middle-class women wrote for other middle-class women, who bought books or borrowed them from Boots' library. Nicola Beauman, the author of a fascinating study entitled *A Very Great Profession: The Woman's Novel 1914–39*, was inspired to begin her research into women's novels when she noticed that Laura Jesson, the heroine of the film *Brief Encounter*, travelled into town every week to change her library books.[33] Such books are yet another repository of images of women.

The 1920s and the 1930s saw a technological revolution in communications. The two dominant new forces were radio and cinema. Radio is examined more fully in chapter 5, but it had its part to play in shaping the image of the housewife: it is worth noting that it was the one non-commercial agency in operation.[34] Cinema-going too is discussed more fully under leisure in chapter 5. Film technology progressed rapidly in the inter-war years. The flickering, noisily projected, silent films of the 1920s gave way to sophisticated sound films in the 1930s: sound was introduced in 1928 but many local cinemas took time to install the new equipment. Many women in Britain went to the cinema several times a week with working-class women going more often than middle class. Both working-class women and men went primarily to see American films.

All these agencies provide a wonderful store of images of women. The attributes a housewife should possess are most clearly set out in women's magazines, household manuals, novels, films and newspapers.

The early numbers of *Woman's Own* give a clear exposition of the idealised image of the housewife as it had evolved by the early 1930s. The Christmas number for 1932 contained an apparently unsolicited contribution from 'one of our readers', Mrs V. N. G.[35] It was a full page feature entitled, 'I am so happy', illustrated with a drawing of a family – pretty woman perched on the arm of chair in which sits a handsome besuited man, at whose feet play two laughing children, a girl and a boy; the caption to the illustration reads, 'A husband, a cosy home and kiddies – what more can any woman have to make her perfectly happy?' The order is significant – handsome husband, pretty home and then children: this was the model of domestic bliss. Mrs V. N. G. tells her story. She recounts her romance with Jack: at first she tried to resist his charms and took a job 200 miles away but then, realising the error of her ways, she turned up at the door of his office:

> 'Jack,' I said, 'I've been a fool. Do you still love me?' He stared at me and his face went white. My heart sank to my boots because I thought he had changed his mind. He said nothing but signalled a passing taxi and bundled me in. The next minute I was in his arms and for the first time in my life I knew perfect peace and happiness.

Then came setting up home. After that encounter they waited

two years before marrying. Those two years were spent in her father's garden shed – making furniture and upholstery. 'At the end of the two years we had the loveliest furniture and the most marvellous curtains and counterpanes, woven by my own fair hands.' After marriage Mrs V. N. G. carried on working until she became pregnant. We are reminded of the reality of the hard times of the early 1930s by reference to the fact that Jack had had a wage cut. Nevertheless Mrs V. N. G. was looking forward to life blossoming forth with Jack and the babies. Her basic philosophy was to be happy with her lot and 'not waste time sighing for the moon'. A second illustration acts as an endpiece: it shows a large detached country house. The illustration belies the text: anyone who could afford a house like that would not have to make furniture in the garden shed. Central to the housewife fantasy is pretending to be richer than you are.

Fundamental to the image of the housewife is that she is confined to the private sphere. Men belong to the public sphere and can bring into the household their broader world view. The housewife who is addressed in Fay Inchfawn's *Homely Talks of a Homely Woman*, a pseudo-religious mixture of homily and practical advice, needs 'John's' breeziness and wider outlook: she frets if the butcher is late in arriving or a tablecloth is torn in the wash or the maid breaks a pan. To John such annoying circumstances are like impudent persons who jostle you on the pavement:

John does not waste time in jostling. He steps into the road. Then the John whom I know best always sees the other person's point of view. He suggests that the butcher has his own worries to contend with. That the washerwoman had an accident, and the tablecloth may have been rotten. That it must be so horrid for Jane to be scolded for what she probably could not help.[36]

Housewives were confined to small spaces and the danger was they became small-minded. Housewives needed John too to keep the household on a firm financial footing. Poor Jill, 'who could do most things but arithmetic – decidedly not', marries accountant, Ray, in a short story by Anne Gordon (1933).[37] Ray expects Jill to come to him each week with an open purse for him to fill but he demands full household accounts. Jill is compelled to go out to work secretly, as a milliner, in order to balance the books. It all comes out in the end – and luckily Ray was very understanding – 'You're the most wonderful, most marvellous little wife that ever a husband was lucky enough to marry, and hang figures – we'll do them together next time.' Jill was lucky. The magazine confession feature on a young wife, headed 'I got into debt', told a harrowing real life story of a woman hounded by creditors and the courts.[38] She worked her way out of debt by economising in the household – by cooking cornish pasties out of scraps of meat and eating mackerel instead of salmon. Working her way out of debt 'made' this young woman: 'And thank goodness Bill never knew! He still thinks I am a financial genius'. This kind of dishonesty between husbands and wives is common in the magazines: women are encouraged to manipulate men.

Women's magazines are full of household tips – how to get sea stains out of brown boots, hints on potted meat making, how to make lampshades. Home-making was elevated to a science. Leonora Eyles, a remarkably sane columnist for several papers, likened running a home to, 'running a big business, army or factory'.[39] Wives were encouraged to take a pride in their domestic role but there was a narrow line to tread lest she should fall into the sin of being house-proud. On the one hand she was urged by magazines and manuals to keep a strict regime of cleaning and to purchase the right tools for the job – A. M. Kaye's household manual listed twenty different kinds of brooms and brushes[40] but, on the other hand, magazines warned against the danger of being obsessed by housework. Ursula Bloom's 'Houseproud' is a homily against falling into this trap:

> Esther adored her home. She had always been the workaday sort, business life had galled her terribly, for she was so utterly domestic. She had longed for the joy of arranging dimity curtains, of fixing crisp blue china against a panelled wall, of burnishing brass. House-proud, she longed for her own little niche.[41]

After the honeymoon, 'she put her whole soul into polishing the linoleum' and there was no time to sit hand-in-hand with Jim in the evenings because she was always cooking, washing up or knitting and mending. But the polished linoleum was both Esther's downfall and her salvation: she slipped on the polished surface, sprained her ankle and was confined to bed, where Jim looked after her! Romance returned to their marriage and Esther had learned her lesson. The story concluded: 'Housepride is a secret vice. It is a big barrier that wants tearing down. They had been lucky that fate had helped them'.

Many sane articles encouraged women to involve husbands in household chores. An article entitled 'Let him help about the house' cautions women against training lazy husbands – and sagely points out, 'At first he will be only too eager to help you with the dishes.

Don't make the mistake of refusing! In a year or two he won't even offer!'[42] The housewife was however positively encouraged to take a pride in her appearance. 'Looks do count after marriage' wrote the beauty expert in the first issue of *Woman's Own*: it is a woman's duty to look her best at all times. The housewife was advised – 'Never let him see you in a grubby apron, a bedraggled apron or a shabby old working frock': instead she was to make herself three gingham overalls, plus matching dust-caps. She was to bath *after* and not before cleaning: she had even to make her own bath salts (bicarbonate of soda plus sandalwood). There was a great deal of harping on about post-marital beauty. The 26 November 1932 edition asked, 'Should a wife make up?'; the article is mainly concerned with how a wife should get her husband to agree to her wearing make-up and, of course, she must never make up in front of him.[43] Husbands, who were to be enticed into reading columnists' advice by leaving the magazine lying open at a particular page, were urged to put the sweetness back into married life by buying their wives flowers and sweets; as columnist Mrs Eyles said, 'a bunch of violets is the price of a packet of fags'.[44]

Husbands needed to be attentive to their wives since housewives often suffered from 'nerves'; they appeared to do so increasingly as the 1930s progressed if the amount of column inches devoted to the topic is any indication.[45] The problem of 'nerves' is clearly related not merely to the house-bound condition of many young wives, but to being house-bound with young children. The housewife was also a mother. There was great concern by the British state and other bodies about the dangers of a fall in population in the 1930s. It was predicted in 1936 that by the year 2033 England and Wales would have a population no larger than London.[46] Given this and many other alarmist statements, it is interesting that media agencies did not put *even more* emphasis on motherhood. Advertisements appealed directly to mothers, and women's magazines are packed with features on childcare, child health and children's clothing. Manuals on childcare proliferated, with the stern child expert Dr Truby King emerging as the chief authority. Motherhood was the accepted aim of marriage and this assumption was implicit in the media's projected image of the housewife.

The housewife also received a new prominence in the novels of the inter-war period. Women novelists began to write about the ordinary lives of middle-class housewives and their day-to-day problems such as bringing up children, paying bills or dealing with servants. Mrs Miniver in Jan Struther's book of that name, written in 1939, had her day full:

Every morning you awake to the kind of list which begins: –

Sink-plug. Ruffle-tape. X-hooks. Glue . . . and ends: – Ring
plumber, Get sweep. Curse laundry. Your horizon contracts,
your mind's eye is focused upon a small circle of exasperating
detail. Sterility sets in; the hatches of your mind are battened
down.[47]

E. M. Delafield, the prime exponent of the new-style domestic
novel, gently satirised the kind of life she herself led – mother,
Justice of the Peace, lecturer to Women's Institute groups, best
friend of the vicar's wife. The 'Provincial Lady' series makes witty
and compelling reading. In *Diary of a Provincial Lady* (1930) she
describes with great wit the 'hard pressed' life of the heroine and her
dealings with her almost totally silent husband, her two children, the
kitten, mademoiselle, the cook and the house-parlourmaid. The last
two named are always threatening to leave the household and the
Lady's preoccupation with 'the servant problem' reflects the reality
of the times. In fact Ethel, the house-parlourmaid, does resign and
cook threatens to:

> March 4th – Ethel, as I anticipated, gives notice. Cook says
> this is so unsettling, she thinks she had better go too. Despair
> invades me. Write five letters to Registry Offices.
>
> March 7th – No hope.
>
> March 8th – Cook relents, so far as to say that she will stay
> until I am suited. Feel inclined to answer that, in that case,
> she had better make up her mind to a lifetime spent together
> – but naturally refrain. Spend exhausting day in Plymouth
> chasing mythical house-parlourmaids.[48]

Films, like novels, more usually end than begin with wedding
bells. Hollywood films had far more interesting images of women
to project than housewives![49] But wives did appear widely in the
1920s and 1930s: sometimes they were figures representing a sort
of archetypal goodness as in F. W. Murnau's silent classic *Sunrise*:
it has only three characters – 'the wife', 'the man' and 'the woman
from the city'. Wives in westerns were similar agents of goodness
persuading cowboys not to fight. Wives were also silly, lightweight
socialites in de Mille or Lubitsch domestic comedies. They exper-
imented with falling in love with men other than their husbands
but the grass was never greener on the other side of the hill. The
Hay's Office Production Code (1934) greatly restricted any female
sexual liberation that had been apparent in films of the late 1920s.
By 1936 Lubitsch made *Desire*, where Marlene Dietrich played a
jewel thief who is redeemed by public confession and by marriage

to solid citizen car manufacturer Gary Cooper; Cooper and Dietrich set off into the sunset – to a happily married life in Detroit.[50]

One British film distils the essence of a wife's role. *Victoria the Great* (1937), directed by Herbert Wilcox and starring Anna Neagle and Anton Walbrook, was one of the most popular films in Britain in 1938. It opens with Anna Neagle receiving the news she is to be the new queen; hitherto dominated by her German mother and her uncle, Leopold King of the Belgians, the young woman throws off their control and prepares to rule independently, subject to the wise advice of Lord Melbourne. It is the sex reversal of roles that makes this film so interesting. Victoria has to make all the first moves towards Albert – inviting him to England, asking him to dance and proposing to him. Once married Albert is confined to what is normally a Victorian woman's role – running the household and playing the piano. Albert, of course, resents his emasculated lot and digs in his heels when she refuses to let him even discuss politics at a soirée at the palace. Affronted, he runs to his room and will not come out again until Victoria has submitted to his will. She knocks once at his door and Albert asks, 'Who is there?' She answers, 'the Queen'. She knocked a second time and this time in response to his question, 'Who is there?' she replies, 'Victoria'. But on the third knock and in reply to the third identical question, she says, 'Your wife, Albert'. Albert opens the door and thereafter Victoria became his *'kleine Frau'* and they shared the concerns of state together.

Hollywood stars were perceived to live outrageous love-lives. Fan magazines were full of gossip and the news of the latest Hollywood divorces. Women's magazines however preferred to emphasise the domestic bliss and homely values of the stars. In 'Peg Trots Around Hollywood', a weekly column in *Peg's Paper*, the star Barbara La Marr is quoted as saying, 'People envy wealthy beautiful women with many admirers, but the person to be envied is the girl with just one sweetheart who marries him and has a little family to work for.'[51]

Woman's Own assured its readers that Hollywood stars are 'just like you at home': Joan Crawford, then married to Douglas Fairbanks, spent her evenings by the fireside making rugs.[52] On another occasion, in similar homely vein, the magazine ran a double page spread on 'loves that have lasted'; we are informed that Hollywood had silver weddings too and we are shown long-married couples – Mr and Mrs John Barrymore, Mr and Mrs Edward G. Robinson and Mr and Mrs Eddie Cantor.[53]

Whilst the housewife was praised, other images of women were either ridiculed or condemned outright as dangerous or undesirable.

The best known of these images is the flapper. She is associated with the swinging images of the roaring twenties but in fact the word dates from before the First World War. In the 1890s it had meant a young prostitute but had come to mean, just before the war, any girl with a young boyish figure.[54] The flapper craze for skinny young, almost transsexual, women had first caught on in Germany, where she was called a *backfisch*. It reached England about 1912 and the word 'flapper' at that point had jolly and friendly connotations: it was used to describe the comradely sort of girl who would ride pillion on the 'flapper bracket' of a motorcycle. In the words of the Dapper Flapper song,

> She is oh, so tender
> Figure so slender
> She loves chocolate creams
> and me . . .

The flapper of the 1920s is superficially identified by her clothing, her manners, her social life and her sexual freedom. Flappers wore their hair short in shingles, bobs, bingles and Eton crops: it was a major culture shock for many people to see women for the first time with short hair. Flappers actually vaunted their shorn locks. A reviewer of Constance Talmadge's performance in the film, *Goldfish*, in 1924 remarked: 'Miss Talmadge is obviously proud of her barber, for there are close ups which show the cut at the back of her head and also at the sides . . . '[55]

Advice columns and film columns in working-class girls' magazines discussed the issue of 'the bob or not' throughout the decade. Flappers departed from conventions in their clothing by shortening their hemlines, wearing the new loose garment called a jumper and by wearing make-up, though not many of them would actually have gone out without a hat. In 1930 *Peg's Paper* told its working-class readers that Clara Bow (the It–Girl) saves money on 'millinery by joining the hatless brigade'.[56] Flappers danced the new dances – fox trot, one-step, Charleston, the black bottom – to the new American music. They smoked cigarettes and they drank cocktails. Flappers did 'silly things' – especially the Bright Young Things, London's smart set of Oxford bagged young men and flapper women. The Bright Young Things went to lots of parties, had midnight scavenger hunts and paper chases, and played 'Follow My Leader' over the counters at Selfridges. And, of course, flappers were sexually wanton: the myth of the flapper has her sleeping around in total sexual abandon.

Contemporary film depictions of the flapper however show that the flapper revolution was essentially 'one of style and not of morality'. In the 1919 British film *The Irresistible Flapper*, the heroine does all the flapper things which outrage her old-fashioned parents but essentially she is a brick: she saves her married sister's life and reputation by rescuing her from the dubious charms of a matinée idol.[57] Colleen Moore, one of the best known Hollywood flapper actresses, wore bobbed hair and short clothes, smoked cigarettes, drank cocktails and danced the new dances in *Flaming Youth* (1923), but when pursued by an admirer on a yacht, she escaped by jumping into the sea: it was a Victorian act.[58] In *Wine of Youth* (1924) the notion of a 'trial honeymoon' is mooted but the liberated flapper is never compromised and ends up merely snuggling up to her husband-to-be.[59] The idea that wanton women do not get husbands is just as strong in flapper films as in nineteenth-century stage melodrama. Films portrayed flappers across the social spectrum. Gloria Swanson, Eleanor Boardman, Colleen Moore and Constance Talmadge usually played middle- and upper-class flappers, but many other actresses played smart, quick-witted, modern girls who worked as shop assistants, maids and factory workers.

But if the image of the flapper sounds just light-hearted fun it was not. The flapper was the heir to the New Woman of the 1890s and by the early 1920s 'flapper' was a term of abuse which could be used against independent women who sought to consolidate upon women's wartime gains and upon the partial suffrage victory of 1918. Flapper denoted flightiness and irresponsibility. It was flighty and irresponsible of working-class girls to wish to continue working after the war. The press raged against ex-munition workers who collected dole at labour exchanges and wanted other work in industry. (See chapter 3.) The press also campaigned against equal franchise for women on the grounds that young women were too frivolous and irresponsible to vote. Some women over thirty had been granted the vote in 1918 but it took a further ten years of campaigning for women to get the vote on the same terms as men at twenty-one. In 1927 the *Evening Standard* attacked 'Votes for Girls' and 'Votes for Flappers'.

By 1927 *Punch* offered a definition of the flapper: 'Flapper is a popular press catchword for an adult woman worker aged 21 to 30 when it is a question of giving her the vote under the same conditions as men'. One hears very little of flappers after 1928![60]

Women are depicted as sex symbols in every age. In the interwar years no medium did this more widely and with greater effect than the cinema. Vamps, flappers, and 'It' girls flickered across the screen in the 1920s; in the 1930s the screen goddesses addressed their audiences in tough American or sultry European accents. The flapper was frequently seen in films and the screen brought to 'life' British novelist Eleanor Glyn's 'It' girl: Eleanor Glyn invented 'sex appeal' and Clara Bow personified it in the film *It* (1927). This film is a variation of the working girl flapper theme but with much greater emphasis on sexual attraction: 'With "It",' the movie informs us, 'you win all men if you are a woman'.[61] In *It* Clara Bow makes the leap from shop assistant to boss's wife. Clara, 'the hottest jazz baby in films', was in reality ruined by scandals and nervous illness; her Brooklyn accent debarred her from making the transition to sound movies.[62] Bow was cute and she was sexy. The late 1920s and early 1930s saw the emergence of the screen-goddesses, the mega-stars, the larger-than-life beauties. There was nothing cute about them. Marjorie Rosen and Molly Haskell, writers of two fascinating accounts of images of women in Hollywood movies, give detailed attention to the goddesses – Harlow, West, Garbo and Dietrich. Harlow and West projected images of tough, fast-talking peroxide blondes; neither was a stereotyped, passive female. Mae West was aggressive in her sexuality and drawled out one-liners, which ensured that the forces of moral purity lined up against her. The censors pounced on lines like 'Is that a gun in your pocket, or are you just glad to see me?' When posters advertised Mae in *It Ain't No Sin*, Catholic priests carried placards saying, 'It is'. The film production code, which attempted to clean up Hollywood, virtually finished Mae off. Scandal and illness led to the end of the other best known of the platinum blondes, Jean Harlow. Harlow exuded sexiness in such films as *The Public Enemy* (1931), *Goldie* (1931), *Red Headed Woman* (1932); she became Hollywood's number one bad girl. Like Mae West, her amoral and tough brand of sexiness flourished in the pre-1934 Hayes production code days. Harlow died young. She died in 1937 at the age of twenty-six. The relaxed style of the early 1930s, when Hollywood permitted women to have sexual appetites, also accommodated within it some of the great screen performances of the two inscrutable European goddesses – Garbo and Dietrich. Garbo was – for example Queen Christina in the film of that name (1933) – sacrificing all for love, and Dietrich was the wicked nightclub singer in *The Blue Angel* (1930). Garbo was vulnerable while Dietrich was calculating and deadly, but both possess mystery. British stars were simply not in this league. It was Garbo and Dietrich who set standards of beauty and dress to be emulated by British girls – not Gracie Fields or Jessie Matthews.

Positive images of career women are plentiful in the cinema of the 1930s. Molly Haskell suggests that this was the result of the 1934 production code's prohibition of sexy women on screen. The most popular career for these screen working girls was journalism. Joan Crawford was a reporter in *Dance Fools Dance* (1931), Loretta Young in *Platinum Blonde* (1931) and Jean Arthur played the sharp, street-wise reporter against Gary Cooper's country bumpkin writer of verses for birthday cards in *Mr Deeds Goes to Town* (1936). The

latter has a complicated plot but it ends with the love match of
Arthur and Cooper. In *Front Page Woman* (1935) Bette Davis is a
reporter on a city paper while her fiancé works on a rival paper.
The fiancé mocks women reporters and Davis refuses to marry him
until he recants, which he does when she clears an innocent man
of murder, gets a confession from the real killer and a scoop. The
apogee of the professional woman in film was without doubt quick-
talking Rosalind Russell. Though made a little later, *Take A Letter
Darling* (1942) belongs in spirit to the Paramount Studios' sex skir-
mishes of the thirties. Rosalind Russell plays an advertising executive who employs Fred McMurray as her personal secretary. In this
case the secretary ends up marrying the boss, but by casting a man
in the role of secretary the film highlights many of the demeaning
practices usually inflicted on female secretaries by male bosses.
Perhaps because film is the medium of fantasy we find so many
strong images of professional women, even if they did have to fit
with convention and marry the hero.

   Fiction too, especially detective fiction, featured daring, independent young women. Two of Agatha Christie's heroines from the
1920s – Tuppence (the intrepid female half of the Tommy and
Tuppence duo) and Lady Eileen Brett – would take on underworld
thugs and foreign agents without a backwards glance. But not all
fiction by any means glorified the career woman. A. S. M. Hutchinson's *This Freedom*, a best seller in the early 1920s, became a by-
word for the danger to home, family and to women themselves of
women taking up careers.[63] The author shifts his standpoint and
sympathy around at will. At first we are led to be sympathetic
towards Rosalie, brought up in a male dominated household, and
to her ambitions and her passions – Lombard Street and the English
Constitution. But when Rosalie becomes a banker *and* marries we
are made to lose sympathy with her. Worst, Rosalie has three
children and still continues to work successfully. She has to witness
her children going to the dogs for want of maternal guidance before
seeing the error of her ways and giving up the bank. This lengthy
novel dealt with the same subject matter as many a woman's magazine story – namely the conflict between marriage and work. The
difference was that the temptation of outside employment in the
magazines was normally limited to being a milliner or a secretary.

   The spinster in these years was portrayed as an undesirable image.
The word had derogatory connotations. It implied failure because
spinsters were seen as having failed to marry. There was much talk
in these years of 'excess' and 'surplus' women. In the years following
the First World War, which had decimated the male population,
the numbers of single women increased dramatically: the number
of 'excess' women to men in the population increased from 664,000

in 1911 to 1,174,000 in 1921 and still remained at 842,000 in 1931.[64] Newspapers discussed the problem of 'surplus women' and advocated nineteenth-century style emigration schemes for them. Some feminists, notable campaigners against the exploitation of marriage such as Cicely Hamilton, championed the cause of spinsterdom[65] and others were prepared to simply make the best of things.[66] The strongest anti-spinster statement coming from these years, which were characterised by a strong anti-feminist feeling, comes from the writer Ludovici:

> From the outset, therefore, it is as well for everybody to bear this in mind in regard to spinsterhood in general, namely, that since the spinsters of any country represent a body of human beings who are not leading natural lives, and whose fundamental instincts are able to find no normal expression or satisfaction, it follows . . . that the influence of this body of spinsters on the life of the nation to which they belong, must be abnormal, and therefore contrary to the normal needs and the natural development of that nation.[67]

His views were hysterical and extreme and he lamented that other people were far too soft on spinsters. Ludovici himself complained that public attitudes tended towards – 'Oh, but it isn't their *fault* if they are spinsters – why say such hard things about them?' and 'What would you do with them poor things? They must live!'[68] These protests denote the wider public attitude that spinsters were to be pitied. Even the feminist Vera Brittain, mother of politician Shirley Williams and friend of spinster Winifred Holtby confided to her diary, 'Oh that University Woman's Club – full of grim looking desiccated spinsters in appalling tweeds. Heaven preserve Shirley from an academic career.'[69] To the popular perception single women remained a problem: small wonder feminists preferred the term 'bachelor girl'.[70]

Fictional representations of the spinster abound. There are young women whose chances of outside happiness are crushed by overbearing mothers: this was the lot of Alex in E. M. Delafield's *Consequences* (1919) and of Joan in Radclyffe Hall's *Unlit Lamp* (1924). Winifred Holtby produced some positive role models such as the schoolteacher in *South Riding* (1935) and she also produced a very affectionate portrait of an elderly spinster in *Poor Caroline* (1931). The archetypal spinster of these years was the clergyman's daughter and both F. M. Mayor's *The Rector's Daughter* (1924) and George Orwell's *A Clergyman's Daughter* (1935) present sympathetic portraits of such women, even if Orwell's book is deeply male chauvinist.

The most striking thing about lesbian images in the inter-war years is how remarkably few they were. This is scarcely surprising, however, given the great hostility towards women who loved women. The toleration of passionate friendships between women as innocent attachments which had existed in the Victorian era, was replaced by homophobia and public anger against lesbians.[71] The sexologists had done their bit. Krafft Ebbing and Havelock Ellis attributed sexual inversion to hereditary taint and congenital weakness: they wrote of the 'true invert', the mannish lesbian. Sigmund Freud attributed lesbianism to childhood trauma. All viewed it as undesirable. Havelock Ellis described the true invert as disdainful of feminine artifices of toilet and pursuits such as needlework; she was, he said, mannish in bearing, in directness of speech and in habits such as cigarette and cigar smoking.[72] The characteristics sexologists attributed to lesbians tally with those ascribed to the pre-First World War New Woman and the behaviour of the New Woman was redefined as lesbian. The fear of being labelled sexually deviant was a new device to keep women in their place. The feminist movement had provided a meeting place for lesbian women or women who preferred the company of women. The First World War provided opportunities for many more women from a wider spread of social classes to live and work together. In the inter-war years most of British society was united in a condemnation of this perversion and even lesbian writers internalised these values and struggled with their inclinations. Small wonder that images of lesbians from this period are so appalling.

Many lesbian images from this period are crude caricatures. Clemence Dane's *Regiment of Women* (1915) provides us with a classic stereotype of the predatory, vampire lesbian in Clare Hartill, the senior mistress in a girl's school. An adolescent girl, whom Clare has *made* to love her, commits suicide and a young teacher, Alwynne, though 'whitened' by her contact with the vampire is rescued by the love of a good man. Victoria Vanderleyden wants to eat her would-be young victim, Gillian, in Naomi Royde Smith's *The Tortoiseshell Cat* (1925); the woman-eating Kim, in G. Sheila Donisthorpe's American novel *Loveliest of Friends* (1931) devoured the victim Audrey; Francis Brett Young's character Miss Cash in *White Ladies* (1935) is described by one of her young pupils as ageless – 'you see, she's a vampire. She lives on blood'.

Other lesbian novels belong almost to the Victorian/Edwardian era of passionate friendships. In writing *The Unlit Lamp* (1924) Radclyffe Hall did not consider that she had written a lesbian novel and this book caused no outcry. Winifred Holtby's *The Crowded Street* (1924) may also be placed in the same category. But the innocence of such novels was an anomaly in the post-war world and could scarcely continue after the publication in 1928 of Hall's bombshell, *The Well of Loneliness*.

The Well of Loneliness is the classic lesbian novel, the 'lesbian Bible'. It remains the best known novel in English on the subject and its role is seminal to the history of lesbianism in Britain. In reading it we are reminded that the study of images is in itself an integral part of the study of reality. Judged against positive novels of the new women's movement, *The Well* is indeed a chronicle of doom and gloom. But the historian's task should be to relate the book to the context of its own time, to analyse the images within it in the light of the knowledge of the limited range of lesbian images available and to assess its impact upon women's lives.

Radclyffe Hall's intention was to make a plea for toleration for the lot of the lesbian. Because of this she chose to portray her lesbian as a born invert trapped from birth and doomed to unhappiness. Hall considered that the way to evoke public sympathy was to make the reader feel sorry for the central character, the queerly named Stephen Gordon, who could not help what she was, namely, the classic invert à la Krafft Ebbing and Havelock Ellis: 'Stephen's figure was handsome in a flat, broad shouldered and slim flanked fashion; and her movements were purposeful, having fine poise, she moved with the easy assurance of the athlete.'[73]

Stephen was the archetypal country gentleman, the heir to large estates; she possessed the love of the land and the stern sense of honour of her class. But Stephen's congenital blight, if not her very femaleness, was to force her away from her beloved estates at Morton to a life in a foreign city, Paris. Through hard work and sheer talent she rose to become a famous author; she was also incredibly rich. But even as a rich and successful woman she would not rival the happiness of the poorest man. She falls in love with the wife of a neighbour in England, the feminine and untrustworthy Angela. Angela's husband denounces Stephen to her mother and with only her faithful governess as companion Stephen takes up residence first in London then Paris. She becomes a great literary success but it is the war that brings about a great change in Stephen's life: she joins an ambulance brigade and meets others of her kind:

> And now quite often while she waited at the stations for the wounded, she would see unmistakable figures – unmistakable to her they would be at first sight, she would single them out of the crowd as by instinct. For as though gaining courage from the terror that is war, many a one who was even as Stephen, had crept out of her hole and come into the daylight, come into the daylight and faced her country: 'Well, here I am, will you take me or leave me?' And England had taken

her, asking no questions – she was strong and efficient, she could fill a man's place, she could organize too, given scope for her talent. England had said, 'Thank you very much. You're just what we happened to want . . . at the moment.'[74]

It was the war too which brought about Stephen's meeting with the femme Mary Llewelyn. After initial hesitations, caused mainly by Stephen's concern for Mary, the two become lovers and live in Stephen's opulent home in Paris. Theirs was a loving sexual relationship though Radclyffe Hall indulged in no torrid sexual descriptions. There is only ' . . . and that night they were not divided'. Stephen and Mary are forced to look for understanding company in the *demi-monde* of Paris salons and gay clubs. It is the awful warning of what that life was doing to others that strengthened Stephen in her resolve to sacrifice her love for Mary to Mary's own happiness. She nobly engineered that Mary should leave her for a fine man. The book ends with Stephen alone yet with a vision of legions of others rising up behind her.

The novel caused an enormous stir in Britain. It was banned as obscene and the publicity occasioned by the trial shows clearly the hostility towards lesbianism: 'I would rather give a healthy boy or girl a phial of prussic acid than this novel', proclaimed *The Sunday Express*.[75] But lesbianism became a topic of discussion in some circles at least. High-class or artistic lesbian women were dismissive of *The Well*. Romaine Brooks described it as, 'a ridiculous book, trite, superficial', and Vita Sackville West called it 'a loathsome book'. It is fashionable nowadays to emphasise the negative impact of *The Well*, but one cannot help thinking that for many ordinary women with lesbian feelings *The Well* made a positive contribution to their lives. Its author had shown great courage in writing it. She had presented a model of two women living together as a couple and she had given a glimpse of a world of gay clubs, even if the first of these did not end happily ever after and the second was depressingly depicted. There could be alternative endings and may not excitement have risen in the provincial woman's breast when she thought of clubs where she might meet others of her kind? In the club scenes Hall, despite the emphasis on the sadness of such places, introduced us to a younger generation of confident lesbians, such as, 'Dickie West, the much discussed woman aviator'.[76] Isolated lesbians in Britain would read the accounts of real life heroines with growing interest. One might suggest that the publication of *The Well of Loneliness* had the positive effect of making life less lonely.[77]

But if literature was a little less than sanguine, what about film images of lesbians? Very few films of the inter-war years dealt explicitly with lesbian sexuality. Leontine Sagan's, *Madchen in Uni-form* (1931) is exceptional. It deals with love rather than sex between pupil and teacher. Set in a Prussian academy for officers' daughters, the film is an indictment of Nazism, of the education of girls for motherhood and of narrow heterosexuality. In the home market version the film ends with the compulsory suicide of the pupil Manuela, but in the overseas market version Manuela is saved by the teacher and by her school friends. Lesbian women had generally to be satisfied with brief glimpses of lesbian scenes. Garbo is having an affair with her maid and kisses her passionately in an early scene in *Queen Christina* (1933). Louise Brooks danced and flirted with another woman in *Pandora's Box* (1929). Women impersonated men and introduced intriguing hints of sexual ambiguity: Katherine Hepburn was disguised as a young man in *Sylvia Scarlett* (1936) and played a pilot in full gear in *Christopher Strong* (1933), whilst Dietrich dressed in elegant drag for her stage numbers and flirted with women in her audiences in *Blonde Venus* (1932) and *Morocco* (1932). Yet such scenes were relatively very few indeed, given the huge output of Hollywood films. Women therefore identified with strong, resilient and hence perhaps 'masculine' women in films where those women played independent characters – even if their sexual involvement in the film was heterosexual. Joan Crawford, Bette Davis, Katherine Hepburn, Marlene Dietrich and Barbara Stanwick were all such women with whom other women might identify.

Finally, there were the feminist heroines, as celebrated by *The Vote* and *Woman's Leader*. This positive image was formulated and for the most part promoted by women. Behind it lay not only a desire to celebrate women's achievements but an urge to provide strong role models for younger women to emulate. There is a touching quality to the enthusiasm of editors of feminist magazines to provide detailed accounts of the lives of women who were then breaking new ground. *The Vote* enthused about 'A Woman Housing Engineer' – Mrs G. H. Wilson – who was engaged in building houses in Halifax;[78] about 'Our Women Mayors', on which it ran a lengthy series chronicling careers such as that of Councillor Miss Lucy Dales, first woman Mayor of Dunstable, whose nomination to that office was opposed by only one council member – her father;[79] about Scotland's first Woman Advocate, Miss Margaret Henderson Kidd, MA, LPD, the first woman barrister in Britain to appear at the Bar of the House of Lords.[80] *The Vote* may almost be accused of getting bogged down in its glorification of women 'firsts' – not only mayoresses but channel swimmers and athletes – but to make such an accusation would be churlish and to fail to recognise the great need for these counter images of women at a time when the image of housewife was so widely promoted by the dominant media agencies. Not only are the written accounts in *The Vote* valuable in correcting the dominant image, but the visual imagery is striking. It is very refreshing to see two healthy good-looking young women shaking hands before leading their crews in the First Oxford v Cambridge Women's Boat Race (1927)[81] and it is quite amazing to see the business-like Gloucester policewoman, one of Britain's first mobile police, astride her powerful motorbike.[82] But no image of women's emancipation caught the public imagination more than that of the aviatrix. It is no accident that the famous *Punch* cartoon of June 1928, entitled 'Free and Independent' and issued to mark the full enfranchisement of women, showed a young woman pilot in breeches striding towards her own aeroplane and declining the services of the three party leaders to act as her pilot.[83] In 1930 *The Vote* devoted its front page to the aeronautical exploits of 'Lady Bailey' DBE: World's Champion Woman Aviator. 'I wanted to go to the Cape to join my husband so I thought I would fly.' Such was Lady Bailey's explanation for her 18,000 mile flight from London to the Cape and back, for which she was awarded the Britannia Award for 1929.[84] Her flight was in fact the longest yet performed by any woman or man. In May 1930 another, much younger woman became an international celebrity and heroine. Amy Johnson from Wakefield flew from Croydon to Darwin in Australia in nineteen and a half days.

> Amy, wonderful Amy
> How can you blame me
> For loving you?

went the song of the day. Amy was not only a male fantasy figure but one of the most inspiring role models for young women in the 1930s. In 1932 the American Amelia Erhardt became the first woman to fly the Atlantic solo.

The odds were stacked against British women and girls following in the adventurous flightpath of Amy Johnson or Amelia Erhardt. The great majority of British women accepted the dominant and single desirable image held up to them and became home-based wives and mothers. Magazines and other media agencies, not to mention the more powerful state agencies, had done their job persuasively. By 1930 Winifred Holtby, horrified that a majority of women civil servants had voted to maintain the marriage bar, which meant compulsory dismissal on marriage, asked:

> Who are the girls who have voted for the marriage bar? Nine out of ten swing daily to their offices in suburban trains and

trams and buses, carrying in their suitcases a powder puff and a love-story or *Home Chat* . . . they think on foggy mornings when the alarm clock goes, that they loathe above everything the scramble to the office. They think if only they could marry and have a little home of their own all will be well.[85]

Winifred Holtby was perceptive in realising the media's influence on the aspirations of young girls. But the process of turning them into housewives started far earlier. Schools in Britain provided an education, which for working-class girls at least, was heavily weighted in favour of preparing them for their future roles as wives and mothers. The education of girls in these years is very closely linked with the back to the home theme.

2

EDUCATION

The education on offer in England and Wales in the inter-war years comes as a shock to those educated in the post-Second World War system, as set out in the 1944 Education Act, and even more so to those brought up in the era of comprehensive schools. It is as though we are looking back far more than sixty years.

The education system in England and Wales, or more accurately, the education pyramid, was clear cut. It was intended to provide for the education of all children up to the age of fourteen: the Education Act of 1918 had raised the school leaving age to fourteen (without any exemptions) and this reform came into force, unlike other innovations of the Act such as the provision of nursery schools and day release schemes for fourteen to sixteen year olds which bit the dust in the interest of economy. The inter-war education system was shot through with class differences. At the bottom of the pyramid lay the elementary schools, which provided education until a young person left school. The great majority of all children, and an even greater majority of girls, received the whole of their education in an elementary school: this meant spending the whole of their school lives in the same building with perhaps a change of floor to mark their passing to the upper level of elementary education. The 1926 Hadow report recommended the division of elementary education into primary schools for children up to the age of eleven and 'modern' schools for those between eleven and fourteen. In practice less than 30 per cent of pupils were transferred to senior schools – the term modern did not come into use. The elementary system was a state system and was free. Secondary education was fee-paying throughout the whole inter-war period and was reserved for a minority. Even state secondary schools (later to be known as grammar schools) charged fees. Only 14 per cent of all children obtained a secondary education: half of these obtained free places, having won a scholarship. This free place system was the only route to improvement open to working-class girls and boys. 'Secondary Education for All' was the cry of the Labour party and of many enlightened people but this did not come about until the passage of the 1944 Education Act. Families who could afford it educated their children, daughters as well as sons, outside the state system. There were private, fee-paying schools which offered education of widely divergent quality and there were the girls' public schools, patronised by the daughters of the wealthy, which offered an academic education, preparation for Matriculation and university entrance. Higher education was limited to even fewer girls. Training colleges offered an opportunity for further study and a professional qualification to some working-class girls who had come up through the free secondary school place route. University education, with the exception of a few indomitable working-class high fliers, was achieved mainly by girls from fee-paying independent and public schools; young women were very much in the minority in the universities, which remained largely the preserve of ex-public school boys.

Most elementary schools were grim reminders that educating the poor was a solemn business. The colossal stone edifices erected to carry out this function, following the establishment of School Boards by the Act of 1870 (England and Wales) and Scotland (1872), were architecturally akin to prisons and asylums. A great many are still in use now and they were certainly the norm in the inter-war years. Towering two and three storey buildings of red brick or grey stone, set in bleak asphalt playgrounds, hedged at the back by low level lavatory sheds and the whole encompassed by high walls and railings, formed the setting in which girls and boys spent every day of each school year. In 1932 1,500 elementary schools were still on a 'black list' of unfit buildings compiled in 1924. Rural schools, often containing just one or two rooms, were likely to be equally as bad as urban ones. Inside, schools were often ill-lit, ill-ventilated and ill-heated. Large high-ceilinged classrooms, sometimes partitioned into smaller units, were crammed with row-upon-row of heavy oak and iron desks, of the sort where two children sat on a bench attached to the main structure of the desk. The inter-war years saw stringent economies in education: the British economy in the 1920s and 1930s is discussed in chapter 3. In 1921 the 'Geddes Axe' fell. This inflicted deep cuts on the education service and class sizes were fixed at a minimum of fifty. In 1922, 28,000 classes in England and Wales contained between fifty and sixty children (often mixed ages) and 5,000 had *over* sixty in them. By 1934 there were still 6,138 classes with between fifty and sixty children but only fifty-six classes with over sixty pupils in them. In the course of the period progressive authorities tried to limit class sizes: London council schools were organised on a forty to forty-eight children in a class basis whilst *infant* classes were for the most part restricted to forty-six![1] Economies in the early 1930s led to cuts in teachers' salaries and a general shortage of money meant that in many schools children shared old and tattered textbooks, passed down from one generation of school children to another. There were some schools which enjoyed considerably better facilities. The movement of some of the population out of large cities into new housing estates (see chapter 4) meant that new schools were built. These new pleasant, light and airy schools often had special facilities like gymnasia and canteens. But the great majority of girls and boys continued to attend the Victorian fortresses in the towns and the ancient schools in the country.

The education of most working-class girls was limited to the elementary sector. Here the quality of education might vary according to factors such as whether the school was mixed or single-sex, or the methods and characters of the teachers, but there was one common element: the education given to working-class girls was designed to turn them into wives and mothers.

There was considerable variety with regard to mixed or single-sex education. Some schools were mixed with girls and boys being taught together up to the age when they left school at fourteen: other schools taught girls and boys together until the age of eleven and then segregated them in separate single-sex senior departments; yet other schools educated girls and boys separately in both primary and post-primary departments. Many schools taught the basic 3 Rs, leavened only by a smattering of religion, English, history and geography, taught in stultifying ways: children endlessly and mindlessly recited multiplication tables and learned by rote the names of the rivers of France and the names and dates of the kings and queens of England. In other schools more progressive methods prevailed and dedicated teachers used what they called 'new realistic methods'; they took pupils on nature rambles, on visits to factories, castles, museums and dockyards. Seventeen girls from the top class of an elementary school in a poor district of London saw the sea for the first time on a school trip in 1928 and five of them saw a cow for the first time in their lives.[2] By the mid 1930s some teachers were making use of radio broadcast lessons.

But above all it was the character and disposition of individual teachers which determined the quality of a schoolgirl's experience. Many women looking back on their schooldays recall very unpleasant and unkind behaviour by teachers. 'You could get some really nasty lady teachers then,' one Lancashire respondent told Elizabeth Roberts and related how a teacher had smacked her so forcefully on her knuckle that it turned blue.[3] Some teachers deliberately humiliated poor working-class girls and chastised them about the state of their clothing or their personal cleanliness. One Fulham woman spoke to me, clearly still with great bitterness, of a needlework teacher who refused to allow her to make an organdie tea-apron for her mother because her hands were dirty from laying the fire at home.[4] Other kindly and imaginative teachers transformed the school experience of girls. Winifred Foley enthused over Miss Hale's reading to the class in her village school in the Forest of Dean:

> She took us out of the classroom, over the hills and far away with *Uncle Tom's Cabin*, *Black Beauty*, *Lorna Doone*, *Treasure Island* . . . Learning new words was like having a key to free the imprisoned thought I'd been unable to express. And Miss Hale was always ready to listen.[5]

A factory girl in the early days of the Second World War remembered affectionately the lantern slides that her headmistress used to bring back from her holidays abroad and her talks about famous women.[6]

Individual schools and teachers varied too in their attitudes towards punishment. Whilst some schools were fairly benign, these were probably in a minority, and others enforced strict discipline by quite brutal means. Casual slapping of girls' legs and knuckle rapping with rulers appeared to be commonplace – but caning was a more formal process, to be done in front of the whole class by the teacher or by the head teacher in her or his study. Punishments were recorded in punishment books. In one Birmingham school the girls were variously punished in the early 1920s with either one stripe or two for 'naughty talk out of school', 'deliberate disobedience . . . ie going into the boy's playground', 'smiling after a scolding', 'using a wrong word' and 'writing in the lavatory'.[7] Ethel Manning recalled: 'I have seen a headmistress cane a child who was already hysterical.'[8] Both girls and boys were caned, though what for a boy was seen as an act of bravado was for a girl a mark of shame.

The common element which characterised the education of senior elementary school girls throughout England and Wales was the heavy emphasis placed upon the teaching of domestic subjects, in order that they might acquire the essential life skills to equip them to be competent and thrifty wives and mothers. There was nothing very new about this. The teaching of domestic subjects had expanded rapidly in the 1880s and 1890s. The Department of Education's Code of 1875 had awarded grants to schools for scholars in the higher standards who passed examinations in two subjects designated as specific subjects, and in 1878 the Code made domestic economy a *compulsory* specific subject for girls, awarding grants first for cookery and then for laundry work. The number of girls in England and Wales qualifying for the cookery grant rose from

37,597 in 457 schools in 1882–3 to 134,930 in 2,792 schools in 1895–6.[9]

The years before the First World War gave two further boosts to the teaching of domestic economy. The outbreak of the Boer War which spotlighted the deplorable physical state of many of Britain's young men – 8,000 out of 11,000 volunteers in Manchester were declared unfit – led to the establishment of the Inter-Departmental Committee on Physical Deterioration to enquire into national standards of health and fitness. The report made by the committee in 1904 laid particular emphasis, and indeed blame, on the ignorance of working-class wives in the matter of nutrition and hygiene. The Board of Education consequently appointed women inspectors in Domestic Subjects to ensure that girls were properly trained in domestic arts. The other spur came from a concern over infant welfare. Between 1910 and 1916 the Local Government Board issued regular reports on infant mortality which was a cause of considerable concern: working-class mothers were this time blamed for infant deaths.[10] Sir George Newman, as Chief Medical Officer to the Board of Education, emphasised that the remedy lay in educating schoolgirls for motherhood. The First World War, with its huge loss of life, further exacerbated the situation and brought forth renewed cries for an intensive domestic education for girls.

The Board of Education encouraged the teaching of domestic subjects throughout the inter-war period. Senior elementary schoolgirls devoted a considerable amount of their time to domestic science lessons. In London in the mid 1930s girls spent two afternoons a week undergoing cookery instruction for forty-four weeks a year in the last two years of their school life. Whereas 45,000 girls had attended cookery centres in London in 1904, by 1931, 70,000 girls attended 325 centres.[11] Dorothy Scannell's cookery lessons in London in the mid 1920s seemed basic in the extreme; the blackboard in the classroom always read, 'A nourishing meal for a poor family of six, three fresh herrings, 2lb of potatoes . . . If a pudding is needed and able to be provided then a suet pudding with black treacle'.[12]

Llewellyn Smith, who looked at London cookery centres for his *New Survey of London Life and Labour (1935)*, may have seen similar lessons as he concluded that cookery teaching was 'good and practical'.[13] However there was a widespread discontent, usually articulated by middle-class people, about the quality of cookery lessons in schools. In 1937 the Board of Education set up an inquiry 'to consider the aims of instruction in domestic subjects, and particularly cookery'. At the same time the Board issued a circular to local education authorities to improve cookery teaching facilities. It stated the reasons lying behind this as being the need to increase housewives' knowledge of good diet and the link between this and 'the national scheme for the promotion of physical fitness'.[14] Domestic 'Science', as it came increasingly to be regarded, involved more than cookery. Elementary schoolgirls attending one domestic subjects centre in South Wales laid tables, cleaned stoves, dyed blouses, cleaned felt hats, boiled collars and cuffs, cleaned brass, made beds, mended broken china and 'brought in children' to bathe and tend.[15] The increasing emphasis on child welfare in these years is seen too in the development of links between schools and welfare clinics. In 1924 *The Times* reported that twelve and fourteen year old girls in Darwen, Lancashire, were 'undertaking a new experiment for equipping girlhood for the natural duties of life': thirteen and fourteen year old girls were attending local maternity centres to pick up tips on child rearing.[16] In Penarth, South Glamorgan, senior girls spent one afternoon a week in the local infant welfare clinic.[17] Another development of the inter-war years was the provision of specially built flats in which girls practised the housewifely arts. Caston Senior Girls' School in Perivale, Middlesex, opened its model, four-roomed flat in 1939. The headmistress told a *Daily Herald* reporter,

> We aim to make the modern girl a little housewife when she leaves school. Each girl will be mistress of this little home in turn. She will make the bed, cook the meals, clean house, launder, sew and knit – in fact, act the little house-proud wife.[18]

She was being taught to be the ideal housewife of the magazines who appeared in chapter 1. Girls from Hannah Street School in Barry, South Glamorgan, accompanied by the domestic science teacher visited a new council house estate. There the clerk of works pointed out labour-saving devices, special merits of the new style semi-detached houses, and the drains.[19] In short the evidence very clearly points to the fact that senior elementary schoolgirls were being educated for marriage and motherhood. The Board of Education frequently said so quite openly. But the Board was far more cagey in linking domestic training with domestic service, but that link was perceived to exist by many people.[20] When Lady Rachel Howard and the Hon. Lady Meade Featherstonhaugh complained to the Board of Education that teachers in Sussex were discouraging girls from entering domestic service, the Board immediately undertook an investigation into the quality of domestic subject teaching in Sussex.[21] Finally many girls thought that what they learned in domestic subjects in school was a waste of time and that they learned more from their mothers. A small proportion of elementary schoolgirls in the large cities was selected to attend free central schools, where they stayed up to the age of fifteen and obtained an education geared to the labour market – in the case of girls, mainly in commerce. But the latter were in a minority.

Secondary education for girls in the 1920s and 1930s is quite a different story. Firstly it must be stressed that secondary education was reserved for a privileged minority. Being entirely fee-paying, secondary education could be bought for the daughters of the rich and the well-to-do in girls' public schools, which included such illustrious establishments as Roedean and Benenden. It could be bought too in 'maintained' schools, which received grants from local authorities, and after 1902 in the municipal and county secondary schools which were paid for by local authorities out of the rates.[22] In 1907 a system of free places in schools receiving grants from public money (ie 'maintained' and the local municipal and county schools) was introduced: it stipulated that up to 25 per cent of places should be awarded free of charge to pupils from local elementary schools who passed an examination at the age of eleven. This provided 'the ladder of opportunity' to girls and boys of the working class. The number of children of both sexes who obtained a secondary education increased greatly but even so by 1935 only 119 children per thousand in England and 223 per thousand in Wales passed into secondary education.[23] There was a great increase in the number of girls who obtained a secondary education from 185,000 in 1920 to 500,000 in 1936, but girls attending recognised secondary schools were far outnumbered by boys.[24]

Secondary education was designed to provide for the eleven to eighteen age group. The public schools for girls, like the great majority of other girls' secondary schools, were single sex. The education offered in them was however modelled on the education available to boys. This represents the victory of the Victorian women educators to achieve for girls a near-identical academic curriculum, in which the emphasis was put on hard work and intellectual achievement. In both boys' and girls' schools art subjects, as opposed to sciences, predominated, although girls' secondary schools placed rather less emphasis on the classics and tended to veer towards modern languages. In short, girls' schools provided a sound, general academic curriculum which was in every way as demanding as that followed in boys' schools. Pupils were prepared to sit and pass examinations and the syllabi and requirements of the School Certificate (taken at about sixteen years of age) and the Higher School Certificate (taken at eighteen) dominated what was taught.

In 1926 girls attending the North London Collegiate School, originally established by the pioneer educator Frances Mary Buss in

1850, were taught classics, mathematics, science, history, English, modern languages, art, music and gymnastics by teams of well-qualified graduates, many of whom had degrees from Oxford or Cambridge.[25] The school prospectus stressed that it taught mathematics rather than arithmetic, that girls should learn a second foreign language – either Latin or German (since French was begun in the junior section) – that upper fifth girls sat London Matriculation exams, that the sixth form students, then numbering forty-seven, could read for 'Higher' in science, mathematics, classics, history, English and French and that an advanced course in art was also available. There was also a course in domestic arts for girls over sixteen – the difference being that this was for the non-academic wing of the sixth form. Pupils went on from the North London Collegiate to Cambridge and to London University.

The stated aims of girls' public schools and of county secondary schools make very clear how they saw their functions. The aims of the County Secondary School, Fulham, were 'to give to girls a well-grounded and liberal education and the ideals of the great Public Schools, and prepare them for public examinations, open scholarships to the Universities, the Civil Service and home life'.[26] Benenden School, founded in 1923, aimed 'to give a broad, general education, and to make the girls realise the value of sound and thorough work'. The curriculum there was designed 'to enable girls to qualify for a career, and at the same time to stimulate in them interests which will enable them to live a full and useful life at home'.[27] There is no doubt that the emphasis in these girls' secondary schools was academic. They were not training young women to be wives and mothers and certainly not to do their *own* cooking and laundry work, though to train a girl to enjoy herself at home, or use her time usefully at home, was no bad thing given that at least some ex-pupils would never be required to earn their own living. The teaching of domestic subjects in girls' schools was compulsory but clearly not all heads and teachers were in favour of it; it appeared in secondary schools because of Board regulations.

It is quite clear that the heads and teaching staff of many girls' schools were primarily interested in providing an academic education for girls and for turning out a new generation of career women like themselves. But this was scarcely in accord with the prevailing view of the times that a woman's place was in the home, and the schools were not allowed to have it all their own way. In 1920 the Board of Education set up a consultative committee to consider whether greater differentiation was desirable in the secondary school curriculum for girls and boys. The Board was looking for a strong statement to support its own policy of favouring different curricula for girls and boys: in 1919 the Board had already stated that 'the educational requirements of boys and girls, like their capacities, are not identical'.[28] But the Board was in for a disappointment. The committee found very little difference psychologically or academically between girls and boys but they did find a difference in the function of the two genders: boys would support families and girls would run households. On the whole their findings were totally equivocal and non-committal. Even on the issue of girls growing up to be home-makers, the committee said it would be unwise to base differentiation of the curriculum on work done now by men and women since 'experience suggests that the division of work between the sexes has changed frequently in the past, and the range of employment followed by women is likely on the whole to increase'.[29] In fact it recommended that 'the prudent course would seem to be to keep open as many doors as possible from the school into the world, and to avoid any policy based on the idea that certain occupations only can be successfully undertaken by men or by women'.[30] The mixed messages emanating from this report, which had even suggested local solutions to whether the curriculum should be differentiated, did mean that they could be interpreted as all things to all people.[31]

The academic education given to girls came under threat in these years. Girls' schools were seen to be educating blue-stockings and sporting Amazons, of the sort admired by the feminist magazines discussed in chapter 1, and contact with only spinster teachers was considered vaguely worrying; the last point is ironic enough since local education authorities enforced a marriage bar on teachers, which compelled women teachers to resign on marriage. The activities of girls' secondary schools did not accord with the 'back to the home' movement of the inter-war years. There were moves to increase the amount of time spent on domestic subjects and even to make domestic science a compulsory subject in the school certificate.[32] The actual structure of this examination and the place of domestic science in it is complex but the reaction to this proposal was clearly expressed by the National Union of Women Teachers:

> A girl taking five subjects for the London Matriculation examination, as a preliminary to a professional or business career, would have to spend one fifth of her time on a subject which would have no bearing on her work, and if later she were competing with young men for a post, her certificate would have only four fifths value of those of her rivals.[33]

Such efforts to push girls' secondary schools along the domestic road of the elementary schools were scorned. Most girls' secondary schools regarded the subject as sub-academic and a waste of time.

Penny Summerfield's study of girls' secondary schools in Preston and Blackburn shows 'the relatively unimportant place which preparation for domesticity occupied in the schools' agenda'.[34] Domestic subjects were viewed as suitable only for the less able, and academic girls thought time spent in making marmalade cakes or unwearable knickers a waste of time.

Yet another potential threat to girls' schools came from a rising tide in favour of co-education. The *Report of the Consultative Committee on Differentiation of the Curriculum for Boys and Girls Respectively in Secondary Schools* had raised the issue of co-education, but among the teachers who gave evidence to that committee it was men rather than women who supported it. Co-education was identified in these years with a number of alternative schools such as Summerhill and Dartington Hall and it was viewed as liberal and progressive. It was perceived by some people as a means to quash female homosexuality (fear of which was fanned by some of the vampire imagery of anti-lesbian novels). Stella Browne, who was greatly influenced by Havelock Ellis and Edward Carpenter, was convinced that 'Much of the unhealthiness of sexual conditions at present is due to the habit of segregating the sexes in childhood and partly in later life, and making them into "alien enemies" to one another'.[35]

But the threat to the single-sex world of girls' schools was not realised in the inter-war years. The Board of Education, a body run by men educated in single-sex boys' public schools, wanted no truck with co-education and so the islands of matriarchy within a sea of patriarchy survived.

What singled out girls' secondary schools, and to a certain extent women's colleges, was that they were autonomous women's worlds. Nowhere else did women have as much power. Headmistresses ruled over all-female establishments and these were imbued with a definite ethos. This is most clearly seen in the girls' public schools, particularly boarding schools, but it echoed throughout the whole of girls' secondary education. Schools demanded loyalty to a corporate identity: one wore the uniform of the school, one worked for the school, played for the school and did not let the school down. Girls' schools borrowed the whole paraphernalia of the house and prefect system from boys' public schools but cut out its nasty excesses such as fagging. It was the world of Angela Brazil, with crushes and pashes on teachers and senior girls, Swedish gymnastics and team games – hockey, cricket and lacrosse. Kirsty, the games captain at Seaton High in Angela Brazil's, *The Luckiest Girl in the School*, embodies all that is best in the system,

Kirsty was a capital organizer. She soon recognized a girl's capacities, and she had a knack of inspiring enthusiasm even in apparent slackers. She worked thoroughly hard herself, and insisted that everybody else did the same. Her motto for the term was the athletic education of the rank and file. It was very self-sacrificing of her, for she might have gained more credit by concentrating her energies on a few, but for the ultimate good of the school it was undoubtedly far and away the best policy to pursue.[36]

Schoolgirls in secondary schools could read about girls like Kirsty and the adventures of the upper fifth in weekly story books. The *Girls' Own Paper* was the chief such magazine aimed at middle-class girls and whereas it gave serious attention to careers and careers advice it had no time for romance and marriage. A far wider network of magazines like *School Friend*, *Schoolgirls' Own* and *Girls' Crystal* aimed at elementary schoolgirls, but these were read by secondary schoolgirls too. These magazines, whilst not dealing with romance or marriage, ignored careers too. Elementary schoolgirls passed on more quickly than their secondary school peers, to the more lurid romance papers described in chapter 1.[37]

Secondary education remained the preserve of a minority in the inter-war years. Access to any form of further or higher education was even more limited. There had been a gleam of light in the 1918 Education Act which had proposed the establishment of day-continuation schools for fourteen to sixteen year olds. These schools provided a general education in English, history, geography, mathematics, art and science as well as technical education geared to the labour market: the latter followed the familiar gender differentiated lines, engineering drawing for boys and for girls needlework and housecraft. Nevertheless continuation schools did offer young people an opportunity to acquire some further education. Employers, believing they had a right to cheap juvenile labour and access to 'tiny fingers', were opposed to continuation schools and indeed these schools were one of the first victims of the economic crisis of 1922; by the end of that year only the continuation school at Rugby was left.[38] Although the issue of continuation schools was raised again in the mid 1930s as a cheaper alternative to raising the school leaving age to fifteen, nothing was done and the vast majority of girls and boys left elementary schools at fourteen. The only hope for working-class girls in this situation was to attend an evening class and acquire skills in some marketable area. Helen Forrester, whose elementary education was virtually non-existent, worked hard in her evening class and was greatly indebted to the dedication of the teachers. She recalled:

I was so behind that I needed dedicated helpers. And the teachers gave me that help. The bookkeeping teacher taught me the simple arithmetic which I have forgotten through long absence from school. The English teachers gave me essays to write, in addition to the business letters they demanded from their other pupils . . . [39]

All over the country there were Local Education Authority classes in which young women sweated over shorthand and typing in order to gain access to better paid and more respectable employment. But it took a great deal of energy and a strong sense of purpose for women to take advantage of these classes and those provided by the Workers' Educational Association. The establishment of a residential college for working women in 1919 was a radical new departure. Originally sited at Beckingham, the college moved to Surbiton in 1926 and was named Hillcroft. Founded under the auspices of the education committee of the Young Women's Christian Association and funded by donations from the sausage and ice-cream tycoon, Mr Wall, and from women's colleges and girls' schools, the college aimed to provide an education for life for working-class women who had left school at fourteen or earlier. It offered courses in history, politics and institutions, social administration, psychology, economics and literature as well as 'how to read the newspapers' and 'how to listen to music'. The college was not vocational but aimed to enrich the lives of working-class women through education. By 1939, 400 students had passed through the college; they had come from industry, from offices and domestic work.[40] One of the destinations for some of the students after leaving Hillcroft was teacher training college and these colleges, which offered the most accessible form of higher education to working-class girls, require some attention.

Teacher training in the inter-war years, for those wishing to become elementary school teachers, meant completing a two year course in college. There were many such training colleges throughout England and Wales and in 1926 they were formed into regional groups, each centering on one of the universities, which validated college courses. Frances Widdowson's work on women's elementary teacher training from the first half of the nineteenth century to the outbreak of the First World War, shows a distinct class shift in the composition of trainee teachers: elementary teaching ceased to be primarily a working-class preserve in that period and passed into the hands of girls from the lower middle class, to the daughters of small shopkeepers and clerks but not of doctors or clergymen.[41] There is much work to be done on the training of elementary school teachers in the inter-war years, and the class origin of girls going in for teaching in these years remains unclear. In some areas training college was the goal for working-class girls; reaching Glamorgan Training College in Barry was the ambition of intelligent daughters of miners from the South Wales valleys. Other colleges, especially those specialising in Physical Education, attracted girls from public schools. Bedford College drew in girls from Cheltenham Ladies' College and one student commented, as late as the 1940s, 'I don't remember anybody without the right accent doing well'.[42]

Training Colleges were run like girls' boarding schools: girls wore uniforms, played games and displayed an *esprit de corps* more usually associated with schools. An ex-student from Glamorgan College showed me a group photograph where students sat around their tutor Miss Evans and held up a placard which read 'Evans' Perkaninies'. At Bedford, under the principalship of the formidable Miss Stansfield, students regarded themselves as 'Stanny's Stues'.[43] Discipline was strict in all the colleges and authoritarian principals demanded total obedience. An ex-pupil of Edge Hill College in Lancashire had complained that they were 'sometimes treated like children, sometimes as nuns, sometimes as servant girls'.[44] A Bedford student enrolling in 1938 thought that she had gone to boarding school and lost all freedom.[45] As late as the 1950s Glamorgan College students had to be back in college by 10 p.m. at night and when I spoke to an ex-student of the college she told me that having served as a sergeant in the Second World War, she was subjected to the same discipline as a schoolgirl. Mixing with young men was frowned upon and one of the effects of a college training was to extend the schoolgirl phase of a young woman's life and leave her, compared to young women in jobs, relatively immature.

The struggle to obtain university education for women on the same terms as men had been an important part of the nineteenth-century women's rights' movement. Before the turn of the century women were admitted to read for degrees in the universities of London, Wales, Scotland, Manchester, Leeds and Liverpool. Oxford only opened its degrees to women in 1920 and Cambridge not until 1948. In fact there was still great antagonism in some quarters to women receiving a university education. Professor Gordon of Leeds University was of the opinion 'that a mistake had been made in accepting and imitating an education designed for men' and said that he would like to see universities for women only.[46] There were some real reversals too in these years. Despite the work women doctors had done in the war, many London medical schools closed their doors to women (see chapter 3). The women's colleges at Oxford and Cambridge, although demonstrating their academic distinction, faced a continual problem of poverty. Virginia Woolf, on being invited to Cambridge in 1928 to deliver the lecture later published as *A Room of One's Own*, contrasted the lavish luncheon she received at a men's college with the meagre dinner at a women's.[47] Winifred Holtby, who was acutely conscious of the poverty of women's colleges, left the royalties of her novel *South Riding* to Somerville for scholarships.[48] At Oxford and Cambridge some archaic regulations persisted but such anomalies as chaperoning were abolished. Life at Oxford offered delicious opportunities – to acquire knowledge, to make friends, to meet a peer's son. As Barbara Pym wrote, 'Oxford really is intoxicating'.[49] Provincial universities however, kept a tight rein on the young women in their charge. Students at Aberdare Hall, University College Cardiff, were never out after 11 p.m. at night, but ex-students recall with great affection their time in the hall and their academic education.[50] University education was of course the preserve of a very few. Middle-class girls, often the daughters of professional men, profited most. Only very exceptional working-class girls could, with the aid of scholarships, get to university. When a girl's or young woman's education ended, the next step for many but not all, was to enter the world of work.

3

EMPLOYMENT

The First World War had seen a massive expansion of job opportunities for women. They had worked on the railways, trams and buses, on the land, in munitions, in engineering, in banks and in offices. They had taken over jobs previously done by men and filled new vacancies created by the war. Between July 1914, just before the outbreak of war, and November 1918, the date of the Armistice, the number of women workers increased from 3,277,000 to 4,936,000.[1] This represents an increase of 1,659,000, of which no more than 150,000 could have been accounted for by normal population growth.[2] But this did not last. When the war ended women were dismissed from the workforce in large numbers. A year after the Armistice some 775,000 women had left their posts,[3] largely due to the Restoration of Pre-War Practices Act (1918) which restored jobs to men and to the cessation of demand for munitions and wartime services. By 1921 the female participation rate in the workforce was 2 per cent lower than that for 1911. Feminist hopes that the war had flung open the gates of job opportunities for women were quickly dashed, though over the whole period between the wars the number of insured women workers increased more rapidly than that of men. I shall survey statistical change in women's work later, but at this point it is necessary to examine what happened to women workers in the period immediately following the end of the First World War.

When the war ended women were dismissed from the labour force and expected to re-enter traditional women's employment or, better still, to return to the home, 'their proper place'. No longer were these women 'our gallant girls' and 'heroines': public opinion shifted rapidly and dubbed them 'pin-money girls', 'scroungers' and 'slackers'. The actual process of dismissals was swift and began well before the war ended. As early as February 1918 some 8,000 women munitions workers had been dismissed[4] and Mary Macarthur and the National Federation of Women Workers (NFWW) began 'to think that so far as women are concerned, something like demobilization had begun on a small scale'.[5] By March the *New Statesman* spoke of ten to twenty thousand sacked women munitioners.[6] Most of these women received just one week's notice and, after a fight by the NFWW, a free rail ticket home although at this stage of the war there were still openings for women in other national services and recruiting meetings were held by the WAAC and the Women's Land Army in TNT factories.[7] These sackings were just the thin end of the wedge and by November 1919 some three quarter million women war workers had been laid off.[8] In fact 1918 and 1919 are characterised by exceptionally high female unemployment. On 31 January 1919 the Ministry of Labour stated that 425,000 women in Britain were unemployed:[9] by March 1919 over half a million women were officially admitted to be unemployed.[10] Lady Rhondda, in a letter to the *Daily News* of 15 February 1919, painted an even more depressingly realistic picture:

Sir, – There are over half a million women workers at present receiving unemployment allowances, *and there are probably an additional million of industrial women at present out of employment.* In whole areas, such as the North East Coast, there is practically no employment for industrial women. A period of unemployment on the cessation of war contracts was recognised to be inevitable, but what is the government doing to find employment for this great army of efficient women workers in peace-time occupations?[11]

The answer to her question was – very little, other than to encourage women into hated domestic service.

Women did not accept being slung out of work with equanimity. A demonstration of 6,000 women munition workers mainly from Woolwich arsenal marched to the House of Commons two days before the Armistice: 'Shall Peace bring us Starvation?' read one of the banners.[12] A similar huge demonstration took place in Glasgow of women munitioners protesting at being laid off.[13] Many women tried to hang on to wartime jobs. In Cardiff women had been taken on as tram conductors in 1915; they held on until 1920 when complaints of the kind 'women are being kept on to the detriment of ex-servicemen, who are walking the streets' prevailed.[14] In Bristol in 1920 the tramways company dismissed the 'tram girls' after ex-servicemen attacked its vehicles.[15] Women clerks and typists sought with more success to hang on to their positions. During the war women had filled many new as well as existing posts in the Civil Service and they consequently looked forward to a Civil Service which gave equal opportunities to women and men: in this they were to be disappointed by government policies of favouring ex-servicemen.

When the war ended women's organisations, some trade unions, suffrage and other political groups demanded recognition of women's right to work. A conference on 'Women's Right to Work' was organised in Manchester in September 1919 by the Women's International League. It passed bold and fighting resolutions demanding that women might enter any trade or profession, equal pay for women, the raising of women's minimum wage rates, and condemning 'the wholesale and needless dismissal of women from government employment without any provision for their future welfare'.[16] It was spirited talk but any optimism entertained by delegates was misplaced in 1919.

The immediate post-war period was confusing for women. On the one hand came recognition of aims, struggled for over decades, and conceded by the authorities in recognition of services rendered in the war and out of fear of a revival of militancy once the war ended. In February 1918 the Representation of the People Act gave the parliamentary vote to women over thirty who satisfied a property requirement or who held a university degree. The limitations on the franchise were absurd but even so the Act enfranchised far more women than some of the proposals for which suffragists had fought so hard in the pre-war days. This act passed easily through parliament, in strong contrast to the stubborn and bitter hostility earlier proposals had met with. Other successes followed. In November 1918 The Eligibility of Women Act was passed, allowing women to stand as MPs. In 1919 came the Sex Discrimination (Removal) Act which, in theory at least, removed barriers to women's entry into the professions: it had the immediate effect of opening up the legal profession to women. All this was cause for elation but other signs pointed to a return to the pre-war status quo. We have seen how quickly the visual imagery of advertisers and the copy of story writers changed at the end of the war from depicting wartime working women to presenting stay-at-home housewives and mothers (see chapter 1). Feminist aspirations however were not so readily crushed and indeed the inter-war period was to see significant gains for career women, but the revived notion that women's place was in the home was clearly in evidence in the immediate post-war period. Nowhere was this more sharply demonstrated than in attitudes to unemployed women in the period following the Armistice.

Official state policy coerced women back into the home – their own or somebody else's: this may be clearly seen by examining how labour exchanges, under government directives, operated the scheme of 'out-of-work donation', to which women war workers were entitled. The press, and the public opinion it purported to represent, were outraged that women wished to hang on to factory work when what the nation needed most was wives, mothers and domestic servants. The operations of the labour exchanges and the angry ravings of the press in the period immediately following the end of the First World War were closely interrelated.

The 'out-of-work donation' scheme came into operation shortly after the Armistice and was designed as an emergency measure to support civilian workers who had lost their employment due to the cessation of hostilities. Civilian workers, especially in munitions, had been laid off many months before the scheme came into effect; previously only women in insured trades, as defined by national insurance legislation, qualified for benefit and that was a meagre 7s per week. The government dragged its heels in announcing the implementation of out-of-work donations. On 6 November, five days before the Armistice, the *Daily News* warned, 'if serious trouble is to be prevented the government must immediately announce the date at which special out-of-work pay will begin, and must undertake to reckon it from the day on which a worker was discharged'.[17]

First payments were made on 6 December 1918 and the rates were more generous than had been mooted even a few weeks earlier.[18] Such an increase was partly due to agitation by the National Federation of Women Workers. Under the scheme, women were entitled to weekly benefit of 25s for thirteen weeks. In order to qualify, unemployed workers had to attend the labour exchange daily and be available for work. The conflict came over the issue of what sort of work the women were available for. Officialdom viewed domestic service as fit work for practically any women who signed on: the women had other ideas. Over and over again in these years and later women were denied benefit for refusing posts as domestics. The shortage of domestic servants, labelled by the middle class the 'servant problem', had become acute: middle-class women, who had been prepared to put up with lack of help during the war, were no longer willing to do so. It was considered an outrage that unemployed women would be living it up on their donations whilst mistresses struggled, servantless, at home.

But it was abundantly clear that most working-class women had no intention of submitting to the 'slavery' of service. One woman who had been in munitions for two and a half years and who reported to the White City employment exchange, said, 'I feel so pleased that the war's over that I'll take any old job that comes along': but when domestic service was suggested she replied (with a laugh), 'except that'.[19] At another employment exchange only one woman out of three thousand entered her name as willing to enter service.[20] At yet another an official entered a room in which forty women were waiting for offers of work and asked, 'Who is for domestic service?'. No one replied. All forty women were immediately handed forms informing them they were not eligible for benefit.[21] The system was one of compulsory domestic service. There are many cases of women being offered domestic work at a mere pittance and, if they refused it, losing their benefit. Dorothy Jewson of the NFWW, writing in March 1919 when 650,000 women and girls were out of work, cited the case of a girl offered a live-in domestic post at 8s 6d a week for a nine and a half hour day; because the girl refused this, her benefit was stopped.[22] At Portsmouth labour exchange a woman was struck off the books for refusing work at 8s a week for a ten and a half hour day (seven days a week), and another for refusing full-time domestic work at 1s a day.[23] Even if a woman took one of these jobs and gave it up because she could not live on the money, she lost her benefit. To enter service was to enter an 'uninsured' area of work and therefore to lose further benefits. A London woman, who struggled for three weeks in a laundry at piece rates, found that she could not earn more than 12s 9d a week by working as hard as she could; when she gave it up, she was denied benefit.[24]

Women did have a right of appeal first to a local court of referees and beyond that to a government appointed umpire. The local referees, who rarely included women members, were uncompromising in their attitudes towards women who were not willing to become servants, but the umpire's decisions were more enlightened.[25] Further steps were taken to ensure that women should disappear from the donation lists and enter service: in May 1919 a second registration of unemployed women recorded women by their pre-war and not their war work, and reclassified some 17,000 women as domestics rather than industrial workers.[26]

The press was quick to attack women for even claiming their unemployment benefit when there were jobs available as domestic servants. The *Daily Chronicle* of 6 December 1918, the first day on which out-of-work-payments were made, ran an article headed, 'Unemployed in Fur Coats'. A *Chronicle* reporter went to the Acton exchange, where large numbers of women from the great shell factory at Park Royal and the camp kit and gas mask makers from Shepherds Bush had come to register, and found women in 'well made fur coats' who refused 'to consider posts as "generals" or cooks even at tempting wages'.[27] The *Daily Chronicle*, like other papers, was obsessed by the women's appearance. The next day it reported amongst the crowds at the exchange 'young girls with elaborately curled hair, wearing expensive fur coats'.[28] By 1919 the feminist magazine *The Vote* could somewhat snootily say that to be wearing a fur coat that year had attached to it the stigma of being a munitions worker.[29] The *Evening Standard*, whilst reporting with some glee a crackdown on ex-domestic servants who refused to return to service, painted what was then a familiar picture of well dressed irresponsible women living it up on out-of-work donation. Under the heading of 'Slackers with state pay' and the sub-heading 'want luxurious days to continue', it informs us,

Their wages have run up to £2 and £3 a week. Fur coats, high topped kid boots, gramophones, every night off, and Sundays in many cases free, have given them higher moral[e] and not readily, especially with weekly gifts of 25s for walking to the employment exchanges, are they going to take on the shackles of domestic work.[30]

Reports of war wages were frequently grossly exaggerated whilst the dangers of working with explosives in a shell factory were totally ignored in the post-war press. Over and over again the inference is that women did not really need the money – they were frittering it away. The Daily Telegraph, whilst asserting that the vast majority really did need the money, told of one woman who, when handed her donation of 25s, remarked, 'that will just buy a teddy bear for my baby'.[31] The Western Mail declaimed that young Welsh girls, who had left to work in areas where there were large munitions factories, had come back home to claim their donations and consequently, 'Seaside places and other holiday centres throughout the country are said to be now reaping a harvest from young women who are out for a good time on their savings as munition workers, and their donations'.[32] The press constantly accused women of being unpatriotic for not returning to their pre-war jobs, especially in domestic service; women, who had not gone out to work before the war, were expected to abandon waged work altogether.[33] The Aberdeen Free Press urged women to accept work offered by the labour exchanges rather than 'to loaf idly about the streets, receiving money which tax payers have to provide'.[34] In Wales one reader was willing to blame the probable total extinction of the nation on the lack of servants. A 'young wife' wrote to the Western Mail: 'Young wives are not going to undertake the responsibilities of motherhood when they cannot get servants on reasonable terms and conditions . . . no maid, no motherhood'.[35]

It was not only industrial workers who were dismissed in 1918 and 1919. Women civil servants too were dismissed wholesale: women who had been willing to enter such office work in the war were regarded in the post-war world as 'hussies', 'with 3 inches of powder on their noses', when they refused to do the decent thing and make room for ex-servicemen.[36]

The out-of-work donation scheme, originally timed to end in May 1919, was extended for a further six months at the reduced rate of 15s for women. In November 1919 some 90,000 women registered as available for work, only 30,000 of whom were eligible for benefit. By the end of 1920 some 103,000 women were registered but the figure means little: by this time many did not bother to register and had simply disappeared back into the home.

The employment of women has to be set in the context of the economic situation, but any study of the economy of the inter-war years comes face to face with a central paradox. That paradox is reflected in two views of those years. The popularly held view is that these were years of slump and depression, of mass, long-term unemployment and unbearable social distress; it was the world of Walter Greenwood's novel *Love on the Dole* (1933) and of newsreels of the Jarrow Marchers. This popular view is based on the grim reality of high unemployment. A brief review of unemployment statistics confirms this picture. According to the national insurance statistics, *at least* 10 per cent of the insured workforce was unemployed for the whole period between 1921 and 1938.[37] In 1931 over 21 per cent of the insured workforce (2.5 million workers) was unemployed and in 1932 over 22 per cent. But not all workers were insured – domestic servants and public employees, for example, were not. If we look at percentage rates of unemployment for *all* workers insured or not, the *percentage* falls – in 1931 to 15.5 per cent (since unemployment was highest among insured workers) – but the *number* increases to nearly 3.3 million men and women: of these 781,000 were women.[38]

The economists' view of these years is quite different. Economists point out that the inter-war years were not years of continuous depression but years of ups and downs. Immediately after the war there was a short boom lasting until the end of 1920; this was followed by a slump, but in 1924 economic growth picked up again and continued until 1929. The years 1929 to 1932 were years of severe economic depression (the Slump) but these were followed by a recovery lasting until 1937, which was in turn followed by a mild down-turn in 1938. The advent of war in 1939 changed the picture altogether. In fact, viewed as a whole, the inter-war years appear from the statistics as years of fairly good growth performance, with an economic growth rate about the same as the second half of the nineteenth century and much higher than the period 1900–1920. Other economic historians are far less cautious and would see the inter-war years as having a growth rate far ahead of that of the nineteenth century.[39] The paradox remains: this was an era of high unemployment and a time of growth. The explanation for this lies in regional differences in Britain and the emergence of 'two nations', a concept which has become familiar in the 1980s.

It is very important to stress the regional character of the Depression in Britain. The areas hardest hit were those which had a concentration of Britain's staple heavy industries: ship-building, iron and steel, coal and cotton textiles. A long-term fall in demand for the products of these industries, which were intended primarily for export, was caused by a world slump after 1929 and led to very high unemployment indeed. In South Wales, with its dependence on coal mining, unemployment in 1934 reached astronomically high proportions – 74 per cent of the male workforce at Brynmawr, 73 per cent at Dowlais and 66 per cent at Merthyr were registered as unemployed.[40] South Wales, central Scotland and northern England were devastated. In 1934 the government officially designated these areas as 'depressed' and attempted, largely in vain, to attract to them new industries.[41] Yet in other parts of Britain the economy was growing and felt the depression only slightly. The South East and the Midlands became sites for what contemporaries termed the new industries – electrical engineering, motor-manufacture, food-processing, food-canning, chemicals and synthetic fibres.[42] These new industries applied new technology and new production methods and were powered by the new power source, electricity. Many made entirely new products such as radios, refrigerators and electric cookers. These new goods were made primarily for British consumption. In Luton in 1934 unemployment was only 8 per cent and 5 per cent in Oxford and Coventry. Two Britains existed and the only hope of many in down-and-out Britain was to migrate to an area of the buoyant new Britain and they did so in their thousands: between 1921 and 1931 nearly a quarter million people left South Wales.[43]

How did the economic developments of the inter-war years affect women? The answer to this question must again depend on regional variations. The depressed areas, the areas of old heavy industry, were areas of primarily male employment where women had very low activity rates. This was true, for example, of the coalfields of South Wales and Durham: in 1935 there were only 5 females per 1,000 insured males employed in South Wales.[44] H. A. Marquand in a lengthy survey of this area stated, 'South Wales is a region where there is normally little industrial employment of female labour.'[45] The investigators who prepared the report for the Pilgrim Trust, entitled *Men Without Work* (1938), said of the problem of unemployment in the Rhondda and in South West Durham: 'Here there is no problem of the unemployment of women, but only of the effect on women of the unemployment of men'.[46] The same investigators in looking at Liverpool, where young girls worked until marriage, did nevertheless perceive that 'the brunt of this unsatisfactory state of things (i.e. unemployment) is borne by the woman who does not marry young and may be left a spinster, or who has to be the main support of her family . . . '[47] Today's historians have too often viewed unemployment as an issue which affected women only in their capacities as wives and mothers. Even in areas where there was traditionally little work for women, apart from domestic service and shop-work, unemployment also affected women – especially young women – as workers; for them the answer was migration to the more prosperous regions. The story of women's employment in those areas where the new industries were located was quite different. The new industries created new jobs for women. It was women who worked on the assembly lines, mainly as semi-skilled labour, making new appliances for sale on the home market.

The chief sources of statistical information regarding employment are the decennial census reports and the tables of insured workers compiled by the Ministry of Labour. Both have their limitations. Census figures exist for 1921 and 1931 but no census was taken in 1941 because of the Second World War. Even if there had been a census in 1941, the war itself had so dramatically altered the employment patterns of women in Britain that this missing census report would have been describing an exceptional wartime situation rather than showing a picture of change over the preceding decade. The other main fault of census reports as a source on women's work is that they simply did not register a great deal of women's casual or seasonal work. The statistical tables compiled by the Ministry of Labour and published in the *Ministry of Labour Gazette* or *The Abstract of Labour* statistics only included *insured* workers;[48] domestic servants, the largest single category of women workers, were not insured and therefore do not appear in the figures. Nevertheless even with these limitations, it is possible to draw a fairly comprehensive statistical picture of women's work in Britain between the wars. It is important not to get bogged down by a mass of statistics but simply to pose the questions one needs answered to them.

How economically active were women? i.e. what proportion of women worked and what percentage of the total labour force did they represent? Table 1 sets out the statistics.

It is important not just to show the statistical information for the inter-war years in isolation. A glance at Table 1 shows that women were marginally less economically active in 1921 than in 1911. The table shows too some growth in women's economic activity rate between 1921 and 1931. The real increase however was to come much later. It should also be noted that the figures given in Table 1 cover a whole range of regional variations: in Wales, for example, the economic activity rates for women aged over fifteen were 1911 – 27.6 per cent; 1921 – 23 per cent; 1931 – 21.52 per cent and 1951 – 24.95 per cent. These rates were so low because much of Wales was dominated by heavy industry. Table 1 shows percentage figures. In terms of numbers, the number of women over fourteen who were

Table 1 Women's contribution to the labour force 1901–71

| | Economic activity* | | |
	% of men	% of women	Women as % of total labour force
1901	83.7	31.6	29.1
1911	83.8	32.5	29.7
1921	87.1	32.3	29.5
1931	90.5	34.2	29.7
1941	-	-	-
1951	87.5	34.9	30.8
1961	86.2	37.7	32.5
1971	81.4	42.8	36.5

* Economic activity rates are for those of working age at each census as follows:
1901–11 persons aged 10 or over
1921 persons aged 12 or over
1931 persons aged 14 or over
1941–71 persons aged 15 or over

Source: C. Hakim, *Occupational Segregation*, Research Paper no. 9, table 13, London, Department of Employment, 1979, p. 25.

gainfully occupied was 5,036,727 in 1921 and 5,606,043 in 1931; the total female population over the age of fourteen for those years was 14,959,282 and 16,410,894 respectively.[49]

How old were most women who participated in the inter-war labour force? Table 2 clearly shows us that the female labour force was a young one.

Table 2 shows how dramatically the age profile of women in the labour force has changed over the century, but for the inter-war years the picture remained one of a very young workforce. In both 1921 and 1931 69 per cent of the female workforce was under 35. Linked to the question of age is that of marital status. What proportion of women workers were single, married, divorced or widowed? Table 3 sets out the information.

The long time span covered by Table 3 again enables us to see a dramatic change in the marital status of employed women. In the inter-war years the typical woman worker was not only young, but she was single. The high proportion of single women in the workforce tells us two things. Firstly many women (but not all) gave up

Table 2   Age structure of female labour force 1901–71

| | Percentage of working women aged | | | Total number of working women (millions) |
	Under 35	35–59	60 and over	
1901*	73	22	5	4.2
1911*	71	24	5	4.8
1921	69	26	5	5.0
1931	69	26	5	5.6
1951	52	43	5	6.3
1961	45	49	6	7.0
1971	40	52	8	8.3

* Figures for 1901 and 1911 estimated from data for the 55–64 and 65+ age groups.
Source: C. Hakim, *Occupational Segregation*, Research Paper no. 9, table 6, London, Department of Employment, 1979, p. 10.

Table 3   Composition of female labour force by marital status 1901–71

| | Percentage of working women who are | | | Total % |
	Single	Married	Divorced or widowed	
1901	78	13*	9*	100
1911	77	14	9	100
1921	78	14	8	100
1931	77	16	7	100
1951	52	40	8	100
1961	40	52	8	100
1971	28	64	8	100

* Estimates based on data for ever-married women. Source: Census reports for England and Wales 1901–1971.

Source: C. Hakim, *Occupational Segregation*, Research Paper no. 9, table 7, London, Department of Employment, 1979, p. 11.

work on marriage and secondly in the inter-war years a high proportion of women remained single: in the age group 15–59, 40 per cent of women were single in 1931, compared to 23 per cent in 1971.[50] However the participation rate of young married women in the workforce increased in the inter-war years and caused comment by contemporaries.[51] Between 1921 and 1931 there was a 5 per cent increase in the number of married women under twenty-four in paid employment.[52] It is not possible to account for this by any single factor, but high male unemployment in depressed areas may have spurred young married women into taking any job they could find and new opportunities for young married women in the more prosperous regions may also go some way to account for this. The decline in the participation of widows in the workforce may be explained by the introduction of widows' pensions in 1925.

Finally, what work did women do? Table 4 shows the occupational distribution of women from 1901 to 1951. It is again necessary to examine a fairly wide time span so that women's patterns of

Table 4   Occupational distribution of women, percentages in major occupational groups, England and Wales, 1901–51

	1901	1911	1921	1931	1941	1951
Personal service	42	39	33	35	-	23
Indoor domestic	33	27	23	24	-	11
Other	9	12	10	11	-	12
Clerks, typists etc.	1	2	8	10	-	20
Commerce and finance	7	9	10	11	-	12
Professional and technical	7	8	7	7	-	8
Textile goods and dress	16	14	11	9	-	7
Textile workers	14	13	12	10	-	6
Metal manuf. and Engineering	1	2	3	2	-	3
Storekeepers, Packers etc.	-	-	2	3	-	3
Transport etc.	-	-	2	3	-	3
Paper, printing	2	2	2	2	-	1
Food, drink, tobacco	1	1	2	1	-	1
Leather, fur	-	-	3	1	-	1
Agriculture	1	2	2	1	-	1
Unskilled/unspecified	-	-	1	3	-	6

Source: E. James, 'Women and Work in Twentieth Century Britain', Manchester School of Economics and Social Science, XXX, Sept. 1962, figure 2, p. 291.

employment in the 1920s and 1930s may be seen in relation to earlier patterns and later change.

From Table 4 we see that women were in fact in three main occupational groups. Personal service was the largest single group, containing as it did domestic servants as well as, for example, waitresses. Between 1921 and 1931 this area, greatly encouraged by government policy, actually grew but was to fall into sharp decline after the Second World War. The second largest group of women workers was employed in textiles and the clothing industry: both the numbers of women in textile production and in clothing-making had fallen from the pre-First World War figures, falling further in the inter-war period and continuing to do so after the Second World War. The third group to note is clerks and typists, taken together with commerce and finance: the inter-war years built on the gains of the first decade of the century and women increasingly entered some form of office work.

There were important factors which hindered women's participation in the workforce. There was much talk in this period of women 'taking men's jobs'; this was particularly strident during the Great Slump of the early 1930s. This antipathy to women workers found reinforcement in certain state and local authority policies, which attempted to ensure that women's place was in the home. Protective legislation squeezed women out of some occupations which they had done successfully during the war. New protective legislation of the 1920s, consolidating some older legislation and introducing some new forms of protection for women and young persons, fixed hours of work at forty-eight hours per week, prohibited Sunday work and night work and excluded women from certain dangerous trades, for example, using lead paint and lifting heavy weights.[53] There were arguments for and against this legislation put forward by women. On the debit side it was argued that women were disadvantaged in favour of male employees by fixed hours; the night work clause hindered women from being telephonists and electrical engineers, and the lead paint clause prevented women from becoming house painters. The inconsistency of such legislation, which protected industrial women, is easily seen when one notes that there was no prohibition against domestic servants, clerical or shop workers working at night or against nurses lifting heavy weights. Trade unions too excluded women from certain processes and jobs in, for example, printing, the boot and shoe trade and on the railways. Labour exchanges had since the end of the war tried very successfully to push women into domestic service, the only really apposite work for women. In 1931 the Conservative government cut unemployment benefit to married women by imposing the Anomalies legislation, already passed by a Labour government. The new rule stipulated that unless a married woman had paid a certain number of contributions *since* marriage, she was not entitled to benefit. This totally disregarded contributions she had paid when single. This had the effect of disqualifying very many married women from benefit. Marriage bars cut short the careers of other women; this was true of civil servants, teachers, doctors and nurses.

Domestic service was the largest single source of employment for working-class women. It had been in the nineteenth century and remained so in the inter-war years. In 1911, 39 per cent of working women were in service; in 1921 service still accounted for 33 per cent of all working women and by 1931 that figure had risen to 35 per cent. Yet viewed from the perspective of the middle-class employer 'the servant problem' was one of the great issues of the 1920s and 1930s: 'Throughout the country distraught and injured mistresses are giving free expression to their feelings with regard to the servant class in general, a class that has suddenly dwindled to astonishingly small numbers and has begun to demand unheard-of conditions', observed one writer in the *Woman's Leader*.[54] One problem was getting servants; another was keeping them. We have seen how Laura, in E. M. Delafield's *The Diary of a Provincial Lady*, lived in dread of losing her cook or her house parlourmaid. Middle-class women felt tyrannised by the new more confident type of servant who emerged after the First World War:

> There is no freedom with unwilling service, ill performed, higher wages demanded than can be paid, principles of cleanliness and orderliness violated, appearances having to be kept up and rigid rules adhered to for fear 'the girl will give notice'. It is tyranny,

observed one middle-class writer.[55]

The conditions prevailing in service go a long way to account for the unpopularity of the job. Wages were wretched. Although newspaper advertisements for parlourmaids and cooks in larger households offered wages ranging in the mid 1930s from £50 to £65 a year, in reality many people paid their maids between 12s 6d to 15s a week.[56] Hours were very long: fourteen hour days were not uncommon. Time off was very limited: one half day per week and alternative Sundays was still quite usual for a general household help. Jean Beauchamp quotes a typical case of a resident maid in the mid nineteen thirties:

> D. does all the work of a small house, including the washing and ironing. She works from 6.30 a.m. till after 9 p.m. with

one half-day off a week and alternative Sunday afternoons.
She sleeps in a tiny bedroom which is very hot in summer
and bitterly cold in winter. Her wages are 14s a week, and
her food is weighed out for her in niggardly portions by her
employer.[57]

Ex-servants I have spoken to, say that to be in the house was to
be on duty. The workloads were very onerous. One young Welsh
woman, who took a domestic job in a nursing home in Bristol
where there were seventeen people to be waited upon and only two
domestic workers (including herself) said of her workload,

> I had to get up at 6.30 a.m. and clean the grates and lay the
> fires, take early morning tea, help cook prepare breakfasts,
> scrub the steps and all these kinds of jobs had to be done
> before breakfast and then your cleaning came after breakfast.[58]

The actual experiences of women interviewed are always difficult
to tally with complaints by employers of the tyranny of their servants. The experience of being in service varied from household to
household. On the whole, wages were higher and conditions were
better in larger households which employed, if not a retinue, then
a number of servants. Most servants however worked in one-servant
households run by shop-keepers or small businessmen. But regardless of the size or type of household, domestic servants resented the
absolute control of their employers, the deference exacted by them
and the de-personalising nature of their experience. Servants with
'fancy' names would be renamed by their employers as plain Mary.
Margaret Powell (née Langley), who has written extensively of her
life 'below stairs', recalled how she handed a letter to her employer
– the grand lady of a large house in Hove – with her bare hands.
She was told, 'Langley, never, never never on any occasion ever
hand anything to me in your bare hands, always use a silver salver.'[59]
The inhumanity and insensitivity of this remark made her cry and
she wanted to give up the job on the spot; but, of course, she could
not. One Rhondda woman recounted her experience as a domestic
in London, where she was starved on the grounds that the daughter
of the house was dieting:

> I was starved to death there. She (the employer) locked every-
> thing up and gave me three lumps of sugar for one day and a
> small pat of margarine . . . and for my dinner every day I had
> half a bag of potato crisps for three weeks and yet I was
> cooking for them but being what-do-you-call, being slow, I
> suppose in those days I wouldn't think of taking anything.

That's one thing that was always drummed into us; don't you ever take anything that doesn't belong to you. She said her daughter was dieting and she wouldn't diet if I ate.[60]

It was small wonder that women would take any job *except* domestic service. Two parliamentary investigations and reports – 1919 and 1923 – sought to solve the servant problem. Both the *Report of the Women's Advisory Committee* on the domestic service problem (1919) and the *Report to the Minister of Labour of the Committee Appointed to Enquire into the Present Conditions as to the Supply of Female Domestic Servants* (1923) recommended better training conditions, and higher status for servants, but neither was implemented. The government sought to direct unemployed women into service through insurance legislation and the operations of labour exchanges. Any training for unemployed women was almost exclusively domestic. The Central Committee for Women's Employment (CCWE), set up in the First World War, was granted half a million pounds in 1920 to train women in such varied fields as journalism, horticulture, hairdressing and domestic service, but as Jane Lewis notes, by 1921 the committee's grant was tied exclusively to domestic training.[61] Throughout the 1920s the Central Committee and the Ministry of Labour were in conflict about the type of courses on offer, but the financial upper hand of the Ministry dictated that whatever body organised the courses those courses would be in domestic service.[62] 'Homecraft courses' were introduced in 1921: they ran usually for thirteen weeks in residential centres and women entering them had to give a written undertaking to enter service. The CCWE even put on Home-maker courses, which were not intended to produce servants but to keep up the morale of unemployed women and make them better housewives. The Ministry of Labour would only fund courses to increase the supply of servants; between 1924 and 1939 it funded Home Training Centres organised by the CCWE. Yet another way in which women were 'helped' into domestic service was through the 'Outfit Scheme', to enable women to make or purchase a uniform for service.

The depressed areas were particularly targeted as being supplies of cheap domestic labour. The Industrial Transference Board (1928) was established to retrain labour and assist with movement to other areas. Domestic service training centres were set up particularly in these areas. In 1931, for example, non-residential courses were on offer in South Wales at Aberdare, Cardiff, Hengoed, Maesteg, Merthyr Tydfil, Neath, Pontypool, Pontypridd, Swansea and Ystrad; in Scotland in Glasgow, Aberdeen, Arbroath, Greenock, Cowdenbeath, Alexandria, Leven, Clydebank and Hamilton, and in the North East in Annfield Plain, Bishop Auckland, Blaydon,

Blyth, Durham, Gateshead, Huddersfield, Jarrow, Leeds, Newcastle, Sheffield, South Shields, Stockton, Sunderland, Rotherham and Middlesborough.[63] Young Welsh girls trained at Ystrad, Rhondda were placed in houses and hospitals not only in Cardiff and Bristol but Islington, Leyton, Hendon, Basingstoke and Brighton: in 1929 some of them were paid 7s a week.[64]

Young girls from the depressed areas faced loneliness and isolation in London and the large English cities. They also, as the National Vigilance Association records show, faced moral dangers. These records make harrowing reading and reveal how misleading job advertisements turned out to be when the girl arrived. One girl from South Wales arrived at a bachelor's home in the Midlands to find only a see-through partition separating her 'bedroom' from his and a nude photograph on her side of the partition.[65] NVA station workers frequently had to rescue young girls from exploitative households and send them home by train, care of the guard. Desperate times led many very young girls to seek jobs in London in order to send money home: of sixty-odd Welsh domestic servants interviewed by Anne Jones in a recent research project all of them sent money home. Still the advertisements for CCWE courses asked, 'Are you Unemployed?' and answered 'Domestic work is a skilled occupation and offers steady employment, good wages and living conditions'. Testimonials reinforced the message: 'I have never once regretted leaving work in the chemical factory to take service', said one, and 'it is by far the best and happiest situation a girl can take', said another.[66]

Of the old industries, textiles employed by far the largest number of women. In 1931, 812,807 women were occupied in the manufacture of textiles in Great Britain. This figure includes women cotton workers in Lancashire, silk workers in Cheshire, jute workers in Scotland and linen workers in Northern Ireland and represents 34.5 per cent of women in paid work.[67] Textiles, like other old, staple British industries, was hard-hit by the economic depressions of the 1920s and 1930s. The cotton industry, which had been the top exporting industry of the nineteenth century, had thrived in the post-war boom of 1919–20 and then slumped dramatically in the early 1920s; it was never to recover. The loss of cotton's overseas markets and competition from rayon, the new man-made fibre, meant a serious contraction in the industry and with it job losses. By 1930 only 54 per cent of the industry's looms were in use and Lancashire's unemployment rate, male and female, was 45 per cent compared to 17 per cent nationally.[68] Of the 812,807 women registered as cotton workers in the 1931 census, cited above, 156,669 were unemployed.[69]

In the weaving section of the cotton textile industry women

enjoyed a greater degree of equality with men than in other industries. Weaving had long been accepted as women's work. It was
skilled work and male and female weavers received a common piece-
rate; trade unions were open to both men and women. Yet despite
this apparent equality, male weavers earned more than women weavers. In 1924 an inquiry showed women earning on average 28s 3d
and men 47s 0d; in 1931 a second inquiry showed women's average
earnings as 27s 3d and men's as 45s 3d.[70] The differential in wage
rates can be explained both by women working fewer looms than
men and by fewer women working as overseers. Men generally
worked two looms more than women. In hard times, when orders
were short, employers put the workers on fewer looms – two or
three instead of four or six; but even working a reduced number of
looms the weavers still had to work a forty-eight hour week. Jean
Beauchamp, whose study of women workers was published in 1937,
tells of the effect of cutting the number of looms worked on individual women weavers' wages. The wages of Mrs X, who had been
earning 29s–36s a week, dropped to 19s 3d and 17s 9d in certain
weeks.[71] She noted that even though wages fell, stoppages remained
the same – 1s 3d insurance, 2d to the local infirmary and 3d per
loom for cleaning. Bad material meant even further losses in income:

> There's many a time when we play for warps, standing at two
> looms all week for half the wage; then it may be bad twist
> and you're bending all day long taking ends up and yet earning
> nothing, for when your loom is stopped so is your money.[72]

Reduced wages were bad enough, but in 1932 employers sought to
increase the number of looms worked which would have led to
greatly increased pressure on those in work, and large-scale unemployment. This ploy resulted in the first major cotton strike of the
century.[73]

The cotton industry employed a large proportion of married
women. In 1931, 41.13 per cent of all female weavers were married.[74] It had been common in the nineteenth century for pregnant
women to work at their looms right up till their confinement; in the
inter-war years women ceased work earlier. On confinement women
lost their work and had to take their chance that work was available
when they were ready to go back. Children were looked after by
relatives or friends but such services had often to be paid for.
Elizabeth Roberts' investigation into women's lives in Preston shows
the pattern of married women's working lives in the early twentieth
century: 'Oral evidence,' she writes, 'certainly reinforces this picture
of a mother working to support her children when dependent and
then "retiring" from full time work as they started earning and

contributing their wages to the family budget'.[75] But Roberts also points out that family size influenced the woman's working career. Usually women gave up working before the birth of a fourth child – childcare was expensive.[76] In the inter-war years unemployed husbands provided another source of childcare. In Macclesfield, where many married women worked in the silk mills, the local newspaper, *The Courier*, ran an article on an unemployed man who stayed home to mind the baby and do the housework and another, entitled 'Busy Women – Idle Men', showed women going off to the mill and men staying at home with the children.[77] Macclesfield was unusual in having a council day nursery but the cost of 7s per child a week was heavy.[78] Housework might be cut down by buying-in dinners and bread and sending out the laundry but the cleaning and bedmaking remained. According to Beauchamp such chores were shared by the family, but she found no instances of textile workers employing charwomen to clean their homes.[79]

Factory work, even amidst the clattering of looms, provided an opportunity for sociability and solidarity. They are qualities which emanate from contemporary photographs of mill workers and which distinguish factory work from the isolation of domestic service. Girls and women talked to each other about what was going on locally, about cinemas, about boy friends and about games of rounders. A member of the mass observation team of social observers, who took a mill job, reported that they did not talk about politics.[80] There were 'footings' – departmental feasts to mark special occasions like the Jubilee, the Coronation, Christmas or a wedding. Nor did factory girls look particularly scruffy going to and from work. George Orwell on his epic of discovery into darkest England noted that the 'first sound in the mornings was the clumping of the mill-girls' clogs down the cobbled street'.[81] The mass observer noted only two women wearing clogs. Most women wore outdoor shoes to work and changed into old shoes in the factory. They wore their overalls ('pinnies') to work but these were covered by quite smart rain coats.

Women worked in other old industries too, usually in gender-segregated jobs. Many of these industries were introducing new technological techniques and machinery but they were still subject to the economic depressions of these years. Amongst the industries where women were to be found in large numbers were clothing, boot and shoe manufacture and the potteries. But women worked too in the 'new industries' of the period, in the highly mechanised factories of the South and Midlands, producing new consumer goods for the home market. These industries, more than the old, set the pattern for the future of women's work.

The booming new industries of the thirties either made entirely new products, such as radios, refrigerators and electric lamps, or they applied mechanised production methods to existing products, for example, ready-made clothing and processed food. The new factories utilised electricity as their power source and consequently did not have to be located near coalfields. They produced goods for the home market and therefore did not have to be near ports. Most were located in the Midlands and South East within easy reach of London, which was the chief market. Such factories were often built on new-style trading estates and on the edge of towns and cities – such as General Electric and Austin Motors on the outskirts of Birmingham.

Employers, and these were primarily a handful of very large firms, preferred cheap women workers. It is difficult to establish accurate numbers of women employed in the new industries. Miriam Glucksmann, who has conducted detailed research into the employment of women in the new industries, put the figure at between one half to three quarter million in the 1930s. This was out of a total five and a half to six million women workers.[82] The numbers employed were relatively small but the important point is that this represented a rapidly expanding area of female employment. In electrical engineering female employment increased by 123 per cent between 1921 and 1931 – the greatest increase being in the London area.[83] In this industry women's employment grew much faster than that of men and the proportion of women to men also increased. In the Greater London area the numbers of women employed in electrical cables, wire and electrical lamps rose from 13,950 in 1923 to 22,910 in 1930 (or 64.2 per cent over seven years); male employment in the same industry also increased but much more slowly from 24,790 in 1923 to 29,110 in 1930.[84] The obvious reason for this state of affairs was that women were cheap and nimble-fingered; they were located in the semi-skilled area of the workforce, whereas adult men, for the most part, did skilled and more highly paid jobs. In the engineering industry as a whole the proportion of skilled workers fell, whilst that of semi-skilled rose.

The female labour force in the new industries was very young. Using the example of electrical engineering, it is possible to see just how young. Of some 50,000 women employed in 1931, 35,500 were under 24; of these 11,500 were under 17.[85] Contemporary observers were quick to point out the non-progressive nature of these jobs. They could in no way be regarded as training for better jobs; as John Gollan noted, 'Young labour has become the basis of the industry and the practice of sacking at eighteen when higher rates of wages require to be paid, with the taking on of a new younger and cheaper set of youth labour, is widespread.'[86]

The wage differentials in an electric lamp factory in 1937 were

15s per week for girls leaving school, 27s 6d at eighteen and 30s over twenty-one.[87] There are no precise figures for the percentage of married women in the new industries. The workforce was predominantly single, given its youth, but increasingly married women chose to stay on at work. Many of the girls employed in these factories were local but there were also many young girls from the depressed areas.

Women were engaged in thousands of repetitive tasks – wiring up radios, fixing collar studs onto shirts, cutting out chocolate shapes like almond whirls and marzipan squares, sewing the leather bucket seats of cars, fixing pockets onto the inside of car doors, spreading the cream in sandwich biscuits, filling tubes with toothpaste, and canning meat and fish. These industries employed the new technology of the conveyor belt. Sometimes these conveyor belts were immensely long. At Philip's Mitcham works forty-five women sat along a conveyor belt nearly half a mile long assembling radios. Each operative had forty-five solder joints to do.[88] The striking thing about this kind of work was the speed of the operation and the stress that it induced in the workers. Jean Beauchamp pointed this out:

In a big chocolate factory in Birmingham piecework has been abolished and the girls have been set to work on a conveyor. They now pack, on the conveyor, 60 to 63 dozen boxes of chocolates in the time in which they formerly packed 25 to 30 dozen.[89]

The clothing industry introduced conveyor belts too. The following is a contemporary account of the operation of a conveyor belt in a factory which made school and sports clothes:

In trouser-making there were nineteen girls on a belt. Eighteen are seated 'staggered', nine each side of a moving belt marked off in sections, each with the appropriate machine. One girl stands at the end 'fixing' the trousers which she has to put one at a time on to each section of belt. Each of the other girls picks the trousers off the belt as it passes, performs her operation and puts them back on the next section. The belt is moving at such a speed that each section takes exactly a minute and a half to pass the girl. In that minute and a half the garment has to be picked up, the operation finished and the garment put back. By this means each girl does the operation forty times an hour, forty trousers are completed for pressing and finishing and a total of nearly 2,000 garments a week is handled by nineteen girls.[90]

The introduction of conveyor belts into a factory meant the end of piecework rates. It also involved a considerable loss of earnings for the workers. The trouser makers, who would have formerly been paid piecework rates of £4, were paid 32s 6d.[91] A fall in the wage packet was a source of great anxiety to these women, but even after all these years what women most remember was the strain of conveyor belt work. One woman in a shirt factory recalled,

> At the end of each hour they would turn off the machines for five minutes for anyone to go to the toilet, so in that five minutes you'd have to hurry up and try to catch up with your work because you're putting everyone else out.[92]

Another woman who assembled radios said, 'if you wanted to go and wash your hands there were girls who had to take your place so that the line could keep moving'.[93] Other factories made no provision for workers leaving the belt to go to the lavatory; there were only short breaks morning and afternoon. The conveyor belt was stress-inducing in itself but the introduction of the American Bedaux system – a system based on time and motion studies, which fixed the time and rate for each job, was even more so. The rate-fixer expected workers who would do one operation in a few seconds to keep this up for hundreds of operations. In 1932 Lucas factories introduced the system but the terrific speeding up led to many girls collapsing from the strain.[94] Women workers at Lucas went on strike against the Bedaux system but the management reintroduced it under another name – the Point System – and promised higher wages. As one woman worker there said, 'we paid for this in loss of fingers, loss of health – we just couldn't cope with it – lots of us had to go to hospital or lose time by staying home. I was absolutely dead beat at the end of the day.'[95] A co-worker at Lucas said, 'Our fellows say they don't know what's the matter with us. Mine said he might as well have a wooden woman. We're that tired by the end of the evening we are fit for nothing.'[96] The strike at Lucas was unusual. Such 'new industries' were generally worked by a non-unionised workforce; at Lucas only two to three hundred women out of 12,000 were union members.

Shop work, or retailing, was another growth area. Women had taken over many male jobs in shops during the First World War and the number of female employees in shops continued to increase in the inter-war years. The number of female shop assistants in 1921 was some 346,000 but by 1931 it was over 394,000.[97] Shop workers were mainly single – a sort of marriage bar operated. Of the 394,000 female shop assistants in 1931, 91 per cent were single.[98]

Shop work enjoyed a higher status than domestic service or factory work. As Mrs R. G., a former Hull shop assistant put it,

> If you were a shop assistant, you never wanted to be a factory girl. We used to look down our noses at them although they got more money . . . If you had a job in an ordinary shop and you got taken on in a department store you felt yourself lifted up a little bit.[99]

Mrs R. G.'s comment differentiates between the types of shop in which women worked, and a social hierarchy of shop workers did exist. Department stores, which carried on the resplendent tradition of their Victorian and Edwardian origins, headed the league, followed by chain stores, renamed 'multiples', a term which in the inter-war years extended from grocery stores to include shoes, furniture and cheap ready-made clothing; drapers' shops and private grocery stores came next and at the very bottom was the corner shop. Restaurants and tea shops should also be included in this section: the latter may have had an air of gentility but, in fact, waitresses were amongst the worst paid and most exploited of women workers.

Shop work, no matter what the type of shop, was characterised by long hours. Shop owners were happy to see the shop stay open late at night; even large stores would stay open until after 9 p.m. Marjorie Gardiner worked in a classy Brighton millinery shop, which opened from 9 a.m. to 7 p.m. Monday to Wednesday, closed at 1 p.m. on Thursday (for the statutory half day), stayed open 9 a.m. to 8 p.m. on Fridays and 9 a.m. to 9 p.m. on Saturdays. As she said, the shop assistants had to be in for 8.30 a.m. every day, and apart from the legally compulsory half-day closing the shop stayed open as long as there were still customers there.[100] She was working at least a sixty hour week. The co-operative stores alone seemed to operate a forty-eight hour week in the 1930s. An investigation of 1931 reported that the normal hours worked in the retail trade were fifty-six hours in boot and shoe shops, seventy-five hours in bakers' shops, and seventy hours in newsvendors.[101] Corner shops were the worst culprits. The following case was cited to the 1931 committee:

> A young woman who worked in an icecream and confectionery shop in South Shields, where the hours were 70 a week, exclusive of meals, was very rarely able to leave the shop until 12 midnight and spoke of the dark and lonely walk home when the tram service had ceased.[102]

The Shop Act of 1934, which did not in fact come into force until 1937, cut shop hours for juvenile shop assistants (those under eighteen) to forty-eight hours per week, *exclusive* of meal breaks; it also allowed fifty hours per year (in practice unpaid) overtime. Only the Second World War, with the need to conserve energy and to black out, brought about closing of shops at teatime.

Wages varied according to the type of store but women consistently earned less than men. The following figures date from 1924 and in fact represent average wages for women and men in grocery, drapery, catering and butchers' shops. At eighteen both females and males earned an average 18s per week; at eighteen to twenty years old the earnings were 25s for women and 29s 6d for men; over twenty-one years old – women 34s and men 62s 6d.[103] For the most part women and men in shops did the same work but women were paid far less. In Lewis' stores in 1937 adult male assistants earned 52s 6d while women earned 37s 6d for a newly negotiated forty-eight hour week (exclusive of meal breaks).[104] The Shop Assistants Union regarded the Lewis' agreement as a triumph but in shops all over the country wages were far, far below this. The following list was collected by the union in 1935:

Town	Position	Age	Weekly Wage s. d.
Sheffield	Assistant, grocery	19	12 6
Belper	Assistant, grocery	25	25 0
Pontefract	Manageress, confectionery	22	18 0
Leeds	Assistant, confectionery	38	25 0
Boston	Assistant, drapery	18	14 0
Newport (Mon)	Assistant, drapery	19	7 6
Sth. Shields	Manageress, boot & shoe	21	9 0
Sth. Shields	Assistant, boot & shoe	18	7 0[105]

Other conditions of work and the working environment varied from shop to shop and ranged from the opulently carpeted and decorated London department stores to the seedy corner shops. But even apparently chic shops treated their employees very harshly. In the Brighton milliner's where Marjorie Gardiner worked, the assistants froze because the doors were always open and they were forbidden to warm their hands on the shop's one tiny radiator; nor were tea or coffee breaks allowed.[106] The sole advantage given by law to female shop assistants, as compared to male, was the provision of chairs, but in practice these were rarely used. Shop assistants suffered from flat feet, varicose veins, anaemia, menstrual troubles and frequently uterine displacements as the result of long hours of standing. Shop assistants lived in dread of managers, floor walkers and store owners. Supervision was very strict. One girl interviewed by Jean Beauchamp worked in a 6d store, where the assistants were forbidden to wear dresses with pockets.[107] These women enjoyed no job security; dismissal was swift and often on the flimsiest of grounds.

Even so, the inter-war years witnessed some distinct improvements over the pre-war period – largely thanks to the union. The living-in system, whereby girls lived above the shop, survived in a few large department stores but it was on a much smaller scale than before the war. The system of imposing fines on assistants for 'failing to call a customer madam' or 'not using paper and string with economy' was a thing of the past but nevertheless strict discipline remained.[108] The union did manage to achieve national wage agreements for workers in certain multiples, but not until the late 1930s. It must also be noted that many employers strongly discouraged union membership and to have joined would have been more than a girl's job was worth.

Finally the plight of waitresses and kitchen workers deserves attention. There seems to have been little difference in the degree of exploitation between genteel copper-kettle-type establishments, Lyon's Corner Houses and transport cafés. George Orwell drew from life when he portrayed Julia in *Keep the Aspidistra Flying* (1936). Julia worked seventy-two hours a week for 25s a week in 'a nasty, ladylike little tea shop' near Earl's Court underground station.[109] In the same period a waitress working in one of London's biggest tea shop firms earned 19s 4d per week plus commission (tips) of 5s 6d:[110] waitresses had to give the first £10 of tips to the company! One London woman, interviewed by Miriam Glucksmann, went to work in Lyon's Corner House as a waitress. The management stressed that she should not talk about the firm because so many girls, coming from Ireland and the north, were committing suicide because they could not live on the money.[111] Kitchen work was if anything even harder. A kitchen hand in a multiple tea shop, working a ten hour day, earned 17s 6d a week plus dinner and a cup of tea. Her take home pay was 14s 6d. She said of her job: 'Cruel work – scrubbing, washing up, scrubbing. I fall asleep in the bus going home each night'.[112]

Office work was yet another area of expansion of women's employment. As far back as the 1870s the dominant trend was feminisation, and the First World War accelerated the shift of clerical work from the sphere of men's work to that of women's work. Shorthand writing, typing and comptometer operating were regarded in the inter-war years as apt work for women. Theresa Davy, in her study of London shorthand typists, quoted one respondent who retained her job as a railway clerk after the war, because 'the men came back and saw girls doing their jobs, so they weren't going to do typing, it was a "sissy" job for them'.[113] The statistical evidence confirms their attitude: women clerks and typists formed 1 per cent of the female workforce in 1901, 2 per cent in 1911, 8 per cent in 1921 and 10 per cent in 1931.[114] But the process of feminisation should not be over-emphasised. Clerical work includes such jobs as accounts clerks and office managers and these remained mainly male jobs. The Civil Service too called an abrupt halt to the feminisation process. Nevertheless, women made substantial inroads into office work and by 1931 women formed 43 per cent of private and public clerical labour in London.[115] However women office workers were not the independent career women as shown in Hollywood movies but wage earners, whose wages scarcely enabled them to aspire to a decent life style.

Office work was seen as respectable work both by the girls entering it and by their mothers. Some offices demanded a 'good education' at secondary level or training in a private commercial college. There seems to be some confusion about which social classes clerks came from. Some writers say that nineteenth-century female clerks were educated middle-class women whilst others point out that most female clerks before the First World War were employed in the lowest commercial sector and were therefore working-class. In the inter-war years it would appear that some middle-class women were employed in, for example, government offices; there were, however, far more female office workers from the lower middle class, the daughters of shop-keepers, teachers or office workers. But the trend of the 1920s and 1930s was for the entry straight from school of large numbers of upper working-class girls into offices.

All this confusion stems from the wide range of work encompassed by the term 'office work'; it ranges from the personal secretary to the managing director of a large company to the girl clerk in a shop or local builder's merchants. Frances Donaldson's account of her office experiences in one of 'the biggest manufacturing firms in England' shows the class range of employees.[116] She herself was upper middle-class, if not downright upper-class, and bluffed her way through on literary merit and the ability to précis (as a substitute for shorthand) as personal secretary to the managing director. Working in this office brought her into close contact with working-class girls. She was struck by their poor wages, poor diet and poor clothes. On one occasion Frances Donaldson was asked by the management, who were offended by the smell of the typists in the pool on hot days, to educate the girls in hygiene. She replied that not to smell is an expensive thing:

One needs to own more than one dress, which, too thin in the winter, is too thick in the summer, and also many sets of under clothes, so that these can be frequently changed. Hot water and plenty of soap are also essential and not easily obtained in working-class houses.[117]

She added too that a few windows in the office would be better than electric fans. The management took no notice of her and the girls continued to earn wages that would not run to many changes of clothes. The typists in this office in the 1930s earned 25s per week. Helen Forrester, who came from a middle-class family fallen on hard times, earned only 10s per week in the same years in Liverpool. She could only afford a 1d bun (with no filling) for her lunch and once a week she treated herself to a 3d bowl of soup.[118] It makes Ethel Mannings' expenditure of 9d on sardines on toast or Cambridge sausage seem wildly extravagant.[119]

Office workers, especially in the private sector, worked very hard for poor wages. Overtime was not paid, yet a typist was expected to stay in the office as late as was required to finish the job. Wages varied between different sectors but what they all had in common was a much lower rate for women than for men. Table 5 from 1929–30 shows the disparities.

Table 5   Clerical wages

Average salaries	Commerce and Industry	Transport	Banking and Insurance	Public service
	s. d.	s. d.	s. d.	s. d.
Males under 25	35 0	40 0	42 6	45 0
Females under 25	35 0	35 0	40 0	40 0
Males 25 yrs +	80 0	85 0	105 0	95 0
Females 25 yrs +	52 6	57 6	65 0	60 0
Males, all ages	65 0	75 0	82 6	90 0
Females, all ages	40 0	45 0	50 0	50 0

Source: J. Beauchamp, Women Who Work, London, Lawrence & Wishart, 1937, p. 57.

The Depression actually brought these wage rates down: by May 1931 women's clerks' salaries had gone down from £3 or £3 10s to 30s and 50s; office girls were starting at 10s to 12s a week and typists earned 20s to 25s.[120]

Working-class women's work in those years was clearly character-ised by low pay and sexual segregation. Small wonder that middle-class women set their sights on gaining admission to the professions and to highly paid jobs on an equal footing with men. In this they had an enormous amount of ground to make up. The nineteenth-century assumption was that a 'lady' could not possibly work for money – an assumption which accorded neatly with the reality that there were no jobs for ladies. Women aspiring to the professions in the 1920s could however draw upon the tradition of the women's movement which had made the right to work, and indeed to an education fitting women to the professions, a central plank of its platform. Ray Strachey wrote in 1936 the following comment on the suffragists' view of work:

> Work, indeed, came to seem almost an end in itself to some of them and they attached a value to earning their own livings which that somewhat dreary necessity does not in reality possess . . . They thought of work as a satisfaction of personal needs, an outlet for gifts and powers, a fulfilment of personal individuality.[121]

The pre-First World War feminists saw earning one's living as bestowing 'freedom' on a woman and the Sex Disqualification (Removal) Act of 1919 held the key to that freedom, the key to the professions. The grandiloquent opening to the act reads,

> A person shall not be disqualified by sex or marriage from the exercise of any public function, or from being appointed to or holding any civil or judicial office or post, or from entering or assuming or carrying out any civil profession or vocation.

The Act decreed that all professional groups, with the exception of the civil service, had to admit women. Somewhat grudgingly they did so – obeying the letter, if not the spirit, of the law. Yet discrimi-nation of one sort or another continued and doctors, civil servants and teachers appealed in vain to the Act. By 1922, in the words of one contributor to *Time and Tide*, the feeling was 'The Act means nothing, we have been hoaxed'.[122]

The 1920s saw the entry of pioneering women into professions never opened to them before and the rise to eminence of individual women in their fields. The press, particularly the feminist press, made a great fuss of each new achievement.[123] Winifred Holtby, surveying a generation of women's achievement, wrote somewhat nonchalantly in 1935:

Today we take it for granted that women should become surgeons, engineers and ministers, that a woman electrician should obtain the contract for rewiring Winchester Cathedral and that a woman architect should design the Shakespeare Memorial Theatre at Stratford on Avon.[124]

The achievements of individual women were very considerable, but when we turn to the figures for women in the professions in the inter-war years the striking thing is how small their numbers were. Catherine Hakim's analysis of women's share of top jobs in 1911 and 1971 shows hardly any improvement over sixty years; the only notable increase was in the number of female doctors.

Table 6   Women's share of top jobs

Percentage of women among total in each group:	1911	1971
Doctors	2	20
Accountants	0.2	3
Architects and town planners	0.08	5
Judges, barristers and solicitors	0	6
Ministers, MPs and Senior Government*	5	12
Local Authority Senior Officers*	5	15

* These two groups were not precisely defined in the 1911 occupational classification and included officers below the senior grade.

Source: C. Hakim, Occupational Segregation, Research Paper no. 9, table 20, London, Department of Employment, 1979, p. 34.

The census categories employed in 1921 and 1931 are too imprecise to give a very useful picture of women's place in the professions. They do however show an overall rise between these two dates. Gillian Darcy extracted the information in Table 7 from the two census reports.

Teachers, who actually declined in number between 1921 and 1931 because of cuts in education, represented by far the largest professional group, followed by nurses; the proportion of women doctors, for example, remained miniscule. It is too difficult to isolate other professional groups from the census information but an interesting source of information exists for the mid 1920s. Charlotte Haldane, an anti-feminist writer, surveyed some thirty professional bodies and asked them to provide information on the number of

Table 7 Women in the professions

Occupation	1921		1931	
	Numbers	% of Total	Numbers	% of Total
Total in professions	348,461		389,359	
Teachers including Music	203,802	58.48	199,560	51.25
Nurses	94,381	27.08	118,909	30.53
Subordinate medical services	6,585	1.88	11,989	3.07
Total	304,768	87.46	330,458	84.87
Librarians	832	0.23	3,439	0.88
Physicians, surgeons, registered medical practitioners	1,253	0.35	2,810	0.72
Social Welfare Officers	1,863	0.53	3,389	0.87
Total	3,948	1.13	9,638	2.47

Source: G. Darcy, Changes and Problems in Women's Work in England and Wales, 1918–1939, unpublished Ph.D, University of London, 1984.

women employed in their respective professions.[125] The figures are set out in Table 8 and might be over-stated.

Women's entry into the professions proceeded at a snail's pace and entry was only the first hurdle; once 'in' there were problems of promotion and pay. The progress or lack of it of women in the law, medicine and teaching deserve attention here.

The legal profession was opened to women by the 1919 Act. Ray Strachey wrote that the lawyers accepted the position handsomely and accepted women with good grace.[126] The first woman to be called to the English bar was Dr Ivy Williams (1922) and the first

Table 8   Haldane's survey of women in professions (1928)

Institute	Total membership	Women members	First women admitted
British Architects	5,949	21	1898
Chartered Accountants	7,458	10	1920
Chemistry	5,186	165	1892
Chemical Society	4,101	84	1920
Civil Engineers	9,936	2	1925
Dental Association	3,501	82	1895
Law Society	10,000	52	1922
Mechanical Engineers	10,040	1	1924
Medical Association	32,010	2,580	1875
Public Administration	2,631	177	1922
Structural Engineers	3,150	2	1922
Others	13,228	446	
Totals	107,705	3,622	

Source: N. A. Ferguson, 'Women's work: employment opportunities and economic roles, 1918–1939', *Albion*, Spring 1975, p. 61.

Scottish woman advocate (barrister) was Miss Margaret Henderson Kidd, MA LLD (1926). By 1926 there were in fact seventy-seven English women barristers.[127] The numbers were not that great but the work done by these women in entering this old profession was indeed pioneering. Entry into the legal profession was not cheap. The training was lengthy for barristers and solicitors and fees were expensive – £150 for the bar in 1927 and premiums of between two hundred and three hundred guineas to enter a solicitor's office. Margaret Henderson Kidd was the daughter of the Conservative MP for Linlithgow and clearly that was the kind of background required for the entry to such a profession.[128] But even money, intelligence and high social status cut no ice with many legal firms who would not have dreamed of actually employing women.

The history of women in the medical profession in the inter-war years is a cautionary tale which prevents us from assuming that women's entry into the professions was one of gradual but sure progress.[129] Elizabeth Garrett-Anderson, the first woman to qualify for entry into the medical profession in England, had done so in 1865. She did this by passing the examinations of the Society of Apothecaries – which immediately altered its regulations so no other woman might follow this route. In 1874 Sophia Jex Blake founded the London School of Medicine for women, but very few teaching hospitals opened their courses to women – despite the opening of the Medical Register to women in the 1870s. By 1917 only a group of 183 rather small institutions, originally staffed by women and specialising in obstetrics, accepted women for medical training. But the shortage of doctors created by the First World War prompted the British Medical Association to apply pressure on other hospitals to accept women. By the mid 1920s there were over 2,500 qualified women doctors. But the London training hospitals had no intention of continuing in peacetime what they had regarded as a wartime necessity.[130] In 1922 the London Hospital decided it would cease training women – on the grounds put forward by Lord Knutsford that, 'the staff have found difficulties in teaching to a mixed audience certain unpleasant subjects of medicine'. Other London hospitals followed suit – St Mary's Paddington in 1924 and in 1928 Westminster, King's and Charing Cross banned entry to women. In London only the Royal Free and University College Hospitals continued to accept women students. A great deal of humbug was talked at the time. In 1928 Sir James Stewart Purvess of Westminster Hospital attacked women doctors for getting married and therefore wasting their training.[131] He made this attack at a time when many public bodies employing women doctors sacked them when they married.

In allied medical professions women fared rather better. In 1928 there were eighty-two women out of 3,500 members of the Dental Association. Women became pharmacists, radiographers and hospital almoners. But by far the largest group of professional women in the field of medicine were the nurses.

Nursing was an exclusively female profession. It was characterised by hard and heavy manual work and was closely akin, in the nature of the job, to domestic service. The First World War, with the influx of semi-trained VADs (literally Voluntary Aid Detachment but used to describe volunteer nurses) drew attention to the anomalous position of trained nurses and led to the establishment of a clearly defined nursing profession. In 1919 the Nurses Registration Act established the General Nursing Council, which devised the rules for registering a 'Registered Nurse'. Examinations for Registered Nurses came into force in 1925. Vera Brittain believed that the VADs had brought about certain improvements in nursing; this group, she said 'refused to submit meekly to authority and to keep their ideas of progress to themselves'.[132] Indeed this may be true, but in the inter-war years nursing continued to be dominated by vexatious rules and petty regulations, which extended to the trainee nurse's off-duty time as well as her time in hospital. By the end of the 1920s the Lancet Commission, in a study of nurses' training conditions, found that attendance at meals was compulsory at 58 per cent of hospitals and in 84 per cent of them the nurse was not allowed out after 10 p.m. without a late pass.[133]

In the mid 1930s nurses normally worked between fifty-six and sixty hours per week.[134] The probationer nurse had a struggle to make ends meet; even with 'all found' (i.e. full board and lodging) a qualifying nurse in 1937 could expect just £65 per annum rising to a maximum of £80 as a staff nurse and £125 as a sister.[135] Nursing demanded dedication. Marriage and nursing were seen as incompatible. In this profession, as in others in these years, the nurse was forced to choose between marriage and a career.

Teaching, especially elementary school teaching, was – like nursing – considered to be appropriate work for women. In fact, the status of teaching had risen in the late nineteenth and early twentieth centuries and the woman teacher had become a respected figure in the community. This rise in status was due to several factors: firstly, more middle-class entrants came into teaching from the 1870s on; secondly, bursaries and the system of teacher training, whereby prospective teachers trained in college and acquired a certificate, replaced the old pupil-teacher system of learning on the job; and thirdly, the Burnham Committee, a new body (set up in 1919, and to last until 1987) announced *national* rates of pay, which in fact represented a substantial increase. The Burnham scale for teachers, although unequal in the remuneration of women and men taken together with the Teachers Superannuation Act of 1918 which set out a revised formula for teachers' pensions, made teaching a well paid job *for women*. Two women teachers, sisters or friends, who shared a home could live a good life with their own house, domestic help, holidays abroad and even a small car.[136] The school mistress couple of the men-depleted 1920s became a regular feature of Europe's more cultured holiday resorts like Florence and Paris. In fact, Frances Widdowson points out that the status of women elementary teachers had risen more quickly than that of their male counterparts.[137] It is certainly true that the numbers of women in teaching rose at a far greater rate than those of men. Between 1875 and 1914 the number of women elementary teachers increased 862 per cent whilst that of men by only 292 per cent. By 1914 women were 75 per cent of all elementary teachers.[138] The war alone brought in 13,000 more women and accelerated the change in the proportion of the sexes.[139]

The Burnham Committee differentiated between female and male teachers' salaries. Women teachers received four-fifths of male rates for the same job, for which they had received the same training. The actual salary paid to a teacher was determined by qualification, scale of post and district of employment. So it is somewhat more useful to look at average salaries rather than scales. (The economic difficulties of these times actually led to cuts in teachers' salaries.) In 1930 the average salary for a certificated teacher in elementary school was calculated at £254 for women and £334 for men – a difference of £80 per annum.[140] Many women teachers had looked with some optimism to the original Burnham scales of 1919 in the hope of equal pay but they were disappointed and continued to be disappointed in this until 1944, when the principle of equal pay was accepted by the government. Actually paying teachers equally took much longer and was phased in between 1955 and 1961.[141] The National Union of Teachers (NUT) was the largest organisation representing teachers and although in 1919 over 60 per cent of its members were women the NUT did little to promote equal pay. Ethel M. Froud of the National Federation of Women Teachers, dismissed the NUT's alleged commitment to equal pay. In 1920 she wrote,

> Equal pay became the paper policy of the NUT – nothing more. There has never been one favourable article in their official organ: no mass meetings in support of equal pay have been organized: no leaflets issued: no attempts have been made to educate the public or Education Authorities or the Board of Education.[142]

The NUT had sold out women teachers in agreeing to the differentiated scales. Women teachers committed to equal pay had set up a separate union as early as 1909, the National Union of Women Teachers (NUWT). The NUWT campaigned vigorously throughout the inter-war years, so much so that when one reads any article headed 'Equal-pay' in an inter-war feminist journal, it is almost invariably concerned with schoolteachers and the activities of the NUWT. The NUWT was prepared to recognise that their male colleagues often had children to support but as its secretary, A. G. Hewitt, explained in 1921, this should be covered by 'some form of endowment of motherhood or family allowances other than the not inconsiderable rebates at present allowed to men'.[143] The NUWT marched, organised mass demonstrations and raised the government's obligation to equal pay in parliament. Some men teachers, on the other hand, were firmly opposed to women earning as much as them. In 1920 the National Association of Schoolmasters (NAS), who were against equal pay, severed their organisation's links with the NUT, which it said, 'was permanently dominated by feminine influence to the detriment of male teachers'.[144] By 1939 the president of the NAS stated his members' refusal to serve under women – 'only a nation heading for a madhouse would force upon men – many men with families – such a position as service under a spinster headmistress'.[145] Their view of spinsters fitted in with the derogatory stereotype seen in chapter 1.

Women teachers failed to gain equal pay in the inter-war years. They were similarly disadvantaged in terms of promotion but there was one outstanding disadvantage which applied only to women: the application of marriage bars. In 1921 some 15 per cent of women teachers were married but in the early 1920s many authorities brought in some form of marriage bar; they would not appoint married women, women were forced to resign on marriage and women teachers who were already married were dismissed. The economic crisis of 1921, with its cuts in public expenditure and the existence of large numbers of unemployed training college-leavers sparked off the introduction of marriage bars in many authorities. The NUT did little to help but the NUWT took up the cause of married women teachers. By 1926 three quarters of Local Education Authorities discriminated against married women. Women in a variety of authorities took legal action to halt this but the process continued. The numbers of married women teachers fell by some 2,500 in England and Wales by August 1922.[146] Teaching, like nursing, became a profession in which women were required to take the veil. 'Public opinion' was against married women working in hard times and there was much hostility to married women teachers and their husbands enjoying a double income. In this climate some couples adopted such subterfuges as pretending not to be married: there are tales of married couples in South Wales, living and teaching as single people in separate valleys, in order that the married woman could keep on her job.

If women teachers' post-war optimism was to prove ill-founded, the hopes of women civil servants in the inter-war years were to prove even more illusory. It seemed that they had reasonable grounds for optimism in 1918. By 1918 there were 235,000 women civil servants or 56 per cent of the total. (In 1914 they had numbered 66,000 or 21 per cent of the total.) But when the war ended women were dismissed in large numbers. By 1919 they were down to 169,869, in 1920, 119,030, in 1923, 76,017 and in 1928, 74,212.[147] The numbers of men on the other hand, and particularly of ex-servicemen, increased rapidly.

This is far from what women civil servants might reasonably have expected at the end of the First World War. Throughout the war they had performed work that was interchangeable with men, an important point in a service which had hitherto segregated women's and men's work. In 1918, buoyant with their own success, aggrieved at the lack of equal pay and highly unionised, they looked forward to an efficient and fairly run Civil Service in which they could take their rightful and equal place. They received great encouragement from the feminist movement and from official bodies where women predominated. The sub-committee of the Women's Advisory Committee of the Ministry of Reconstruction, composed of six women and two men, announced in 1919 that women should be eligible for all grades of appointment on the same terms and conditions as men, that they should enter by the same procedures and that they should have equal pay and promotion with men.[148] What the women of 1918 and 1919 could not fully have expected was the determination of the Treasury (the body responsible for employing civil servants) not to allow women into any but the most subordinate grades and the vigour and deftness with which the Treasury spokesmen fought off 'any threatened interference with their preserves'. It was as Ray Strachey remarked in 1927 'the adroitness of long practice'.[149]

The struggle for equality in the Civil Service was immensely important because the government was the employer and the attitude taken by the government would influence other employers. Meta Zimmick in an informative article examines the shifts and turns by which a reactionary Treasury sought to preserve the Civil Service as a male enclave.[150] The Treasury, she maintains 'did not so much have a consistent policy as an attitude or series of attitudes which it projected on to administrative eventualities'.[151] The Treasury was prepared to shift and manoeuvre to protect the maleness of the service and particularly its top rank, the First Division. Such manoeuvres included ducking out of its obligation under the Sex Disqualification (Removal) Act by adding a clause exempting itself; excluding women from posts abroad; deliberately favouring ex-servicemen; holding very few examinations for executive posts open to men and women; expecting women candidates to be older than men; failing disproportionate numbers of women at the interview stage; and introducing a regrading of posts which actually reinforced gender divisions. The Civil Service, on top of all this, operated a marriage bar enforceable on all grades from 1918. Many women in the lower grades of the Civil Service actually had no objection to this because they received a lump sum on marriage and resignation but women in the higher grades sought its abolition. In fact the Treasury did have the discretion to retain married women in the higher grades but by 1937 only eight such women were allowed to pursue their careers.[152]

The structure and operation of the Civil Service is complex. It is simplest to view it as a pyramid – a pyramid with male executive and administrative grades at the top (theoretically open to women after 1920) and with the broad base of women writing assistants and clerks at the bottom – or, as one contemporary put it, 'women up to a point and men above'.[153]

Finally it must be noted that individual talented and resourceful women made their mark in business, in academic careers and in journalism. Their numbers were not great but they did open more doors for others to pass through in the future. There are two further questions to ask, which relate to women workers as a whole, both manual and professional. Did women, as contemporaries asserted, take men's jobs in the bad times of the inter-war years? And how did unemployment affect women?

Women were frequently admonished in these years for 'taking men's jobs'. With regard to, for example, women clerks, the sentiments which appeared in the *Western Mail* in 1920 in a letter from 'Disgusted', were widely shared. 'These girls have done nothing for their country, but they have done uncommonly well for themselves in many cases'. He (?) went on to complain that men cannot get well-paid jobs as clerks 'because better berths with private firms are being retained by girls taken on during the absence of men'.[154] Fourteen years later when the *News Chronicle* published an article advocating better pay for women secretaries so that they could be not only better fed and housed but better dressed, more self-respecting and therefore more efficient, the very next day a correspondent complained bitterly, 'Better pay and smarter clothes for women: unemployment and patched pants for men'.[155] There may be some truth in this allegation with respect to office work. This was an area of work which continued to undergo a process of feminisation, largely because women clerks came a lot cheaper than men. On the other hand, the Civil Service employed wide and varied stratagems to keep women out and to let ex-servicemen in. It is possible to cite instances where women were employed in industry on processes previously done by men – such as the working of large Hoffman presses in the clothes-making industry – because they were cheaper: whereas men working on the Hoffman press received 1s 4d per hour, girls (under sixteen) received 16s 6d to £1 a week.[156] In the manufacture of ready-made clothing as a whole, the shift to automated processes again 'favoured' women workers; it represented a shift from one male tailor hand sewing a pair of trousers to nineteen girls performing nineteen processes on a conveyor belt to make a pair of trousers. Where there is any truth in the allegation that women took men's jobs (even where one is prepared not to quarrel with the notion of male and female jobs), it was always because women were cheaper. As Jean Beauchamp wrote of the engineering industry,

If the employers can get a woman to do from 30s to £2 a week, work that skilled men used to do for £5, £6 and even £8 and £9 a week, of course they will employ her, even if it means paying her rather more than the usual woman's rate to get her to do it.[157]

The number of insured women workers rose faster than the number of insured men in the inter-war years. But in general as our survey of women's work in the inter-war period shows, women were not taking men's jobs: women did not become ship-builders or miners and they made numerically very little impact on the top professions. Protective legislation, trade union attitudes, government and educational establishment policies saw to that. Marriage bars were in themselves a form of enforced unemployment of women, though they created vacancies for other younger single women. Women did not take men's jobs but many of them were forced into the position of family breadwinner. In a situation which means-tested the income coming into a house of all members of a family, a wife or a daughter could be the sole breadwinner. Given women's low wages, such a role was much more burdensome than for a man in a similar position.

Table 9   Rates of unemployment of males and females 1927–36 G.B. and N.I.

| | ALL INSURED INDUSTRIES | | |
| | Mean unemployment percentage | | |
Year	Males	Females	Rate for females as % of males
1927	11.0	6.2	56
1928	12.3	7.0	57
1929	11.6	7.3	63
1930	16.5	14.8	90
1931 Jan–Oct	22.4	18.4	82
1931 Nov–Dec	23.1	15.3	66
1932	25.2	13.7	54
1933	23.2	11.4	49
1934	19.3	10.0	52
1935	17.7	9.8	55
1936 Jan–Aug	15.6	9.1	58

The table is derived from Beveridge's work.
Source: J. Hurstfield, 'Women's unemployment in the 1930s: some comparisons with the 1980s', in S. Allen *et al.* (eds), *The Experience of Unemployment*, London, Macmillan/BSA, 1986.

All this talk of women causing male unemployment obscures the very real issue of women's unemployment in the inter-war years. We saw the position at the end of the First World War. In March 1919 over half a million women were officially admitted to be unemployed. By the end of 1920 however only 103,000 women were registered at labour exchanges. This was partly the result of a post-war boom but more the result of government strategies in deterring women from even bothering to register. In fact for the whole inter-war period government figures consistently show much higher percentages of unemployment among male than female workers. Jennifer Hurstfield has produced a very interesting article comparing women's unemployment in the 1980s with the 1930s. As in Table 9, her work on the 1930s shows how women's unemployment was consistently played down.[158]

These figures very much play down female unemployment. They only include insured workers: whole categories of women workers, most notably domestic servants, were not insured. Many women only registered if they had a hope of gaining unemployment benefit. We have already seen how, in the immediate post-war period, women were denied benefit if they turned down work in domestic service, which was uninsured. This practice continued. The umpire, who arbitrated in cases where employment exchanges and local tribunals refused benefit, continued to disallow benefit where women turned down posts as domestics. Cotton operatives, normally paid 45s a week, were disallowed benefit for turning down jobs in service at 17s per week in 1921.[159] In fact in 1921 further regulations tightened up the National Insurance Act by adding a clause that the applicant must be 'genuinely seeking whole time employment but unable to obtain such employment'; 'the genuinely seeking work clause' replacing the condition that an applicant be simply 'capable and available' for work now made it even harder for women to claim benefit if they turned down jobs in service.[160] In 1922 the new Insurance Act stipulated that applicants were to accept any job which they were capable of doing and that they no longer had any right to demand that it be a job with comparable pay and conditions to their previous employment. All this left little alternative to women but domestic service. In 1922 the government surreptitiously introduced the means test whereby an applicant's claim for benefit would be turned down if there was deemed to be sufficient income in the household. Alan Deacon's detailed investigations revealed that only 3 per cent of applications by men but 15 per cent of those made by women were refused on income grounds.[161] As Sydney Webb observed, the assumption was

a woman always had some kind of family belonging to her,

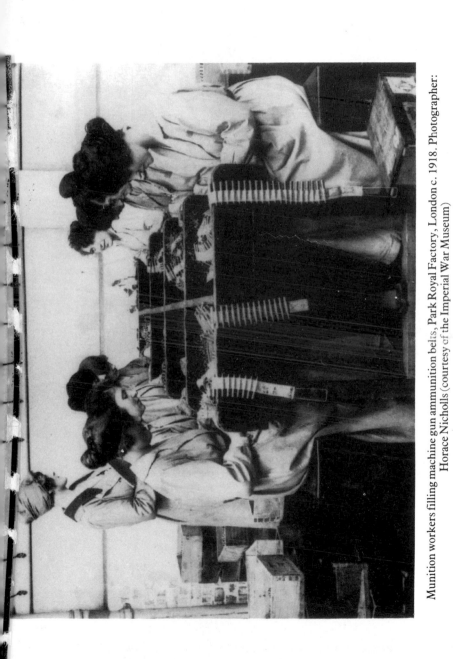

Munition workers filling machine gun ammunition belts, Park Royal Factory, London c. 1918. Photographer: Horace Nicholls (courtesy of the Imperial War Museum)

"'Here's a find,'

I thought to myself when I first tested Rowntree's Cocoa. I was feeling tired after a long day in the yard, but the cocoa soon put new life into me. That was weeks ago, and you'd think the spell of it would wear off after a time, *but I like it more every time I taste it.* As Dad says, 'It seems to grow on one.' It's lucky it's so inexpensive—I've worked it out, and it costs less than a halfpenny a cup."

a Cup of
Rowntree's Cocoa
makes a biscuit into a meal

Rowntree's Cocoa advertisement, *Everywoman's*, 8 February 1919
(courtesy of the British Library)

"Why, how he's grown!"

The Husband: "You don't know how *glad* I feel. I was a bit nervous that you and the kids were feeling the pinch of food. And now to see him look so bonny— it does one's heart good . . . Tell me, how did you manage?"

The Wife: "It was difficult, sometimes, Dad. But when food was short and queues were on, we always used to have a big cup of Rowntree's Cocoa, all of us. It was so strong and nourishing that we got on famously— and we're never going to give it up now."

There are many Cocoas not so good as

Rowntree's
Elect Cocoa

Rowntree's Cocoa advertisement, *Everywoman's*, 29 March 1919 (courtesy of the British Library)

"BESTWAY"

COOKERY GIFT BOOK

Sixth Book

A Book of Delicious Recipes, Easy to Prepare, and Inexpensive in Cost. Every Recipe has its Photograph.

Issued from the office of The "Bestway" Series, Fleetway House, Farringdon Street, London, E.C.4.

An idealised view of the housewife from a cookery book, 1930

Oxford v Cambridge:
captains in first women's
race, *The Vote*, 1927
(courtesy of Mary Evans
Picture Library)

Policewoman on motor
cycle, *The Vote*, 1929

THE VOTE,
JULY 6, 1928.

VICTORY!

THE VOTE

THE ORGAN OF THE WOMEN'S FREEDOM LEAGUE.
NON-PARTY.

VOL. XXIX. No. 976. *(Registered at the U.P.U.)*   ONE PENNY.   FRIDAY, JULY 6, 1928

OBJECT: To secure for Women the Parliamentary vote as it is or may be granted to men ; to use the powers already obtained to elect women in Parliament, and upon other public bodies, for the purpose of establishing equality of rights and opportunities between the sexes, and to promote the social and industrial well-being of the community.

FREE AND INDEPENDENT.

The Three Leaders *(together)* "WANT A PILOT, MADAM ?"
New Voter "NO, THANKS."

Free and Independent, *Punch* cartoon, 1928. Used as cover
illustration for *The Vote*

Evan's Perkanninies, students at Glamorgan Training College, c. 1921

Late evening in the kitchen, 1936. Photographer: Bill Brandt, 1936 (courtesy Noya Brandt)

Women workers in a Lancashire cotton mill

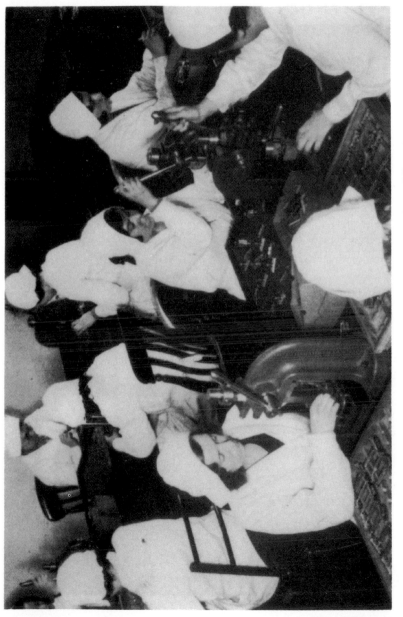

Women assembling razors (courtesy of John Topham Picture Library)

A vacancy for one woman librarian was advertised. This is the queue that turned up, mid 1930s

Working-class house.
The hole was discovered
when the wall was
stripped for re-papering

Semi-detached house,
1930s

Give her Pleasure — Give her Leisure

The 1920's

Give her an
ELECTROLUX
for Christmas

RILETTE

The wonderful Cleaner that every woman covets!

The moment a woman with a house to look after sees the Electrolux suction cleaner at work, she longs to possess it. Such easy, effortless, efficient cleaning of every nook and corner! Dust banished — germs destroyed — the very air of the room sweetened and purified in a few minutes. Hours of labour saved. Dust cleared from under the heaviest furniture without stooping, carpets thoroughly cleaned without being taken up.

There is no cleaner like Electrolux — none so powerful, nor yet so handy and compact. Electrolux is the very last word in up-to-date domestic efficiency.

Give her an Electrolux this Christmas — it means a New Year of leisure and freedom — and not only *one* New Year but a lifetime of them!

The NEW
ELECTROLUX
THE *CLEANER* CLEANER

Advertisement for Electrolux suction cleaner, 1920s

Weighing a baby in the clinic from the film *Health of the Nation*, 1937 (courtesy of Labour Party Library)

Entrance to a fortune teller's booth, Blackpool, 1938. Photographer: Humphrey Spender (courtesy of Humphrey Spender)

Labour women MPs, June 1929. *Back row, left to right:* Dr Marion Phillips, Miss Edith Picton Turbervill, Dr Ethel Bentham, Miss Mary Agnes Hamilton; *Front row:* Lady Cynthia Mosley, Miss Susan Lawrence, the Rt Hon. Margaret Bondfield, Miss Ellen Wilkinson, Miss Jennie Lee

Conservative women MPs, November 1931. *Standing, left to right:* Lady Astor, Mrs Helen Shaw, Mrs Mavis Tate, Miss Thelma Cazalet, Mrs Sarah Ward, Mrs Ida Copeland, Miss Florence Horsburgh; *Seated:* Mrs Norah Runge, Lady Iveagh, Duchess of Atholl, Miss Irene Ward, Hon. Mary Pickford

Welsh women hunger marchers, 1934

and can in times of hardship slip into a corner somewhere and share a crust of bread already being shared by too many of the family mouths, whereas the truth is that many women workers are without relatives, and a great many more have delicate or worn-out parents, or young brothers and sisters, or children to support.[162]

If single women were supposed to slink back into the home and disappear from unemployment statistics, then married women were not really, in the eyes of the state, regarded as unemployed at all. This thinking was clearly shown in 1931 when the Anomalies Act was passed. This Act cut the number of married women who registered as unemployed at a stroke. Before looking at this Act it is necessary to note that in 1930 the Labour government removed the 'genuinely seeking work' clause. Reference to Table 9 will show that this caused the numbers of women registered as unemployed to increase from 63 per cent to 90 per cent of the male rate. Female unemployment became visible, briefly. The Anomalies Regulations (October 1931), however, insisted that a woman should have paid a certain number of contributions *after* marriage. The legislation was aimed directly at married women and again Table 9 shows how after October 1931 the female rate of unemployment fell back to 66 per cent of the male rate. By 1933 it was down to 49 per cent. By April 1933, of 299,908 claims refused under the anomalies legislation, a massive 84 per cent came from married women.[163] Once again the full extent of female unemployment was shrouded from view. As D. Caradog Jones wrote of Merseyside in 1934, 'Any woman, of whom no evidence was recorded that she was seeking work, was also relegated to the non-earning class'; women were 'non-earners' not unemployed.[164]

The dominant notion of the times was that a woman's place was in the home and that feeling was at its strongest in times of male unemployment. The press was hostile to any women working and the idea of married women working was beyond the pale. These attitudes and the legislation that put them into effect should be seen in a European context: there was similar legislation in Belgium, France and Germany.[165] Germany, under Hitler, was to take far more extreme measures to push women out of the workforce as a way of solving the problem of male unemployment. Some British feminists feared similar tactics here.

But what was the experience of unemployment like for women in the 1930s? Many women missed not just the money but the work and the company. J. B. Priestley wrote of one single woman mill worker who was pensioned off – 'wondering how to get through the coming week'.[166] Winifred Holtby spoke to an unemployed woman, laid off after nine years as a skilled perm-winder in an artificial silk factory – 'a grand job', as the woman herself called it: 'I hate this nothing to do,' said the woman. 'I am a strong woman and I can keep this little house clean with two hours work a day.'[167] There is little insight given into the unemployment of women workers in the many social surveys of the time. The Pilgrim Trust's *Men Without Work* is exceptional. In Blackburn and Leicester, where women normally worked after marriage, the investigators stressed the social and psychological effects of unemployment. One fifty-one year old weaver believed that 'she could do fancy weaving perfectly well but is too nervous now'. Another, aged forty-seven, said 'she misses the company, and evidently she feels very keenly that she is too old for work'.[168] Such information gives us mere glimpses into the experience of unemployment for working-class women. We must remember that unemployment hit professional women too, particularly teachers and librarians in local government employment.

Labour women and feminist groups campaigned vigorously throughout the 1920s and 1930s on behalf of women workers. They appealed to government after government for financial help and for training and work schemes. They did not get very far: all successive governments came up with were training courses in hated domestic service. It is small wonder that, given popular attitudes to women working and policies which pushed them out of the labour market (with the exception of domestic service), the centre of life for most women in Britain was the home.

4

HOME AND HEALTH

The home was the most important place for the great majority of
women in Britain. The media attempted to persuade women that it
was their only sphere and the workings of the job market largely
ensured it was. The home was, as contemporary magazines put it,
'the woman's workshop'. Housing, household budgeting and daily
routines of shopping and childcare were central features of women's
lives. I have concentrated very much on married women because
the home was even more important for them than for single women,
though it is important to realise that there was a phalanx of single
women at home looking after parents, brothers and working sisters.
Closely linked with home life, particularly with housing and family
finance, is women's health. Family size, contraception, childbirth
and its dangers, nutrition, disease, ill health and medical treatment
are all important aspects of women's lives. Since the state only took
notice of women when they were pregnant or nursing mothers
most of the information available on health care from contemporary
sources is concerned with married women.

Housing was fundamental to the quality of home life. The work
of nineteenth-century social investigators had brought to light the
appalling housing conditions in Britain's slums and Maud Pember
Reeves' study of the home lives of working-class people in Lambeth,
published in 1913, brought the experience of poverty to the attention of a middle-class audience on the eve of the First World War.
Maud Pember Reeves and her co-investigators from the Fabian
Women's Group were not describing the lives of the very poor or
the down-and-out but of respectable families where the husband
was in 'full work at a more or less top wage'.[1] She describes how
'the London poor are driven to pay one third of their income for
dark, damp rooms which are too small and too few in houses which
are ill built and overcrowded'.[2] A quarter of a century later in 1939,
on the eve of the Second World War, the Women's Health Enquiry
investigated the lives of 1,250 working-class women and reported
that only seven per cent of them were in 'good' housing.[3]
The background of home life for the great majority of working-
class women remained much the same as in their mothers' and

grandmothers' day. Yet there were important changes in housing which affected the lives of many women in Britain and these deserve attention.

One of the chief issues facing the nation at the end of the First World War was an enormous housing crisis. The pre-war housing shortage had been calculated at 120,000 houses. The war exacerbated this situation: house building had been at a virtual standstill while the war was on. Yet the war itself brought home to the government the great need for better housing. The poor health of the conscripts – by 1918 four out of ten were declared unfit for any kind of military service, let alone the trenches – was widely blamed on poor housing. Rent strikes, led by women, took place in Birmingham, Liverpool, Dundee, Aberdeen, Ayr and, most notably, Glasgow in 1915 and focused attention on poor conditions and high rents. During the war there had been a great debate on what kind of housing should be built afterwards, and there was a feeling that those soldiers who were fortunate enough to come home from the front should have 'Homes fit for Heroes'. In 1918 the housing shortage stood at 600,000, five times its pre-war level.

Housing was a woman's issue. When Maud Pember Reeves investigated housing in pre-war Lambeth she had done so from the point of view of the woman who had to manage on 'Round About A Pound A Week'. The government, which had established the Ministry of Reconstruction in 1917 to survey a wide variety of aspects of British life, appointed to it an all-women committee to report on the housewife's needs in the design of new state-built houses. The work of the Women's Housing Sub-Committee is discussed later. Feminist magazines gave a great deal of space to housing from 1918 onwards and as The Vote succinctly put it in 1919 – 'The homes of Britain – this is a woman's question'.⁴ Women's organisations gave housing a very high priority. The Women's Village Councils Movement, founded in 1917, had originally greatly concerned itself with rural housing: by 1924 it had developed into the Women's Housing Council Federation and could claim to represent over 120,000 women.⁵ The Women's Co-operative Guild concentrated on campaigning for high standard, low rent accommodation for working-class families. Other women's pressure groups concerned themselves with the provision of housing for working girls and spinsters. In the period immediately after the First World War the government's response was very encouraging, though it is not altogether clear what its motives were. The British establishment was shaken by the Bolshevik Revolution in Russia 1917. In 1919, in a debate on housing, Mr Bottomly, the MP for Hackney South, told of a conversation he had had in the war with a soldier. The soldier, who lived with his wife and five children in one room without even a pane of glass in the window, had said to Bottomly, 'Now, tell me, sir, what difference it makes to me whether the Kaiser is to rule over England or the present King?'[6] Leonora Eyles in her powerful study *The Woman in the Little House* (1922) reminded the government 'that revolution always begins in towns and cities where housing troubles have reacted disastrously on the nerves of the people'.[7]

The housing shortage hit hardest at the working class but it was felt too by the less well-off sections of the middle class. The practice of sharing houses was commonplace within the working class but new to the middle class. A writer in the *Woman's Leader* in 1921 made a plea to those whose houseroom was more than their needs to take in another family. Putting a good face on it, the magazine expressed the hope that sharing a house would lead to a 'spirit of social accommodation which has been so conspicuously lacking in middle-class English people up to the present time'.[8] The solutions to the housing shortage differed according to class: for the working class, hope lay with municipal or council housing and for the middle class it lay with newly built housing by private developers.

Most people in Britain lived in old houses. Many working-class people lived in houses of the type described by Maud Pember Reeves in 1913. Two families shared a terraced house, sharing a scullery and copper boiler on the ground floor; the house had no hot running water at all and the family living upstairs had no cold running water; each family had two rooms – a kitchen, where they cooked on an open grate and lived, and a bedroom; the lavatory was downstairs in the back yard. In 1931 the census revealed that there were eleven and a half million families in Britain but only ten and a half million dwellings, which meant many families were still sharing houses.[9] Not all working-class housing was as bad as that described by Pember Reeves. Many families rented their own single dwelling but these were almost always dark, cramped, without bathrooms, without electricity (they had gas), without inside lavatories, without separate sculleries with cooking facilities so that cooking was done on the kitchen fire. The worst houses were damp, bug-infested slums. The major English cities had immense housing problems. Leeds had many thousands of back-to-back houses built seventy or eighty to the acre, with one outside toilet to every three or four houses. People in Liverpool were still living in houses condemned in the 1850s and Glasgow had the worst slums in Britain: nearly 200,000 people in Glasgow lived more than three to a room.[10] But not all bad housing was in cities; there were many rural hovels without even an inside tap.

There are two excellent books showing the impact of poor housing on women's lives in the inter-war years. Leonora Eyles' *The Woman in the Little House* was published in 1922 and Margery Spring Rice's

Working Class Wives in 1939. The latter surveys a wide variety of working-class housing and provides many examples of the conditions in which women spent almost all of their lives:

> Mrs W. of Woolwich lives in four rooms on the two upper floors of a four-storey house; 'the scullery in which I cook is on the ground floor and there is no pantry or bathroom which seems somehow to treble my work'. There is one W.C. for the three families of the house.[11]

> Mrs K. of Marylebone has two rooms on the top floor of a healthy old fashioned house with large windows and 'a feeling of space', she has four children and there are eight flights of stairs to the top of the house 'but it is nice when you get there'. The washhouse is on the ground floor and water is fetched from a tap on the second landing.[12]

> A country woman in Essex complains that her cottage is damp and that she has to keep fires going all day long . . . All water to be fetched out of well which I share with neighbour and as house very draughty I can't keep warm.[13]

Rents varied in these older houses but it was not uncommon for working people to pay a third of their income on rent.[14] When George Orwell asked an unemployed miner to record his weekly budget his income was 32s and his rent was 9s 1/2d, twenty-eight per cent.[15] Landlords were not necessarily villains; they were often simply 'the wrong people', as Mrs Eyles said. She described the spinster lady, Miss Minnis, who owned her (Mrs Eyles') rented Peckham house, as living entirely from rents accruing from her five properties on a net income of 25s per week; Miss Minnis could not afford to think of her tenants.[16] For people in such housing the only way out was a rented council house.

Most middle-class people lived in old pre-1914 houses. These ranged from Belgravia, Mayfair and Chelsea to the solid nineteenth-century suburbs of cities and seaside resorts. Whilst some of these were updated and modernised to very high standards, most were Victorian mausoleums, designed to be run by an army of domestic servants. Though these houses were spacious, if not always light, they were draughty, expensive to heat and maintain and involved long distance carrying of coal and water. The efficient running of these houses depended wholly upon a plentiful supply of domestic servants – a supply that was not forthcoming in the inter-war years (see chapter 3). Even middle-class families did not usually purchase houses; in 1931 only one house in five was owner-occupied.[17] The ready solution for the middle class was to purchase a new house or flat which would be infinitely easier to run. Both council housing for rent and new suburban housing for purchase are important features of inter-war Britain.

In 1919 Addison's Housing and Town Planning Act placed the responsibility for remedying housing shortages upon the local authorities and made generous subsidies available both to local councils and subsequently to private builders. 213,000 houses were built under this Act but by 1921 hard times and inflation brought Addison's scheme into disrepute and council house building was curtailed.[18] In 1923 the Conservative government passed another Act which gave a subsidy to private builders and in 1924, Wheatley's Act, under the first Labour government, provided subsidies for houses built either by councils or private builders to be let at controlled rents subsidised from local rates. This Act gave a great boost to council house building and another 520,000 houses were built. But in 1932 the National government introduced a bill to abolish all subsidies for council building in England and Wales, except for slum clearance. The Act was, in Branson and Heinemann's words, 'a bombshell'; it meant that all municipal building, designed to alleviate the shortage of housing, stopped.[19] In Scotland subsidies were not abolished but cut drastically.

The net result of all these Acts was that between the wars 1.1 million council houses were built and large housing estates on the outskirts of every town became new features of the landscape. Bristol provides an example of the progress of council housing.[20] Bristol's first council houses were begun under Addison's subsidy of 1919; council estates were built at Fishponds, Sea Mills, Shirehampton, Knowle and St John's Lane – some 1,200 houses in all. In 1921 the Coalition government cut the subsidy and Bristol council was pressed to sell its new housing stock within a year of the houses being built. By 1923 the housing shortage in the city was acute and some 15,000 new dwellings were needed immediately. The Conservative government's subsidy to private builders of that year did little to help working-class families and between 1923 and 1929 only 1,600 council houses were built in Bristol under this Act. The 1924 Wheatley Act enabled councils to build houses to let at lower rents than previously. Some 7,000 houses were built under this Act. In 1933 this subsidy too was cut off by the National government and the city was forced to curtail its activities to slum clearance. In all, the city had built 14,500 council houses by 1939.

Council housing provided vastly improved standards over the older style houses in which the new tenants had previously lived. The Women's Housing Sub-Committee (1918) to the Ministry of Reconstruction, a group who came from various political positions but who were strongly influenced by Labour women, outlined certain basic demands.[21] The women on this committee, despite some of their own more 'advanced' preferences for such features as communal cooking arrangements, faithfully represented the wishes of the working-class housewives whom they had consulted. These demands were for a separate scullery where the housewife could wash and cook; a separate bathroom; a parlour, where the housewife could relax and take pride in her nice home; such labour-saving facilities as hot water on tap (as opposed to boiling it), and low rents. The ideology underlying these demands recognised that a woman's place was in the home: this squared both with the opinions of many housewives, with prevailing propaganda and with the 'new feminism' (discussed in chapter 6). The Women's Committee influenced another government-appointed committee, the Tudor-Walters Committee, whose report was to set the standards for houses built between the wars. Tudor-Walters did not always live up to the Women's Committee standards – in, for example, the question of hot water on tap – but it did in the fundamentals of scullery, bathroom and parlour.

There were however problems with council housing. The first of these was that the rents were very high and consequently put much council housing out of the reach of working-class people. Sub-letting was forbidden on pain of eviction. In Bristol the first tenants in the Fishponds estate were clerks, artisans, reporters and teachers.[22] In 1923 the *Woman's Leader* enthused about the standards of new council housing but regretted that although such housing was let at an uneconomic rent, it was still out of the reach of labourers and their families.[23] In the late 1930s the Women's Health Enquiry interviewed a woman living in a council house in Woolwich who paid 14s 7d rent out of an income of £2 12s 6d and a woman living in a London county council flat who paid 16s 9d rent out of 41s income, nearly 28 per cent and 40 per cent of their incomes respectively.[24] The usual way in which housewives coped with higher rents was by cutting down on expenditure on food.

There were other problems with living on the new council estates. The estates were a long way from where people worked, which lengthened the time they were away from home and meant having to pay tram or train fares. A Bolton woman slum dweller in the 1930s, in an area already being cleared, said she could not afford to move to a council estate because her three daughters worked in the mill and they would have to pay fares and buy food in town instead of coming home for dinner.[25] Then there was the lack of social amenities on the estate. Many were built without shops. The Sea Mills estate in Bristol was built in 1920; there was no shop there until 1929.[26] Tenants relied on travelling grocers, butchers and bakers who charged extortionate prices. Throughout the 1920s there was not one cinema, social centre or public house on any of the Bristol housing estates.[27] When Mass Observers spoke to women in Bolton about housing estates one said she was sorry for her friend because she was lonely knowing no one there and another woman said she would not move willingly to the estate because she had attended the same church all her life and did not want to give it up.[28]

If social amenities were slow in coming to estates, as were schools and libraries, the one consolation was a garden. Women viewed gardens primarily as places to occupy their husbands but in the evenings, when the housework was done, they helped their husbands in the garden. The garden gate, rather than the interior of a neighbour's home as in some older communities, became the place where women met to talk to one another. One Mass Observer described this new phenomenon:

In the nice weather they will also have an evening session that may go on till the stars come out and Henry Hall's band is ready to close down. The redeeming feature of this incessant chattering is the fact that it is *the only social intercourse existent for women on this estate*.[29]

Council housing provided better facilities and healthier locations and women appreciated this – but it was isolating. People almost felt a responsibility to act well out of some remote fear of the council. Women put their efforts into their homes and where there was spare income began to make new purchases for the home, such as radios and furniture.

The great building boom of the inter-war years took place, however, largely in the private sector. Of some four million houses built in the 1920s and the 1930s two and a half million were built by private builders without any form of government subsidy. Many were built in the 1920s but the removal of subsidies for municipal house building in 1933, an Act which private builders had urged upon a willing government, led to even greater private house building in the 1930s. These houses were primarily built for sale and not for letting. House prices actually fell in the inter-war years. A house of similar style and construction which cost just under £1,000 in 1920 could be purchased for as little as £400 in the late 1920s and in the 1930s. A third of all new houses built in 1931 cost less than £600 and by 1939 nearly half the houses built cost less than this.[30] These houses could be bought with a building society mortgage, then a new method of purchase. Initially building societies asked for a 25 per cent deposit, e.g. £125 on a £500 house. Only middle-class people could afford this. But speculative builders were anxious to sell their houses to people lower down the social scale and reached deals with the building societies so that they lent 95 per cent mortgages to prospective buyers. Mortgage interests were very low, 4½ per cent in 1934. These arrangements meant that clerical workers and better paid industrial workers, earning £4 to £5 a week, could put down just £24 on a £480 house and repay at 13s 6d a week.[31] Repayments started at 8s 10d. George Orwell described the feelings of insurance salesman George Bowling in *Coming Up for Air* as he walked down Ellesmere Road, somewhere in the London suburbs, towards his estate and towards mortgage repayments to the Cheerful Credit Building Society: it was 'a line of semi-detached torture chambers where the poor little five to ten pounders quake and shiver, every one of them with the boss twisting his tail and the wife riding him like a nightmare'.[32]

Orwell always represented the male point of view. He had a point though when he wrote of Bowling and all the other men on Bowling's estate as 'eaten up with the ghastly fear that something might happen before we've made the last payment'.[33]

By 1939 owner occupation had risen from 10 per cent before the First World War to 31 per cent. In 1928, 554,000 people had building society mortgages; in 1937 the figure was 1,392,000. The change in house ownership was dramatic but even these low house prices were far beyond the pockets of most working people and the relatively small proportion of new private housing built for rent (mainly in the late 1930s) was also beyond their range. The new houses were to be seen everywhere in the inter-war years but especially on the outskirts of southern and Midland towns. They stretched for miles out of London along the new arterial roads – along Eastern Avenue, Western Avenue, Edgware Way, the Kingston by-pass, the Great West Road or Rochester Way.[34] They looked brand new and had not mellowed into the landscape. The new houses were mainly semi-detached and what strikes us now is their uniformity – acre upon acre of near identical housing – though builders sought to add variety by a little mock timbering and an assortment of bay window styles. The cartoonist Osbert Lancaster called them 'By-pass variegated'.[35]

The semi-detached houses had a small garden to the front and a much larger one to the rear; access to the rear was gained by walking around the side of the house. The interior plans were very much the same and were variations on 'the universal plan'. There were no long dark corridors and poorly lit rooms as in older terraced houses (see figure 1). The ground floor had a bright hallway, a kitchen overlooking the garden, a living room and a separate lounge – the new word for a parlour; upstairs there were two double bedrooms, a single bedroom, a bathroom and a separate WC. The floor area ranged from c 800 to 1,200 square feet (see figure 2).

Figure 1: Nineteenth century terraced house
        occupied by single family

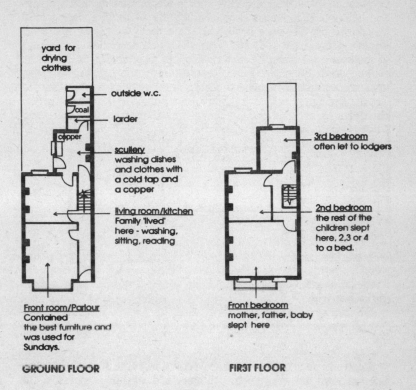

yard for
drying
clothes

← outside w.c.

coal

← larder

copper

← scullery
washing dishes
and clothes with
a cold tap and
a copper

← living room/kitchen
Family 'lived'
here - washing,
sitting, reading

3rd bedroom
often let to lodgers

2nd bedroom
the rest of the
children slept
here, 2,3 or 4
to a bed.

Front room/Parlour
Contained
the best furniture and
was used for
Sundays.

GROUND FLOOR

Front bedroom
mother, father, baby
slept here

FIRST FLOOR

For women the great joy of such houses was that they were light throughout, they had separate well equipped kitchens and enough bedroom space for parents and children to sleep separately. The new homes were easy to clean and care for. They had gas and electricity. Hot water was plentiful. As the Ascot gas geezer company's advertisement said,

> Happy in the morning
> As the water's hot
> We can bath an army
> The Ascot's done the lot.

Figure 2: 1930's Semi-Detached
            House.

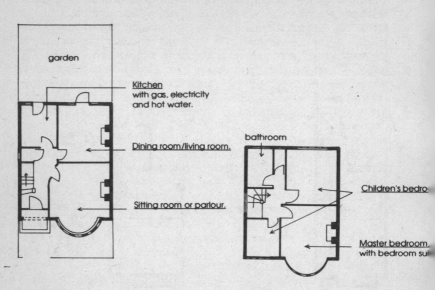

GROUND FLOOR   **FIRST FLOOR**

Electricity meant that housewives could buy labour-saving devices
like vacuum cleaners, electric cookers and washing machines, the
very products other women were assembling in the new industries
of the South and Midlands. Homes became much more attractive
places for wives and mothers to be in; this was just as well since
the building of suburban estates served to reinforce the division
between the public world of work and the private world of the
home.

Finally housing was an issue for single women as well as for
married women. Not all single women lived with their families.
Some were fortunate and were able to obtain flats such as those
rented out by the Women's Pioneer Housing Company, which con-
verted old houses into self-contained flats – but at rents costing
between £30 and £80 a year in 1922.[36] Other, often older, single
women faced difficulties. Whereas a spinster could live before the
war on £1 a week paying 6s to 10s a week rent for a cottage or
seaside flat, by 1924 two rooms were costing 15s and many single

women found themselves paying out half their income to keep a roof over their heads.[37]

Most women in Britain, even in the men-depleted inter-war years, married. Marriage, as we have seen, enjoyed an infinitely higher status than spinsterdom. Working-class women looked upon marriage, as Jane Lewis describes it, as an 'economic and emotional support system'.[38] Men went out to work and women were usually aware of the demands made upon their husbands at work; wives accepted the domestic sphere as their responsibility. Some working-class women performed a dual role: they worked outside the home for wages in full-time employment and accepted responsibility for domestic management as well. Middle-class women were more rigidly segregated into the private world of the home than their working-class counterparts. The early nineteenth century had firmly allotted this limited space to them and although there were much greater employment opportunities for middle-class women in the first half of the twentieth century, the operation of marriage bars in the professions in which women worked returned them sharply to the home on marriage. For middle-class women, who had worked in offices or in teaching and had mixed with many people, their lives shifted abruptly into staying at home, alone, in what could be the isolation of a new housing estate.

The welfare of families depended on the managerial and budgeting skills of the wife. It was a role in which women took pride and for which they were praised. Magazines extolled housewife-geniuses: 'she can make sixpence do the work of a shilling, and she knows all the best places for bargains and her accounts are never a penny out'.[39] For working-class women it was important to get a good husband – a man in regular employment, who would be a good provider and preferably one who would hand over his wage packet unopened as many men did, for example, in the mining and port areas of South Wales. Handing over the wage packet shows how totally responsible working-class women were for family budgets. It is one of the amazing achievements of such women that they were able to stretch an inadequate income to provide for their whole family, although all too often this was done by the woman herself going without. Jane Lewis suggests that the sense of self-worth and achievement of working-class women, who knew that their families' survival depended on their management skills, was lost by the relatively isolated suburban wife of the regularly employed man in the inter-war period.[40]

The level of family income was the single most important factor in determining how well a woman could manage the family budget. At the lowest end of the scale in the inter-war years were unemployed families; unemployment rather than low wages was the greatest cause of poverty in these years. In 1921, for example, an unemployed man received 22s for himself, his wife and two children with each additional child receiving 1s a week; in 1938 the benefit for a family of four had risen to 33s with 3s for each additional child.[41] In 1939 Margery Spring Rice stated categorically, 'No unemployed married man with a family under the Assistance Board, nor any married man in such poorly paid trades as agriculture, receives enough money to buy adequate food for himself, wife or children.'[42]

When she and the Women's Health Enquiry investigated the lives of 1,250 women and their families, she estimated that in no more than a dozen cases would their diets meet any recognised nutritional standards. The family budgets and diets recorded in her survey give us a very clear picture of the hardship and difficulty facing a woman trying to manage on inadequate resources. As she noted, the solution for the woman was to go without herself.[43] Before turning to examine some of these budgets, it is necessary to point out that the second determinant of how well a woman and her family lived was the number of children she had. Although the size of working-class families began to fall in the 1930s, there were still many large families.

The two following weekly budgets are both those of women with unemployed husbands. Mrs N. of Derby lived in two tiny rooms 'in squalid surroundings'. Her income was 29s 3d, which she spent as follows:

	s	d
Rent	4	6
Arrears of rent		6
Clothing Club	3	0
Weekly payment for pram	1	0
Insurance	1	6
2 cwt of coal	3	0
School dinners for two children		10
Baby's food from clinic		18
	15	0

This left 14s 3d for food for herself, husband and three children aged five, three and five months.[44] Mrs T. of Arbroath lived in three tenement rooms with her husband, five children (aged fourteen, eight, seven, three and fourteen months). Her total housekeeping was 36s 9d (including her income from office cleaning). She made regular weekly payments of:

	s	d
Rent	5	6
Coal	3	4
Gas	3	0
	11	10

so that only 24s 11d was left for food and clothing for the family of seven.[45] Both women had very poor diets themselves. Working-class women were criticised for not spending what little money they had for food wisely on nutritious items such as milk and eggs. Cranks wrote to newspapers suggesting diets of carrots and oranges and wholemeal bread for the unemployed. George Orwell stated that the unemployed of Wigan had an appalling diet of white bread and margarine, corned beef, sugared tea and potatoes. These were filling foods and, as he noted, cheerier and nicer than brown bread, dripping and a glass of cold water.[46]

Working-class women used a variety of strategies to balance the family budget. They went out to work, for example, cleaning like Mrs T. of Arbroath or they took in washing. Elizabeth Roberts wrote of women in Lancashire who sold roast potatoes or mugs of cocoa.[47] Within the house women had to be inventive and devise economies – making pillow cases and towels out of flour bags, babies' cots out of banana boxes, or sending out the children to pick up coal fallen from carts.[48] Poverty frequently led women into debt. Pawn shops were for many a last but frequent resort; most of the pawnbroker's business was in advancing money on clothing, bedding, small household items and wedding rings. Women's magazines warned women against getting into the clutches of money lenders. In Liverpool in 1924 so alarmed was the Women's Citizens' Association at the vast numbers of women borrowing from the city's 1,380 registered money lenders (1,100 of whom were women!) in order to pay off rent arrears and doctors' bills, that they pressed for legislation on money lending.[49] In 1924 money lenders charged 1d in the shilling weekly which amounted to 433 1/3 per cent interest and sometimes 2d in the shilling or 866 per cent. In 1927 legislation provided that money lenders must possess a licence costing £15 and interest rates were not to exceed 48 per cent but the law was often broken.[50]

When one reads of the poverty in the depressed areas of Britain or even of cases of appalling conditions in southern Britain, it is difficult to remember that the inter-war years were not years of uniform and unmitigated gloom. The fluctuations in the economy in these years and the regional variations have been described in chapter 3. Overall, economists see them as years of growth, and indeed there are many indications of a raised standard of living.

Food consumption per capita rose in Britain as a whole; expenditure on clothing increased; there was a consumer boom in the purchase of household appliances and of motor cars; we have seen too the rise in home ownership. For many of the middle class there were bad patches in the inter-war years, notably in the early 1920s and in the Great Slump of the early 1930s, but the world of the middle-class woman was aeons away from that of the wife of an unemployed miner. In 1931 the middle-class *Good Housekeeping* realised that many of its readers had been forced to readjust their expenditure because of the Slump. It advised certain obvious retrenchments – fewer visits to the theatre (or cheaper seats), getting rid of the car and entertaining on a simpler scale. The magazine was most insistent that economies should not be made below a certain level on food. Food prices had actually fallen in the 1930s, a fact which enhanced the lives of those in work. *Good Housekeeping* advised in 1931 that from 12s 6d to £1 per head per week should be sufficient to provide an adequate diet.[51] Even the smaller of these sums was more than many working-class women had to feed a whole family. Middle-class women, in common with working-class women, held responsibility for running the household, though middle-class men took charge of some larger items of expenditure.

It is hard for us to appreciate how gruelling the daily routine was for working-class wives. The Women's Health Enquiry's interviewees were usually up at 6 a.m. and on their feet all day until the evening with at best a few quiet hours sitting and mending and perhaps reading the paper. Housework was a never-ending round and many women organised it on a strict weekly basis, for example: Monday – washing; Tuesday – ironing, bed-making; Wednesday – upstairs rooms; Thursday – mats beaten; Friday – parlour. Most working-class homes had no modern labour-saving devices at all. It was a battle to keep small overcrowded houses clean. Door steps had to be whitened with a donkey-stone, flagged and wooden floors had to be scrubbed, linoleum had to be scrubbed and polished; working-class families usually had a few rag mats and some few had carpet squares. Clothes too had to be kept clean – washed with boiling water, heated in the copper (by a fire or gas), scrubbed and rubbed in a tub with a washing board and a bar of hard soap or washed with soda; then rinsed, blued, starched, and hand-mangled. All this had to be ironed with a flat or box iron. The housewife's work load also included shopping, cooking, clearing up, bed-making and looking after small children. No wonder there was so little time for leisure, with its refreshing properties, for working-class women. Housework was much easier in the new style housing of the inter-war period, whether on the council estates or in the new privately built houses: bathrooms and kitchens could easily be wiped down.

Middle-class women faced different problems. The shortage of domestic servants meant that the burden of housework fell on middle-class housewives, who may or may not have had some help from a daily woman. The new range of domestic electric appliances such as vacuum sweepers, kettles, cookers, toasters and refrigerators were designed for their households. Great emphasis was put on modern 'scientific' housekeeping. *Good Housekeeping* magazine, which was launched in 1922, addressed itself to 'the house proud woman in these days of servant shortage' and promised to bring to her attention 'every new invention that is practical and economical'.[52] Advertising increased in intensity as the housewife emerged as an important consumer. Manufacturers of electrical goods wooed them always with the same message – 'Electricity plays the most valuable part in eliminating drudgery' – and Mr G.A. Service promised that gas meant 'goodbye to unnecessary drudgery'. Housewives could reach the new high scientific standards expected of them by buying a host of devices modern then and now museum pieces.

Many of the new appliances were purchased by another recent innovation – hire purchase; vacuum sweepers could be bought for a few shillings a week. Most furniture, wireless sets, motor cars, bicycles and gramophones were bought on hire purchase. Working-class women often purchased household items and clothing through 'check' firms. Checks were purchased from salesmen and then taken to the shop to be exchanged for goods; the customer then paid for the goods over twenty weeks. Working-class housewives normally shopped every day for items of food and cleaning materials. They shopped at grocers, fishmongers, butchers, markets and the corner shop. In working-class areas the Co-op store was a great favourite because it paid a generous dividend of 2s 6d in the pound.

Finally the most time-consuming activity of women in the home was childcare. Falling family size in part helped to lighten this burden but, as in the case of housework, higher standards were demanded. Jane Lewis writes:

> The encouragement given to middle class wives during the inter-war years to devote more time to both housewifery and childcare marked a departure from the ambivalent nineteenth century attitudes regarding the degree of personal involvement in domestic tasks compatible with cultured, lady like activity.[53]

Working-class women had always been 'personally involved' in housework and childcare. Now middle-class women, even more than their working-class counterparts, were made to feel that they had to reach certain high standards of childcare as laid down by child psychologists and medical experts. They were made to feel that there was one right way of doing things.[54] For women living away from their own families and older female relatives this was particularly alarming. It may well be connected with the emergence of the phenomenon of 'suburban neurosis' or depression in women living on new estates.[55]

Another vitally important aspect of women's lives in this, as in any other period, was health. This was not a view shared by the state in the inter-war years. Social and welfare legislation, whilst keen to promote motherhood and increase the population, concentrated on healthy children rather than on fit mothers. It is therefore not surprising that in order to investigate this question we must look to enquiries undertaken by women themselves into women's health rather than to state initiatives. The term health encompasses many issues: fertility and birth control, nutrition, disease and medical services.

Fertility rates declined steadily from the beginning of the century down to the Second World War. The change from the large Victorian family of perhaps seven, eight, nine or more children to the small family of one or two children is quite striking. Of all marriages taking place about 1860, 20 per cent had two children or less, while by 1925 the figure was 67 per cent.[56] The decline in family size in late Victorian times was largely confined to the middle class: the rapid decline in family size in the early part of the twentieth century was even more marked within the working class. Diana Gittins in an interesting study suggests that this decline in family size within the working class cannot simply be attributed to the spread of birth control knowledge but involves a whole variety of factors including the employment of women outside the home, increased expectations of life, and social mobility. However in the inter-war years despite the *general* decline in the birthrate, there were considerable local geographical variations and there were variations from family to family. Rhondda Urban District, a mining area hard hit by the Depression, experienced a decrease in the birthrate between 1911 and 1931 of 53.7 per cent and Burnley in Lancashire of 46 per cent, as against 38 per cent for England and Wales as a whole.[57] Margery Spring Rice and her team of investigators spoke to Mrs D. of Glasgow, aged thirty-six, who had ten children, Mrs B. of Caerphilly, aged thirty-six who had eleven children, but also Mrs C. of Essex who had three children and Mrs D. of Croydon who had only two children.

Birth control may not be the only factor which brought about a decline in the birthrate in the inter-war years, but it did offer women the chance to take some control over their own lives. As Diana Gittins points out, there was no birth control revolution comparable with that of the 1960s, but the inter-war years were a time when contraception was a much publicised issue and when birth control clinics were first established.

Women's attitudes towards birth control and the limitations of family size were mixed. Many women felt that recurrent child-bearing had worn them out physically and emotionally. The letters published by the Women's Co-operative Guild in 1915 showed that many women bitterly regretted having large families. Although this survey of one hundred and sixty members of the WCG did not ask for information about birth control, twenty respondents wrote that they either used or approved of birth control. The following poignant letter to Marie Stopes shows that women who had borne large numbers of children and not previously used birth control were very glad to turn to it:

South Wales
22 March, 1921

(Letter from Mrs R.G.M. to Marie Stopes.)

What I would like to know is how can I save having more children as I think I have done my duty by my country having 13 children – 9 boys and 4 girls and I have 6 boys alive now and a little girl who will be 3 years old in May. I buried a dear little baby girl three weeks old who died from the strain of whooping cough. I have not had much time for pleasure and it is telling on me now I suffer very bad from varicose veins in my legs and my ankles gives out and I just drops down. I am please to tell you that I received one of those willow plates from the News of the World for mothers of ten.[58]

Mrs Eyles bluntly stated that many working-class women had said to her, 'I shouldn't mind married life so much if it wasn't for bedtime', or 'I could put up with anything but the going to bed side'.[59] The first woman who had said this to her was the mother of seven. Fear of pregnancy and successive pregnancies wore women out. Older women had felt that they had little choice but to bear so many children – either from lack of contraceptives or of contraceptive knowledge or because their husbands were opposed to it. But they wanted a better life for their daughters. Stella Browne, the birth control campaigner, reported after a tour of South Wales and Monmouthshire in the early 1920s: 'How often in this tour have elderly women not said, "You've come too late to help me, Comrade, but give me some papers for my girls, I don't want them to have the life I've had" '.[60]

But if many women were anxious to limit their family size, through abstinence or contraception, others were fatalistic. Jane

Lewis quotes a leading obstetrician in the late 1930s who, when he asked women in Aberdeen how many children they would like to have, received the reply, 'Aye, Doctor, I shall have me number'.[61] Other women genuinely wanted and enjoyed large families and Roman Catholic women were sternly enjoined by priests not to limit their family size.

People have used a variety of contraceptive methods since time immemorial. With the exception of the development of the sheath with the vulcanisation of rubber in the nineteenth century, there were, as Diana Gittins writes, 'no dramatic innovations in contraceptive technology until after the Second World War'.[62] In short, the contraceptive methods available in Britain between 1918 and 1939 were all known before that period. The chief methods of birth control used were coitus interruptus (a male method), abortion (a female method) and the employment of a variety of 'mechanical' devices, for example, sheaths, douches, and diaphragms. One of the most striking changes in the practice of birth control in the inter-war years was the greatly increased use of these 'mechanical' contraceptive devices. The middle-class led the way in this but the working-class was quick to follow. The increase of middle-class people using mechanical means of birth control rose from 9 to 40 per cent between 1910 and 1930, whilst figures for the working-class are from 1 to 28 per cent.[63]

Information on birth control was difficult to come by. One might have expected that women who went out to work discussed methods of family limitation with their co-workers, but as Elizabeth Roberts points out in her study of working-class women in Lancashire: 'There is little evidence that women discussed sexual topics in the mill'.[64] The 1920s saw the emergence of a new source of information – birth control clinics. Marie Stopes stands out in the annals of the twentieth century birth control movement. After the publication of her book *Married Love* (1918), which had sold nearly a half million copies by the mid 1920s, she achieved great fame and notoriety.[65] She was reviled by many churchmen but heralded as a saviour by women: she was, as one elderly Welsh woman described her, 'that woman, that Saint' or as Naomi Mitchison put it 'a light in great darkness to many of us . . . '[66] Stopes' *Married Love* had carried hardly any reference to methods of birth control but in response to many letters begging for information she followed it up with *Wise Parenthood* (1918) in which she recommended a small rubber cervical cap preferably used in combination with a soluble quinine pessary.

The long term effect of Stopes' work was to make birth control respectable; by setting contraception within the context of marriage she divorced it from its association with promiscuity and prostitution. Stopes, a eugenicist interested in curbing the breeding of the lower classes, nevertheless performed a great service. Despite opposition from the church and the medical profession, she opened the first birth control clinic in London in 1921. Within the next three years the clinic gave advice to 5,000 women. The spread of birth control clinics is an important development of the inter-war years. In 1921 another birth control organisation, the Malthusian League, opened a clinic at Walworth.[67] Throughout the 1920s the initiative lay with such bodies: the state did nothing. The first Labour government, elected in 1924, would not take up the birth control cause and Labour women had to continue to press the party to act on this issue.[68] In 1924 the Society for the Provision of Birth Control (actually the Walworth centre) encouraged the setting up of new clinics; the first of these to open outside London was in Wolverhampton in 1926.

Throughout the whole of the inter-war period the provision of clinics remained inadequate and there was enormous regional variation. There were great controversies in many areas. The *Manchester Guardian* reported reactions to the establishment of a clinic in Salford throughout the spring of 1926. The Bishop raged against 'these strange filthy things' and against 'the powers of evil' in the Greengate clinic. A protest meeting was held. This time a local canon opposed birth control on the grounds of the declining numbers of the white races and when reminded that the black man was his brother, he replied, 'But I would ask, do you desire him as a brother in-law?'[69] It remained difficult for the great mass of working-class women to gain access to the facilities of a clinic. Many local authorities pressed the government to set up birth control clinics – among them Brighton, Shoreditch, Bootle, St Helen's and Warwickshire. In 1930 a conference of Public Health Authorities held in London demanded that birth control information be given to all those desirous of it. In that year the government gave way in part by conceding that existing Maternity and Child Welfare clinics could give birth control instruction to mothers whose health would be injured by further pregnancies. In 1930 all the major birth control organisations, including Stopes', came together to form the National Birth Control Council and in 1931 this became the National Birth Control Association (NBCA). Stopes did not remain long and was soon off on her independent way again.

Memorandum 153/MCW and subsequent government circulars in the 1930s provided local authorities and regional hospital boards with the power to set up birth control clinics themselves or to assist the NBCA in providing voluntary clinics. There was actually no compunction to do so and there were many local disputes on the issue of birth control clinics in the 1930s between those who were demanding facilities and those who were fiercely opposed to them. In fact, the result of government policy and the activities of the NBCA meant that the number of clinics increased from under twenty in the decade 1921–31 to about sixty in the decade 1931–41 and to about 140 in 1951. The co-operation between the state and the NBCA in the 1930s meant that by the outbreak of the Second World War the idea of family planning had been integrated into the machinery of the state. A fall in population growth in the 1930s and fears of a dwindling population influenced the NBCA to change its name in 1939 to the Family Planning Association.

Provision in Scotland lagged behind England. However, in the mid 1930s two official reports recommended wider provision of contraceptive advice in Scotland. The NBCA sent Miss Holland to Glasgow in 1936; Mrs Grey took over as Scottish adviser to form branches and clinics. In May 1939 the NBCA organised a deputation to the Scottish Office to urge greater local authority action in giving contraceptive advice. In Scotland, in contrast to England and Wales, private practitioners undertook more maternity and child welfare work. As Audrey Leathard points out, by 1939 six voluntary clinics existed but only five out of a possible fifty-five Scottish authorities made any sort of provision.[70]

The sketchiness of the local provision of clinics, and the proviso that maternity and child welfare clinics would only assist women whose health would be injured by further pregnancies, meant that millions of women were denied information and assistance. Birth control remained a difficult subject and women who did visit clinics often did so furtively. Women who had only one child were often suspected of having had an abortion. One of Elizabeth Roberts' respondents said she was insulted like a lot of women who only had one child: it was, 'They know how it's done'.[71]

Abortion was probably the most important female initiative in limiting family size and the most frequently used.[72] Abortion had been illegal since 1803 but most women regarded it as a perfectly legitimate way of dealing with an unwanted pregnancy. As late as 1938 a government Inter-Departmental Committee on abortion reported that 'many mothers seem not to understand that self induced abortion was illegal. They assumed that it was legal before the third month (before quickening), and only outside the law when procured by another person'.[73] Marie Stopes' experience bears out this attitude. She wrote that within three months she had received '20,000 requests for criminal abortion for women who did not apparently even know that it was criminal' and that within three *days* one of her travelling clinics received only thirteen applications for contraceptive instructions but eighty demands for criminal abortion.[74] In 1932 the medical officer of health in Cardiff reported that 'an alternative to birth control is being widely practised, namely self induced abortion, and leads not infrequently to death, and still more commonly to permanent damage'.[75] Women induced abortions by taking hot baths, by drinking gin, washing soda, quinine, rat poison, by swallowing tablets advertised in newspapers (tablets and tabules which 'got rid of blockages' and 'cured *all* ladies' ailments') and using implements such as slippery elm bark sticks and knitting needles.

In 1936 a survey of 3,000 women in Birmingham showed that 35 per cent of them had had an abortion.[76] In 1939 an official surmise of the number of deaths annually attributed to abortion estimated the figure at between 110,000 and 150,000.[77] The 1926 Infant Life Preservation Act reaffirmed the illegality of abortion, except where it could be proved that an abortion had been performed to save the life of the mother. The Abortion Law Reform Society, founded in 1936, although strongly supported by feminists such as Stella Browne (who believed abortion was a woman's right), argued for a change in the law on the grounds of the high incidence of women's deaths from illicit abortions. One legal judgement, made in the 1930s, however, was important. A judgement made by Justice Mac-Naghten in 1938 indicated that it was lawful for a doctor to terminate a pregnancy in order to safeguard a woman's mental health and to prevent her from becoming 'a mental and physical wreck'.[78] This decision left many loopholes and ambiguities in the law, often helping wealthy women procure abortions but was of little help to most women. The whole issue of abortion was not seriously confronted until long after – in the 1960s.

If birth control was fraught with difficulty so was childbirth. The great majority of confinements took place at home. Only women whose husbands were in insured employment received a maternity benefit of £2 after World War I. This money often went on paying for medical attendance. In the 1930s midwives charged between 25s to 50s for a first confinement and 21s to 40s for subsequent ones. Doctors charged at least twice as much. Not only did pregnancy and childbirth frequently damage women's health, but the rates of maternal mortality (women's deaths in childbirth) were scandalously high; at a time when mortality generally and infant mortality specifically were falling rapidly, maternal mortality rose. It rose from the end of the First World War up till 1934: the figures for England and Wales stood at 4.33 deaths per thousand in 1920, and at 4.66 in 1934. In poorer areas the figures were higher. In Wales the rate for 1920 was 5.52 per thousand. Infant mortality too showed great regional variations. In 1935 when the infant death rate stood at 42 per thousand in the Home Counties, it was 63 in Glamorgan, 76 in Durham, 77 in Scotland, 92 in Sunderland and 114 in Jarrow.[79]

Poor housing conditions may well have been linked with the high maternal mortality rate. This factor, together with inadequate income and an over demanding workload affected other aspects of women's health. Although the standard of nutrition of the country as a whole rose in the inter-war years and the consumption of nourishing foods – eggs, milk, butter, fruit and vegetables – increased, this improvement was not distributed across the classes. Official sources were markedly reluctant to acknowledge that the slump of 1931-3 had any detrimental effect on working-class diet: 'The depressed state of industry and the need for national economy does not appear to have exerted, as yet, any measurable ill-effect upon the child population', wrote the chief medical officer to the Board of Education in 1931.[80] In 1933 Sir E. Hilton Young, Minister of Health, told the House of Commons that, 'there is at present no available evidence of any general increase in physical impairment, sickness or mortality as a result of the economic depression or unemployment'.[81] More enlightened observers put the absence of signs of physical deterioration down to the superficial nature of school medical examinations and the lack of fixed medical standards for measuring malnutrition.

The diseases linked with malnutrition were rife: rickets, for example, was widely reported. People had no resistance to diseases because their diet was inadequate. In 1936 John Boyd Orr published his survey *Food Health and Income* and concluded that a completely adequate healthy diet was out of the reach of 50 per cent of the population and that for 30 per cent of the population the diet was seriously deficient.[82] The result of Orr's work and of Rowntree's survey of poverty in York was agitation to feed the children. It resulted in a slight increase in the provision of school dinners and a much greater increase in the provision of subsidised milk for school children. But we must remember that it was women who did without in the family. Margery Spring Rice's work has demonstrated what many people know from experience – that women put themselves last.

Poor housing and poor diet often literally crippled women's lives. The Women's Health Enquiry sample women lived life at least '5 degrees under' and often suffered serious illness. Anaemia, constipation and headaches were an unremarkable part of their lives; of the 1,250 women interviewed 588 were anaemic, 291 suffered from headaches, 273 from constipation and/or haemorrhoids, 165 from toothache, 258 from rheumatism, 191 from gynaecological ailments, and 101 from bad legs.[83] Sometimes remedies were apparently very simple but they required medical treatment and in those days that cost money. One woman said that her eyes hurt when she went out into the light after being in her 'dark smelly kitchen'. She like many others could not afford spectacles.[84] Housing could cause much more serious ailments. Tuberculosis was linked with damp housing. When Lady Megan Lloyd George made her maiden speech in parliament in 1930, she concentrated on tuberculosis and housing in rural areas. She referred to a report made on her own constituency of rural Anglesey, where the death rate from tuberculosis for women was the highest but one on the whole list of administrative counties in England and Wales. For men, however, it came only twenty-second on that black list. There could be only one explanation of that – bad housing: 'The greater risk to health was for the woman who spent the greater part of her life in those squalid, dark, ill-ventilated cottages . . . '[85]

Then there was the problem of 'nerves'. One articulate and reasonably well educated woman explained to the Women's Health Enquiry in 1939:

> The constant struggle with poverty this last four years had made me feel very nervy and irritable and this affects my children. I fear I have not the patience that good health generally brings. When I am especially worried about anything I feel as if I have been engaged in some terrific physical struggle and go utterly limp and for some time unable to move or think coherently. This effect of mental strain expressed in physical results seems most curious and I am at a loss to explain it properly to a doctor.[86]

That respondent could pinpoint the cause of her nervous condition to poverty. There were many other causes and the problem of 'nerves' was not restricted to working-class women. Middle-class women, especially those who felt isolated and housebound caring for young children, were equally liable to 'bad nerves'. *Woman's Own* addressed itself to the problem and stressed women's responsibility to take their nerves under control for the sake of the whole family. It proceeded to give sensible advice on fresh air and exercise:

> Few housewives realise what powers they possess and how much depends on them; how they have within their grasp to make or mar the lives of everyone within the household. They are the pivot – the centre around which this small organisation works and when it is out of gear everything is affected . . . If she takes this nervy condition in hand in its early stages, she will prevent disaster in the future not only from the point of view of her own health, but because she is risking something none of us likes to lose – the power to keep her husband.[87]

Wealthy women, who suffered from 'nerves' in a period when Freud was capturing headlines, had the new option of psychoanalysis open to them.

It is quite astounding to us now that before the establishment of the National Health Service after the Second World War, the great majority of women were not entitled to free medical treatment. The National Insurance Act of 1911, under which manual workers and those earning less than £160 per annum contributed towards unemployment and sickness benefit, benefitted mainly male workers. It entitled them to see a 'panel' doctor without payment, and to free medicine but not to free hospital treatment. The National Insurance Acts were extended in the inter-war years to cover more workers but large groups of employed women still remained outside these acts. Moreover the acts did not cover dependent wives and children. Middle-class people paid fees all along the line – to consult the doctor, or dentist, for medicines and for hospital treatment. For working-class women the cost of visiting a doctor could be prohibitive even at 2s 6d or 5s a consultation. The only women the state 'had time for' were pregnant women and mothers. The National Insurance Act of 1911 had included a 30s maternity benefit: local authorities began to provide health visitors from the early 1900s and increasing alarm at infant welfare, exacerbated by the losses of men in the First World War, greatly enhanced provision for young children. State concern centred around children. From 1918 onwards the state provided clinics for maternity and child welfare but the emphasis was always on the child. In 1918 there were 2,324 infant welfare clinics and by 1938, 3,580. There were only 120 antenatal clinics in 1918 and by 1933 still only 1,417. [88] Health care in schools improved too but once a young girl reached adulthood she was on her own and could only expect free advice for herself if she were pregnant and for about a year after the birth of a child. She had to pay for everything else. So where did women turn for help? The Women's Health Enquiry of 1939 is again useful and gives the following information on where women received help and instruction:

> Of the 1250 women in the survey, these and the remainder have learnt anything they know from Welfare Centres and Ante-Natal Clinics (591 women cite these), the Health Visitor and/or district Nurse (245 cases); Daily Press, magazines, wireless, lectures at Clubs, Church Socials, etc. (217 cases), and their own doctor (67 cases). Eleven women have been nurses or midwives and have had some special training. [89]

The small number of women going to see their own doctor is

striking. No mention is made of consulting female relatives and it is possible that the welfare system began to oust older female networks. Finally no mention is made of another resort of working-class women – quack medicine. Market places were often full of salesmen and saleswomen (dressed as nurses) selling bottles of medicine and tablets – cures for worms, uric acid, constipation . . . for 'every illness of the human body'.

In looking at both home life and health, class differences have shown up very clearly. If we turn now to how women spent their leisure time, either inside or outside the home, these differences are even more apparent.

5

LEISURE

In writing of women's leisure during the inter-war years the first and most obvious point which must be made is that the amount of leisure time available, and indeed the kind of pursuits engaged in, depended upon wealth and consequently upon social class. At the top end of society there were women who could devote their whole lives to the pursuit of leisure: young aristocratic women were presented as debutantes at court, went to fork lunches and to tea at the Ritz, attended balls and nightclubs (where they did the new daring dances), flung themselves into the whirl of the London season, weekended in the country and holidayed on the Riviera or at Biarritz. Older women of this class, though potentially equally leisured, spent much of their time in philanthropic works. Women from the better-off sections of the middle class too filled their lives with social engagements.

Although there was a growing expectation within the middle class that daughters would take up some form of paid employment before marriage, or at least 'do something',[1] it was still unusual for women who belonged to families rich enough to keep them to do any work at all.[2] Smaller family size and a continued, if not always easily-available supply of domestic servants, meant that many middle-class women could lead a leisured life. Frances Donaldson filled her days lunching-out with a friend, playing golf in the afternoon, dining out nearly every evening and weekending in the country.[3] It was not just the upper class and upper middle class who gave themselves over to lives of leisure. Lady Rhondda, in a pamphlet entitled *Leisured Women* (1928), attacked such idle women as a menace to society:

> The school girl of today is allowed to suppose that providing her father has enough money to keep her she will be doing nothing wrong when she leaves school, if she does what would be regarded as the last disgrace if her brother did it − if (in the hope of marriage) she lives at home idly.[4]

Such women, who Lady Rhondda claimed, existed in every suburb and town, spent their lives playing tennis and bridge, dancing, spending money on clothes and reading novels not newspapers; there were, according to the viscountess, even more of these women in the 1920s than in the 1870s.[5] In a later article Lady Rhondda explained that the leisured woman was not necessarily rich – 'she can and does exist on an income of six or seven hundred a year'; in weekly terms this meant between £11 10s and £13 10s.[6] However it is difficult to generalise about the amount of leisure available to middle-class women.

Whilst it is certainly true that the new houses built in the inter-war period, equipped with gas, electricity and labour-saving devices, were easier to run than those of the days before the First World War, it would be easy to overemphasise the amount of leisure available to middle-class women. Young mothers were subjected to a barrage of information on childrearing and there was undoubtedly far greater emphasis on good housekeeping performed by the wife. Of course, working-class young women had their fun too – in the evenings after a day's work in a factory or a shop – but they had far less time or money to give to leisure; paid holidays were far from common. But it is the married woman with children of the working class who had least time of all for 'leisure'. Margery Spring Rice's survey shows time and again the never-ending nature of a working-class woman's work. As one woman from Caerphilly in South Wales, who was on her feet for 16½ hours a day, sometimes more, said about leisure, 'After my children go to bed, I gets two hours rest, if call it rest, I am mending my children's clothes and tidying in those few hours I get.'[7]

Clearly there was great variation in the amount of time given over to leisure by women of differing social classes. There were great differences too in the type of leisure pursuits women enjoyed. Those I shall examine briefly here fall into three main groups – leisure outside the home, holidays and leisure at home.

Cinema-going was the most popular form of entertainment in Britain in the 1930s. Admissions boomed. From the already high annual admission figure of 903 million for 1934, the figure climbed to 990 million admissions for 1939.[8] The numbers of cinemas increased too – from 3,000 in 1926 to nearly 5,000 in 1939 and many of these were large new buildings.[9] Picture-going was a regular feature of people's weekly entertainment. In Liverpool in 1934 some 40 per cent of the population went to the cinema once a week and 25 per cent of these went twice a week or more.[10] There are many statistics to show how often people 'went to the pictures' and we have already seen what a central form of entertainment the cinema was for women. Seebohm Rowntree in his study of York noted that many people went three or four times per week and stated, 'Fully half the people who attended cinemas are children and young people, and of the adults about 75 per cent are women'.[11] Of the East End of London Richard Carr commented in 1936, 'women and young people depend nowadays almost entirely for their entertainment upon the cinema'.[12]

Given that social observers are unanimous in the assertion that the cinema was the most popular form of entertainment for women, what sort of women went? The evidence from a survey conducted in the early 1940s shows that the women who were regular (at least once a week) cinema-goers were young, working-class and educated to a low standard: 81 per cent of women in the 14–17 age group and 45 per cent of women in the 18–40 age group, compared to 76 per cent and 38 per cent of men, said that they went to the cinema at least once a week.[13] A.P. Jephcott in her enquiries into the leisure habits of working-class girls wrote, 'It is not unusual to find a girl of fourteen who goes to the pictures nearly every night'.[14] Cinema-going was cheap entertainment. Working-class girls and boys in South Wales sat in the front seats for 5d and were content 'that they are having the same programme as those in the dearer seats behind'.[15] As to educational attainment, a survey published in 1940 showed that 66.1 per cent of girls (aged fourteen or over) who had received only elementary education, went to the pictures once a week or more, whilst only 32.5 per cent of girls (aged fifteen or over) who had undergone secondary education went once a week or more.[16] A survey conducted in Bolton in 1938 showed one eighteen year old attending sixteen times a month.[17] Throughout the 1920s and indeed the early 1930s the female cinema-going audience was largely working-class but an increasing number of middle-class women became cinema-goers in the 1930s. In the course of the 1930s cinema-going became far more respectable as it was no longer viewed simply as trash for the masses. The introduction of sound in 1928, the building of large, comfortable cinemas in the suburbs, often with restaurants or tea rooms, and the screening of popular novels such as *South Riding* by Winifred Holtby and *The Citadel* by A.J. Cronin made the cinema an acceptable place for middle-class housewives to spend an afternoon. Writers such as Vera Brittain, Barbara Pym and Elizabeth Bowen were frequent cinema-goers.

Cinema-going in the 1930s represented a complete night-out for many people. The luxurious and opulent new cinemas, particularly the Odeons with their marble stair-cases, chandeliers, Wurlitzer organs, uniformed staff and bright lights were indeed dream places. Others were merely cold and grubby flea-pits. Both kinds of cinema sold the same dreams. There were however class differences. The middle-class were more responsive to British films, while the working-class preferred fast American films. In working-class Bolton in

1938 teenage girls ranked musical romances, followed by love films, as their favourites. Women of fifty years of age and over placed musical romances as their first choice and both the teenagers and older women appreciated good history films. Anna Neagle had recently appeared there as *Victoria the Great*.[18] Middle-class women too had liked that film, which brought into the cinema many old people for the first time.

For many women the cinema was no doubt just a form of entertainment but for many others it was the place where one escaped from the daily round of drudgery into the opulent and romantic world of fantasy: 'I go to the films to be entertained, amused, to forget everyday worries and find it a success and should go more often if I could afford it', said a seventy-eight year old woman in the Bolton Odeon.[19] Another younger woman said that the cinema was 'a cheap night-out after a day's work – picture palaces are so comfortable'.[20] An eighteen year old spelt out her reasons for going, and indeed those of many other girls – 'to think that for a few coppers one can enter the world of make believe and leave behind all the worries and cares, well I say "Long Live the films" '.[21] Young women dreamed of becoming film stars and trashy magazines fed the fantasy.[22] *Peg's Paper* not only ran its regular feature 'Peg Trots Around Hollywood' (a mixture of gossip, fashion and beauty tips) but frequently gave over double-page spreads to such forgotten stars as Ivy Duke. Ivy Duke (who 'liked best' kiddies and animals and 'disliked most' swank) advised girls to copy the appearance of the film actress 'that is nearest to your type because it is part of a film star's job to do her hair the way that suits her and to dress to the best advantage'.[23] Film magazines reached enormous circulation figures, particularly *Picturegoer*. It is remarkable too that the feminist *Woman's Leader* introduced a film review column, written by the witty novelist Rose Macaulay, as early as 1921: serious newspapers did not do so for many years. Britain in the 1930s was full of young girls looking like actresses and dreaming of being Greta Garbo or Marlene Dietrich.

Among the young, of all classes, the other most popular form of entertainment in these years was dancing. The inter-war years can fairly be described as dance crazy. There was a frenzied quality in the way in which the wild and jerky new dance steps and syncopated music were taken up from America. The steps were always changing. There were the Charleston, Black Bottom, the Shimmy and many others. Films reinforced the craze: Joan Crawford Charlestoned, Valentino tangoed and Adele and Fred Astaire danced just about everything. The dance boom affected all social classes in Britain. At the top end of society the most striking feature is that dancing went public. Young society women danced in restaurants and nightclubs, as well as at charity balls or at debutante dances arranged for the London season. Fancy dress became the rage within the upper class and baby-romps were very popular: wealthy young women and men, attired as babies, drank gin from baby-bottles and cocktails from nursery mugs. Women in provincial 'society' had a duller time of it but throughout the country dances proliferated – often put on by local organisations such as tennis clubs or churches. Churches were also closely associated with a largely middle-class, arty-crafty revival of folk-dancing. But the main dance boom was undoubtedly within the working-class. Between 1918 and 1925 some 11,000 dance halls and nightclubs opened.[24] Throughout the country the Palais, Mecca and Locarno dance halls, with the local equivalent of the big bands, offered entertainment and hope to working-class girls. In addition to the large commercial dance halls were the evening dances arranged in drill halls, works' clubs, church halls and the booming dance schools, often with roped-off areas for learners.

It is important to realise how popular dancing was as a pastime for young working-class girls. When A.P. Jephcott conducted a survey among young women in London, Manchester and County Durham in 1941, of twenty-seven girls between the ages of fourteen and seventeen dancing emerged as the most popular activity – pipping the pictures into second place. Jephcott's twenty-seven girls had been in one week between them fifty-two times to the cinema and fifty-four times to dances.[25] Of these girls one seventeen year old from Lancashire, a factory worker, went dancing on Monday, Tuesday, Wednesday, Thursday and Friday and to the pictures on Saturday and Sunday. She was exceptional but many young women went dancing once or twice a week to the local Palais or to some sort of social club.[26] The pattern of procedure in both seemed to be the same. Girls usually went to dances with a girl friend, with whom they would dance until invited to dance by a boy. There were no introductions: the boy made his selection from the waiting girls. Girls endured the agony of waiting to be asked. Only in a 'Ladies Excuse Me' – or 'Buzz off' – could a girl invite a boy to dance.

There were plenty of reasons why girls and young women went dancing. The radio and gramophone had popularised dance music and for many young women stooped over a factory bench or typewriter all day, there was the fun of the exercise to music in company. But there is no doubt that the dance hall was the place where young women thought it most likely that they would meet their future partner. Dance halls were imbued with romance. Women's magazines, especially the down-market ones, promoted dancing as the road to happiness. They were full of advertisements for 'Dancing Made Easy' – 'in a short time you can become an accomplished dancer by our amazing chart system – be popular, the envy of the crowd'.[27] Agony aunts told readers that the best way to meet a man was to learn to dance. Stories, aimed at working-class girls, featured transformed factory hands, floating around in the arms of handsome titled men at masked balls:

> A stray petal brushed Mary's cheek and caught in the silken folds of her skirt, and she picked it off and held it in her hand.
> 'Why it is real', she said, wonderingly.
> Sir Nigel laughed.
> 'Everything is real tonight,' he said. 'This is the Ball of Dreams come true.'

It is all a far cry from the bare-boards and wooden chairs in the local drill hall.[28]

Eating out demonstrates an even greater class divide. The upper class, or the simply wealthy, might, in the new order of public night-life, dine at Boulestin's, the Eiffel Tower, the Ritz or the Savoy, as well as attending large dinner parties in each other's houses. For women eating out after a certain hour, there was one proviso: they had to be accompanied by a man, otherwise a restaurant would not serve them. Winifred Holtby tells of herself and the respectable, elderly matron of a public school being refused a cup of coffee in a northern hotel at night and of business women roping obliging men in off the street to fulfil the rule of having a male companion.[29] In 1930 women organised a campaign against this rule but the practice continued. In the mornings or afternoons those who could afford it might drink coffee or tea in one of the growing number of genteel tea rooms. Hundreds of 'Copper Kettles' sprang up run by spinster ladies and lunching with a woman friend was part of the normal routine of middle-class women.

For the working-class eating out, except in a fish-shop parlour on holiday, simply does not come into the picture. This was due not only to lack of money but also to different eating habits. Whereas for the rich there was afternoon tea followed by dinner, which was the main meal of the day for the well-to-do, for the great majority of the population, some 95 per cent of people, there was 'high tea' as the main evening meal followed by a late night supper.[30] Working girls, particularly those employed in offices, might eat out at lunch-time but this was scarcely 'luncheoning'. Ethel Manning wrote in 1932 that it was impossible to make up for a scanty breakfast,

> when one dare not spend more than sixpence, or ninepence at the outside, on a 'meal' . . . the most one can afford is a

cup of coffee, a roll and butter, and a 'Cambridge sausage', or sardines on toast, or a poached egg.[31]

As to women's pub-going it is impossible to be categorical. Much detailed local research needs to be done. Some working-class women did indeed go to pubs. In Bolton, there were many men-only bars or 'vaults'; some women did go to lounge bars and drank guinness, beer or gin.[32] A working-class Hackney housewife described how she went regularly to the pub for a sing-song of an evening. Of her local pub she said, 'It was open to all. Women could go there as well – husbands and wives used to go in'.[33] In the newly built residential suburbs and in the countryside along the new arterial roads, 'road house' style public houses were built to cater for the motor traffic; these were the sort of places a man might take his wife or girl friend.[34] But on the whole, especially in the older industrial areas, public houses were male domains and no 'respectable' woman would be found dead in one.

Throughout the period under review the church played a central part in the social lives of many girls and women. Not only were there church services to attend but a whole host of ancillary activities such as Mothers' Union meetings, youth clubs, Bible classes, whist drives, social evenings and dances. Although the role of church and chapel in people's leisure did decline in the inter-war years in the face of the growing commercialisation of working people's leisure, in the countryside the church continued to be the focal point of life.

In addition to the social activities provided by the churches there were many secular organisations which women could join. The important point emerges here that women's 'leisure' is often connected with some productive activity. Cicely Hamilton in writing of women's clubs, mainly middle-class bodies, stated,

> where a woman's club in England sometimes differs from a man's is in having its more serious, more cultural side; it is not just a place where members drop in to spend their leisure – where they idle in comfort, dine, read the papers or play bridge.[35]

On the contrary, women often attended lectures or participated in debates in their clubs or luncheon clubs. This serious side is to be seen in many other organisations. The Women's Institute, established in 1917, was a boon to country women. At these meetings Institute members were given lectures on 'such simple everyday subjects as fruit-bottling, mending and recovering furniture, home nursing, glove-making and elementary agriculture'.[36] The Townswomen's

Guild was the WI's urban equivalent.[37] The Women's Co-operative Guild was engaged in many serious issues in the inter-war years, for example, birth control, peace and international relations, yet it was also a place of recreation for its members. The Wesley Castle, Birmingham, branch of the Guild, enjoyed the following social activities in 1934: mystery night, summer outing to Manchester, pantomime outing, singing, raffle, drama, social and dance, games, whist drive, outing to Chepstow and the big event of the Guild's year, the anniversary of the branch's birthday celebrated by a tea, games and dancing.[38] Perhaps the one women's organisation entirely given to recreation, though it may have seemed like hard work, was the Women's League of Health and Beauty, whose devotees exercised their way to health. It is testimony to the new awareness of physical fitness of the 1930s that by 1939 the League was second only in its membership numbers to the WI.[39]

Girls too had many organisations which they could join; again these organisations all had at their core some form of educational, moral or civic purpose. In 1933–4 M. Rooff, in a survey of girls' clubs, listed the Girl Guides (membership 474,408), the Girls' Friendly Society (GFS, membership 158,000), the Girls' Life Brigade (40,242), Young Women's Christian Association (26,653), Federation of Working Girls' Clubs (13,670) and such smaller organisations as the Girls' Guildry and the Campfire Girls.[40] The Girl Guides and the Girls' Friendly Society demonstrate well the improving aims of girl clubs. The Guides taught, along with useful skills, *esprit de corps*, character-building and loyalty to the nation, whilst the GFS with its large numbers of servant members taught honesty, thrift and the rightness of the God-given social order. Both organisations provided a ground where the classes mixed: the middle-class often provided the organisation and leadership of the Guide movement and the GFS had not only ordinary members but 'associates', upper- and middle-class employers and their daughters. Many girls' clubs were a mixture of ping-pong, tea and biscuits and debates but they provided a friendly and often stimulating atmosphere even if they were held in poor accommodation. In reply to a survey of clubs made by Jephcott, girls showed that they especially enjoyed ballroom dancing, netball practice, country dancing and club-organised holidays.[41]

In sport there were many developments which reflected women's new freedom of dress and indeed strong sense of self-esteem. Amongst the very wealthy, winter sports became fashionable, as did flying. Plucky rich girls might buy and fly their own bi-plane. Stage personalities who did so were Gladys Cooper, Peggy O'Neill and Margaret Bannersman – perhaps influenced by Queen Elizabeth of Belgium 'who is the owner of a glittering, silvery two-seater that looks fairy like when in the air'.[42] Tennis and golf were played by many middle-class women whilst rambling and cycling became popular within the working class. There is little evidence of a participation in sports by working-class women though rounders was very popular with women in Bolton. Women employed in factories run by benevolent employers, such as Fry's or Cadbury's, had access to excellent recreational facilities. Fry's female employees at Somerdale, near Bath, had opportunities to play tennis, netball and cricket.[43] Some working-class women were enthusiastic spectators of male sports. Speedway racing, a new sport, attracted a female following. Some northern women went to All-in-wrestling to see well-built men, but as one remarked 'the general tone and social standing of All-in-wrestling could be raised and then we women wouldn't feel like gate crashers'.[44]

Even for the very wealthy whose whole lives might be viewed as a continuous whirl of pleasure and leisure, there existed a distinct notion of the holiday away from home. For them the year was divided into certain fixed periods to be filled by appropriately fashionable holidays. The dreary months between Christmas and March would be given over to the newly popular winter-sporting in Switzerland. St Moritz was the most chic of resorts for ski-ing, skating and sleigh-riding. By 1928 trousers were definitely *de rigeur* on the slopes. *Vogue* filled its winter numbers with photographs of the rich and famous in Norwegian gabardine suits or in Chanel *après-ski* wear and the middle-class *Good Housekeeping* treated its readers to drawings of sports costumes by Drecoll, Schiaparelli, or Nowitzsky.[45] The less hardy might choose to travel to the Riviera and spend the mimosa month at Cannes. Cannes, easily reached on the Train Bleu, offered not only tennis, golf and polo but gambling too and, if one tired of Cannes, there was always Monte and Nice. The Riviera also became firmly established as the summer holiday centre for the wealthy chic of Europe. E.M. Delafield allowed her heroine, the Provincial Lady, a fortnight at Ste Agathe where she spent her time amongst socialites sea-bathing and sun-bathing, but the very rich spent the whole season there, and engaged in just such pursuits.[46] *Vogue*'s Diary of August 1927 informs us,

Bathing from rocks is a new found pleasure. When one has seen the rocks at the Cap d'Antibes, terraced down to the sea, each with a little nook shaded by umbrellas under which one has gin fizzes or tea while watching the diving: has seen the aquaplaning and the groups of people sunburned a deep mahogany, it is a scene to rival the Lido. In the way of pyjamas and bathing suits Miss Ina Claire takes the honours. Her Nowitzsky pyjama suit has enormously full trousers.[47]

While sybarites whiled away the summer months on the Riviera or cruised on each other's yachts, other wealthy women were apparently hardier. August was the beginning of the shooting season at home and shooting-parties formed part of the normal season's entertainment. Nancy Mitford maintained that despite the general impression that sports women were 'seen everywhere with dog and gun', women were superfluous on such occasions and forced to content themselves for much of the day with embroidery and bridge.[48] But the inter-war years were also a period of far more adventurous travel by ocean-liner, aeroplane or motor-car. The early 1920s, after the restrictions on travel imposed by the First World War had been lifted, saw a burst of globe-trotting activity by wealthy women and men. Contemporary 'society' magazines are full of illustrations of intrepid titled riders on camels in Egypt and Arabia or posing with natives in South America and Africa.

The middle class too began to venture abroad with increasing frequency, travelling for the most part by train and boat. The most exotic foreign holidays, however, appealing to the more comfortably off, were cruises. They went to the Baltic and to the Mediterranean, stopping at places of interest and were the very stuff of romantic stories and serials in women's magazines. Travel at home for the middle class expanded at a much faster rate. Motoring as a pastime grew rapidly. In 1920 there were a half million vehicles on the road but by 1939 there were over three million of which two million were private cars. The cost of purchasing a car, thanks to mass production, actually fell in this period. In 1931 an Austin Seven cost £118 and a Morris Minor £100. Motoring holidays, as well as Sunday afternoon drives, became a feature of middle-class life. Some wealthier members of this class purchased country cottages as second homes for weekends. Francis and Vera Meynell's *Week-end Book* (1924) was an anthology of poetry and country-lore for town and suburban weekenders. Yet, although motoring expanded rapidly, the train remained the most popular form of transport to holiday resorts. The middle class went to select and quiet resorts – Cornwall became very popular – or shared resorts with the working class but with fairly strict lines of delineation. Ethel Manning recalled Hastings in her childhood. She and her family always went to a 'select beach' well away from the pier, the band, motor-boat trips in the Skylark and Punch and Judy shows. She envied the fun going on on the common beaches and stated, 'the more "select" the beach the duller it becomes, patronized by people who sit sedately in deck chairs instead of sprawling on the shingle, and by stiffly-uniformed nurses in charge of well behaved children'.[49] Ethel Manning and her mother took their annual holiday for three weeks and stayed in a seaside boarding house with good plain cooking. Such a long holiday was beyond the dreams or resources of the working class.

The single most important factor which determined whenever a working-class woman had a holiday away from home was whether she, or in the case of a married woman, her husband, received a holiday with pay. In 1922 only 1½ million manual workers were covered by agreements which included paid holidays. By 1939 this figure had risen to some four million manual workers.[50] The major improvement occurred largely at the end of the period. The 1938 Holidays with Pay Act gave local trade boards the power to fix one week's paid leave for workers. Without pay, a 'holiday' was a time of financial hardship. Many workers joined saving schemes at their factory or office to pay for the new clothes and for the holiday itself. In the late 1930s a man taking his wife for a week's holiday to Blackpool needed at least £8, a sum which few cotton workers, who were prime patrons of Blackpool, could save.[51] Not surprisingly by 1937 only fifteen million out of a population of forty-six million took a holiday of a week or more.[52]

People travelled to the seaside resorts by train or bus. Motor buses and charabancs increased greatly in number in this period and seriously rivalled the railways. At Easter 1938 a Ribble bus left Bolton every five minutes transporting holiday-makers to Blackpool.[53] Blackpool, Bridlington, Rhyl and Scarborough were amongst the most favoured holiday resorts for northerners, especially during the Wakes weeks, whilst Southend and Brighton were the Meccas of southerners.

Blackpool was the queen of seaside resorts. J.B. Priestley, visiting it on his English journey in the autumn of 1933, considered it 'a complete and essential product of industrial democracy'. It was a place for workers at play.[54] Priestley stayed at an expensive old fashioned hotel, with an indifferent orchestra and which charged exorbitant prices. Holiday-makers from the industrial towns stayed in kippax (private) houses, boarding houses or private hotels. The prices ranged (in 1938) from 6s per day in kippax accommodation, to 7s 6d in a boarding house and to 10s for an unlicensed private hotel and 15s for a licensed hotel.[55] Many young girls took accommodation in multi-occupied rooms. When Helen Forrester was sent on a charity holiday to Morecambe Bay she shared a room with five others.[56] In private houses it was common practice for the guests to bring their own food in, which the landlady would cook for them. This had the disadvantage for the visiting housewife of still having to go out shopping for food. Accommodation offering full board was the tired housewife's dream, where she would be waited on for a change. Of course, Blackpool offered opportunities to eat out, not a normal working-class practice at home. Fish and chips was the commonest working-class meal in Blackpool: middle-class restaurants did not even have it on the menu. In 1938 fish, chips and peas cost 6d.[57]

It is interesting to note what working-class women liked most about their holidays in Blackpool. The evidence given to the Mass Observers by women from Bolton is poignant and shows that the women did not ask for much. One respondent said,

Instead of preparing meals for my family, it would be a real holiday for me to be waited on. I would love to stay at a hotel and have *everything* done for me. For 10 years things have not been too prosperous, money has been scarce, and holidays have been make-believes. It would be a *joy* going in to breakfast, washed and dressed in nice clothes, then rising up from the table knowing that some one else would clear and wash up. I am tired. I just want a rest from everything one does and everything one sees for the rest of the year.[58]

Another woman, who had boarded-in for the first time, really appreciated being waited on: 'I have done nothing but laze on the sands or go in the sea and go home ready for my meals, and better still ready for bed at 10.30 to sleep'.[59] A week's reprieve from the round of cleaning and cooking, being served nicely presented meals and, above all, rest and the opportunity to lie-in in the morning, made the Blackpool holiday special for working-class women.

The seaside holiday resort offered a wide variety of leisure activities unavailable to the working class at home. Blackpool offered miles of fun from the Norbreak Hydro to the north to the Squires Gate holiday camp (another innovation of this period) in the south. Beaches, amusement arcades, miles of promenade, putting greens, the fun fair and the three fun-packed piers offered an enchanted world to housewives and mill girls. Palmists, ice-cream vendors, oyster carts, herbalists and contortionists livened up a walk in the balmy air of the promenade, and the Tower with its menagerie, slot machines, restaurants, bars, Reginald Dixon and the ballroom was a haven on a wet day. At night there were theatres, where famous stars like George Formby, Gracie Fields and Stanley Holloway performed. For young women above all there was the dancing in the Tower ballroom or elsewhere. Young girls could pick up men and vice-versa. Picking up with different young men most nights of the week was all part of the fun. In 65 per cent of the Mass Observers' recorded cases on holiday sex in Blackpool, it was the girls who took the initiative in picking up young men.[60]

A week in Blackpool had to be paid for by fifty-one weeks hard work. For many people a holiday meant just a day trip by train or charabanc and for many others, particularly in the depressed areas, there was not even that.

The amount of money a woman had and the social class to which she belonged determined both the comfort of her home and the range of leisure activities which took place within it. Entertainment at home still continued on a lavish scale amongst the wealthy both with regard to the country house weekend and the dinner party. Women's magazines gave advice on dinner parties and dances at home. *Vogue* contained advice on a dinner party for twelve[61] and even the more stolid *Good Housekeeping* gave menus for dances at home for fifty.[62] *Vogue* was quite explicit in stating that servants would cook the meal – it mentions four servants – while *Good Housekeeping* did not specify who would do the cooking but the cost per head of 3s 6d to 5s, and the size of home necessary to accommodate fifty guests, made it clear that the house would have live-in servants or, at worst, daily help. If the Victorian and Edwardian 'at home' was dying out, many ladies spent their time entertaining friends or out being entertained by friends. Monica Dickens, herself a well-to-do young woman, wrote of her employer, who breakfasted in bed, bathed, dressed and then, 'once dressed she was either out seeing people or at home with people coming to her'.[63]

Reading was another form of relaxation to be enjoyed at home. It was supposed to form part of the middle-class woman's day. Rose Macaulay in her parody of advice from mother-in-law to daughter-in-law in *Crewe Train* allocated the morning to reading: 10–11 read the papers and write one's letters: 11–1 serious reading.[64] *The Times* or the *Morning Post* or the more business orientated *Daily Telegraph* would have been considered suitable newspaper reading. From the early 1920s newspapers contained an innovation, which developed into something of a craze and which served to pass many an idle hour – the crossword puzzle. As to novels of the period, some of which I have drawn on in chapter 1 to illustrate images of women, Nicola Beauman's study provides an excellent starting point and reading guide. If the middle-class female reader did not purchase these in the new cheap paperback editions, she could borrow them in hardback from Boots Library; in 1926 Boots ordinary service cost 10s 6d a year and its special service of providing 'books on demand' cost 42s 0d.[65] The women's magazines, discussed in chapter 1, were all, except those devoted exclusively to some female craft, crammed with stories and serials. As to 'serious reading', tastes were not determined by social class. Some factory girls read H.G. Wells, Bertrand Russell and D.H. Lawrence.[66]

Indeed, reading was not a pleasure confined to the middle class. Reading a newspaper, local or national, or perhaps a woman's magazine at the kitchen table in the evening, was one of the few breaks from domestic routine available to the working-class woman. Newspaper circulation expanded rapidly in the inter-war years and the 1930s were characterised by a cut-throat circulation war. New readers, or readers of rival papers, were persuaded to buy the socialist *Daily Herald* by free gifts of such hefty volumes as *Home Doctor*, *Handy Man* and complete sets of Dickens. These were often the only books in a working-class home. The *Express* issued free insurance policies to regular subscribers. A contributor to the Mass Observation team's social investigation, conducted in Bolton in 1938, noted that the newspapers most in evidence in that working-class town were the dailies, the *Daily Express*, *Daily Mirror*, *Daily Mail* and *News Chronicle*. In addition to these were evening papers (often local), local weeklies and most sensational of all the Sunday papers. There were the women's magazines too, designed specifically for the working class. *Red Star*, *Peg's Paper* and *The Oracle*, with their mixtures of vivid and romantic tales and their superstitious nonsense, formed a large part of the reading matter of working-class women; such 'books', as they were referred to by their readers, were particularly popular with women who had received no education beyond elementary school.[67] Many married women of this class simply could not afford any sort of magazine. George Orwell in *Coming up for Air* drew a portrait of the hero's mother, Mrs Bowling, at her leisure; her 'paper' (women's magazine) and the Sunday newspaper were her staple reading:

We used to have tea at six. Mother had generally finished the housework, and between four and six she used to have a quiet cup of tea and 'read her paper', as she called it. As a matter of fact she didn't often read the newspaper except on Sundays. The week-day papers only had the day's news, and it was only occasionally that there was a murder. But the editors of the Sunday papers had grasped that people didn't really mind whether their murders are up-to-date and when there was no new murder on hand they'd hash up an old one, sometimes going as far back as Dr Palmer and Mrs Manning. I think Mother thought of the world outside Lower Binfield chiefly as a place where murders were committed.[68]

On weekdays, in the hour or so before tea, Mrs Bowling devoted herself to her woman's magazine with its interminable serial, its short stories, advertisements and advice columns to readers. She read it throughout the week sitting in an old arm-chair beside the hearth with her feet on the fender and she often dozed off.[69] For a busy working-class woman a quiet hour's read might mean, apart from being in bed, the only time she was off her feet.

Sewing was another, particularly female, 'leisure' activity. One hesitates to regard most needlework as leisure but the fact that it is generally so regarded reinforces the point that women's leisure was often productive. Turning again to George Orwell, one reads this description of a working-class family at leisure, after the day's work is done.

> Especially on winter evenings after tea, when the fire glows in the open range and dances mirrored in the still fender, when Father in shirt sleeves, sits in the rocking chair at one side of the fire reading the racing finals, and Mother sits on the other with her sewing and the children are happy with a pennorth of mint humbugs, and the dog lolls roasting himself on the rag mat.[70]

Mother is the only one in that scene who may be regarded as working. But what was she sewing? Perhaps she was making another rag mat for the dog to loll on or perhaps she was darning socks. The education of working-class girls put a heavy emphasis on sewing in this period so any girls attending a state school could not avoid picking up some sewing skills. Mrs Eyles, however, pointed out that working-class women in the 1920s did not darn as well as they used to and certainly did not apply their darning skills to their own stockings – they just turned the heel or toe under and cobbled them together anyhow.[71] Women in the inter-war years spent a great deal of time and effort making clothes for the families and themselves. The magazines were full of dress and knitting patterns for adults and children. *Good Housekeeping*, which ran a pattern service (readers sent in for the patterns), found that half of the magazine's entrants in a competition made their own underwear.[72] The contemporary *The Big Book of Needlework* devoted a whole chapter to 'Dainty Lingerie' and expected its readers to be making petticoats, knickers and pyjamas in satin, crêpe de chine, spun silk, linen-lawn, cambric and cotton. Clothes were often smocked and embroidered – both very time-consuming decorations. The nineteenth century was the heyday of the sampler, but embroidery continued to be regarded as a highly suitable leisure pursuit for women of all classes. The aristocratic Nancy Mitford regarded a piece of 'work' as indispensable when staying in other people's houses. She gave cheerful advice to other women on how to use embroidery as a barricade – when you are asked to go for a walk, play bridge or do anything else you particularly dislike you can entrench yourself behind it: 'My dear I *must* get on with this wretched work, it is for mother's birthday and I don't see *how* it is to be finished in time'.[73] The *Vogue* readers whom she was addressing in this delightful tongue-in-cheek piece were not to worry if they could not sew because, 'if it is well begun for you at some school of needlework you can always muddle along with the background'.[74] Most of the above remarks apply to knitting too, though knitting lacked the social chic of embroidery. Women knitted a far wider range of things in those days. Magazines and manuals abound in patterns for knitted vests and cami-knickers in two ply wool and dresses and blankets in three ply.

The wireless or radio was an important technological innovation which transformed home life. It was a particular boon to women as a form of leisure because it allowed them to do other things at the same time. Regular radio broadcasts from the BBC, chiefly of music, began in 1922. At first listeners picked up these broadcasts through 'cat's whiskers' or crystal set receivers. In the course of the 1920s valve wireless sets in expensive cabinet models and later table models became widely available. These were powered by batteries or, particularly later (early 1930s), by mains electricity. There were also local stations whereby a selection of radio programmes was transmitted to households for a weekly payment. This system was favoured in the many households without electricity or in areas where there was substantial interference of the signal by traffic or shipping. The cost of listening is difficult to establish. In Oxford in the period 1922 to 1929 the 'Wootophone' cost 49 guineas and a set from the Oxford Wireless Telephone company cost as much as £73. These were imposing pieces of furniture around which the family could sit and listen.[75] Crystal sets could be purchased in 1923 for £2 10s. Wirelesses became cheaper – but never very cheap in the inter-war years. In 1931 Curry's were selling two valve sets at 29s 6d and three valve models at 59s 6d; hire purchase terms were available.[76] In 1922 the licence cost 10s. Early radio achieved a wide reach. In 1931 there were 3,391,042 households holding licences; by 1938 the figure was 8,864,900.[77] Radio entered the homes of millions of people and it held far greater power to influence people than newspapers, magazines or novels. In terms of listening hours, women listened far more than men, largely because they were at home in the day.

Given the potential power of radio, it is perhaps fortunate that the doughty Lord Reith's policy of 'uplifting' cultural values prevailed. There was a constant tension, especially in the early days, between the public demand for entertainment in the form of light music and variety shows and the Reithian policy of serious music and talks. The public, especially on Sunday, avoided 'uplift' and religion by tuning into foreign stations like Luxembourg, Hamburg or Normandy. From the point of view of women in the home who listened to music, to talks and to drama, often while they ironed or washed or cleaned, a whole new world opened up. How many working-class women had been exposed to drama before? Women listened to talks on many subjects that were new to them like English literature, history or biology.

A survey commissioned by the BBC in 1939 and undertaken by two experienced women researchers, Hilda Jennings and Winifred Gill, came up with interesting findings on women's listening habits and the impact of the wireless on family life.[78] Jennings and Gill undertook their research in a working-class area of Bristol. Women there listened regularly to the wireless in the daytime and expressed annoyance when the milkman or other callers interrupted their listening.[79] They found that the interests of women were greatly enhanced by radio. One woman said that after listening to a programme on Byron she had gone to the library to get a biography of him.[80] Another woman, the mother of a family, bashfully admitted that what interested her was 'whales – anything to do with whales or whale-fishing'.[81] Radio talks included items specifically directed at housewives and mothers. The radio doctor was held in high esteem. In short, Jennings and Gill reported that, 'the housewife learns (from radio) what she had no time to get from books'.[82] Furthermore, they pointed out that radio provided women at home with an interest in common with other members of the family. In fact because the mother was at home most of the day she had the advantage over husband and children in that she had additional opportunities for listening. One male contributor to their survey reckoned that radio had enabled the woman to come into her own in organising the family in the evening: she would prepare tea, serving one then another and then she would say, 'Now clear the cloth there's a good play coming on'.[83]

Television was developed in the 1920s and the first transmission took place in 1936. Manufacturers of television sets expected a similar boom to that in radio but this was to be delayed by the coming of the Second World War in 1939. The television audience in the inter-war period was confined to the Alexandra Palace area and never exceeded 10,000 before transmission ceased in 1939.[84]

Leisure constantly reminds us of class difference and the extremes of wealth and poverty of the inter-war years. The final leisure pursuit I would like to mention was one which particularly emphasises these differences. The football pools offered hope to the working-class woman to escape from the hard work and scrimping of her own life into another world – to the world of a lady of leisure. But to many working-class women, and indeed men, a win on the pools promised security against sickness and unemployment and simply a decent standard of living. One woman said,

If I won, first I'd have my front room decorated and buy a

nice carpet for the floor. I would buy a good supply of bedding so that the children would not catch cold through sleeping in what had been washed that day. If there was any left when the holidays came round we should be able to take the children to the seaside for a whole week instead of the half day trips we have to make do with.[85]

It was a modest enough dream. The pools, an innovation of the 1930s, offered all this hope for a 1d stake – though the average bet in the late thirties was 3s. This particular form of gambling suited women because it could be done at home. Woolworths in working-class areas sold little gadgets which forecast solutions to the penny pools: it is sad to see with what eagerness and credulity working-class women bought these things.[86] The pools, apart from the time a woman spent filling in the coupon, offered not so much leisure as a fantasy – a fantasy to be conjured up when standing over a chipped sink in a damp kitchen.

'Doing the pools' might offer the dream of escape into a better world but there were other women, rooted in harsh reality, who were determined to bring about a better world for women and men. Such women refused to be bound by the current wisdom that women's only place was in the home; because they knew that it was only by getting involved in public life that they could bring about change. An examination of women's role in politics in Britain in the 1920s and 1930s is in many ways quite different from the other aspects of women's lives treated in this book, coloured as they are by a great emphasis on domesticity. But even in the realm of politics we cannot escape the central notion of the inter-war years that women's place was in the home. Even feminism itself and feminist theory was affected by the view that a woman's role was that of wife and mother.

6

POLITICS AND ISSUES

The history of women's political activities and the pursuit of women's goals in the twenty year period between the two world wars has been greatly neglected. Traditional history books scarcely give such issues a mention. It is as though 'the woman question' was solved in 1918, when women over thirty were 'given' the vote. Thereafter we are left to assume that women's lot improved and proceeded quietly and inexorably along the road of progress. Larger events, including the economic crisis at home, the rise of fascism in Europe and the growing threat of war (all issues which are presented as having nothing to do with women) crowded women off the stage of history. To a certain extent too, women, no longer so vociferous and insistent in making their voice heard, colluded in this. In this chapter I want to correct a view of history which goes along the lines that women, having achieved emancipation, and therefore feminism having become redundant, got on quietly with their own lives. Even naming the issues here shows how much had to be done and demonstrates that women involved themselves in a wide spectrum of political activities, both women-centred and of concern to women and men.

On 6 February 1918 The Representation of the People Act, giving most women over thirty the vote, became law. It was a great victory and a significant milestone in the struggle for enfranchisement which had begun in the mid nineteenth century. Women had fought for and won the vote through long years of campaigning. On the eve of war there was great optimism in the suffragist camp and in the summer of 1914, having won over much public support, they looked forward to 'another winter of hard work and then to an election which might open the door to their triumph'.[1] Then came the calamity of the First World War. Although not all feminists supported the war, it gave many women an opportunity to prove their worth. As Mrs Fawcett, the leader of the National Union of Women's Suffrage Societies, wrote, 'Let us prove ourselves worthy of citizenship, whether our claim is recognised or not'.[2] The vote was not merely a gift to women for war services rendered: however, the women's contribution to the war rendered it unthinkable that their demand for enfranchisement should continue unheeded. The war certainly changed attitudes in die-hard anti-suffragists. When Edith Cavell was shot by the Germans in 1915, the Liberal Prime Minister, Asquith, said, 'There are thousands of such women, but a year ago we did not know it'.[3] The issue of women's suffrage arose again in 1916 when the problem of servicemen, fighting in the services and away from home, meant that a reorganisation of electoral registers was imperative. A 'conference', or committee, was appointed to deal with franchise issues, and among the electoral reforms it recommended was the introduction of some form of women's suffrage. The enfranchisement of women was to be limited to householders, wives of householders and women over thirty or thirty-five. Labour women were quick to point out that the report omitted the very women most active in war work but the suffrage movement as a whole, fearing that further demands would jeopardise this possible gain, agreed to support the bill on condition that the age limit was thirty and not thirty-five. The bill passed the committee stage in the House of Commons by 385 to 55 votes. It was as Ray Strachey wrote, 'victory without reserve'.[4] The suffragists also managed to get included a clause to extend greatly the proposals for the enfranchisement of women in local government. In January 1918 the House of Lords, which had so often before pronounced a death-knell on feminist aspirations, passed the bill by a majority of 131 to 71.[5]

Other factors ensured the success of the suffrage bill in 1918. Sylvia Pankhurst astutely observed, 'Yet the memory of the old militancy, and the certainty of its recurrence if the claims of women were set aside, was a much stronger factor in overcoming the reluctance of those who would again have postponed the settlement.[6]

A year earlier in 1917 the world had been shocked by violent upheavals in Russia. The Bolshevik revolution in Russia was perceived as a threat to the old order everywhere and British governments in the early post-war years were prepared to undertake social and political reforms in order to stabilise society and avert the threat of possible revolution. Women were to be enlisted into the parliamentary democracy of Great Britain in order that they be transformed from a threat to the state into a stabilising force within it. It was no accident that only women over thirty were enfranchised. On the other hand women were not to be enfranchised on the same terms as men, as they would have become the majority of voters. Finally changes in the voting pattern of groups within parliament, and a changed relationship between the House of Commons and the House of Lords, effected the smooth passage of this bill.[7]

The full enfranchisement of women, on the same terms as men, did not come about until 1928. In the meantime a spate of legislative activity affecting women took place. This legislation included the Eligibility of Women Act (1918), enabling women to become members of parliament and the Sex Disqualification (Removal) Act (1919), opening the professions to women. Other Acts enhanced the position of women as wives, mothers and widows: these included Acts granting women divorce on equal grounds with men (1923), equal guardianship of children (1925), widow's pensions (1925) and the right to legitimise a child by marriage to the father (1927). But ten years after the Representation of the People Act (1918) all women aged between twenty-one and thirty were still voteless, as were a large number of women over thirty.

Contemporary feminists considered that it was only a matter of time before the vote would be extended to women on the same terms as men but time dragged. Suffrage organisations put equal franchise at the top of their agenda and continued to lobby for this aim, but despite such assurances as that made by the coalition government in its election manifesto of 1919 that 'It will be the duty of the new government to remove all existing inequalities of the law as between men and women,' equal franchise had to wait.[8] In 1924 when the Conservatives came into power Baldwin promised to rectify this absurd anomaly. Two years later he had done nothing, and feminists tired of scouring the King's speech at the opening of each new parliamentary session for reference to proposed equal franchise bills. By February 1926 the Women's Freedom League spoke openly of Baldwin's betrayal.[9] In 1927 the Conservative government torpedoed a Labour private member's bill which had exactly the same intentions as Baldwin's proposed – but as yet unmaterialised – legislation.[10] Women were becoming increasingly disillusioned – 'as usual, the Women's Bill has been the first to be tossed aside in the conflict between party issues', said The Vote.[11] When parliament reassembled in November 1927 women paraded outside the House of Commons carrying umbrellas bearing the legend 'votes at 21' and sandwich-boards with the words 'On the same terms as men' – it was an echo of the old days of mass demonstrations.[12] The Evening Standard and the Daily Mail ran silly articles on 'Votes for Girls' and 'Votes for Flappers' but, in fact, in 1927 there were still two million women over thirty who were not entitled to vote because they did not qualify under the 1918 Act. Women kept up the pressure. The Equal Franchise Bill went before parliament in March 1928. It promised an equal parliamentary and an equal local government franchise for women and men. Having the support of all parties, it sailed through the Commons, passed the Lords and became law on 2 July 1928. Emmeline Pankhurst of the Women's Social and Political Union, the great publicist of the suffrage cause, died in June 1928. She was buried on the very day that the Equal Franchise Bill was passed by the House of Lords. Millicent Garrett Fawcett, the great constitutional stateswoman of the cause, died one year later in August 1929, after sixty years of campaigning.

The vote was won – but what happened to feminism in the inter-war years? It is impossible to understand the inter-war feminist movement without comparing it to the character of the movement before the First World War. The suffrage movement had got going in the 1860s and by the first decade of the twentieth century was a truly mass movement. By 1900 not only did the movement possess inspired and dedicated leaders, but it could draw upon a vast army of women ready to lobby parliament, write letters, attend rallies, carry banners, demonstrate on the streets, smash plate-glass windows, blow up pillar boxes, go to prison and do all the myriad administrative tasks the running of a vast organisation entailed. Belonging to the women's movement brought with it a sense of sisterhood and a sense of purpose. Although the campaign had been initiated by middle-class women, by 1900 it had spread to working-class women and many men, through such organisations as the Independent Labour Party and the Women's Co-operative Guild. As Olive Banks wrote of the period 1900–14, 'at this period feminism in its united stand for suffrage, was for the first time truly representative of both middle-class and working-class women'.[13] There were many groupings within the suffrage movement. The chief ones were the National Union of Women's Suffrage Societies (NUWSS), which was a constitutional organisation under the sage leadership of Millicent Garrett Fawcett and the Women's Social and Political Union (WSPU) – the militant branch renowned for its brilliant publicity stunts and its almost para-military lightning attacks on property. The WSPU was led autocratically by Emmeline Pankhurst and her equally charismatic daughter Christabel. A group which split away from the WSPU, the Women's Freedom League (WFL) led by Charlotte Despard, was also prepared to put itself outside the law – in its case by withholding payment of taxes. There were Scottish groups, groups associated with churches and groups linked with various professions and with trade unions. Diverse groups were united in the demand for the vote. The vote was the single big issue but it was not the only issue on which women campaigned. They fought too for higher education, entry into the professions, better working conditions for women, a single standard of sexual behaviour for women and for men. There was a feeling amongst many suffragists that women were superior to men and there was, if not clearly articulated within the suffrage movement, a feminist consciousness which extended beyond the vote into an attack on male-dominated culture as a whole.[14] It is this last point which links the women's movement before the First World War with the women's movement of the late 1960s and the 1970s and it was this attack on the whole edifice of male values and culture which was singularly lacking in the inter-war years.

So what happened to the feminist movement between the wars? Olive Banks describes the whole period 1920–60 as 'years of inter-mission, when for the time at least, feminism seemed to have come to an end'.[15] Winifred Holtby reflected on the last 'six years of lassitude' within feminism in 1925[16] and by 1934 when writing of professional women, organisers and members of women's groups she stated clearly these women 'are now in a minority and they know it'.[17] When Dale Spender asked the journalist and feminist Mary Stott what she had done 'during the time when there was no women's movement?' Mary had stoutly replied, 'There's always been a woman's movement this century.'[18] It is true individual women and groups of activists kept feminism alive in the inter-war years but feminism was no longer a mass movement. Why? What happened to curtail its scale?

The war had clearly shown the division in what had previously appeared as a united feminist camp: Mrs Pankhurst and Christabel had thrown themselves into the war effort while pacifists in the movement campaigned for peace. Mrs Pankhurst and Christabel set up the Women's Party in late 1917 but it foundered within the year and Mrs Pankhurst turned to the Conservative party and Christabel to American evangelism. Labour women suffragists could see clearly that beyond the cause of the vote they had nothing in common with those two. The vote had united women. Now exercise of the vote was to divide them.

Feminism split in the 1920s into two camps. There were those who were 'old feminists' like Lady Rhondda and Winifred Holtby, who regarded feminism as being about equal rights and were there-fore opposed to any form of special protective legislation for women in the workplace. The 'new feminists' such as Eleanor Rathbone, Mary Stocks and Maude Royden concentrated on the special pos-ition of women as mothers; their platform was primarily the welfare of women at home and the main aim of the new feminists was to bring about 'family endowment', or family allowances. Once women had the vote and had achieved their single dominant aim a host of choices lay before them with regard to ways and means of bringing about a better world for women. They did not all make the same choice. Women, like men, voted on party lines. As Sylvia Pank-hurst, who devoted herself to socialism, wrote of the post-war world:

Gone was the mirage of a society regenerated by enfranchised womanhood as by a magic wand. Men and women had been drawn closer together by the suffering and sacrifice of the war. Awed and humbled by the great catastrophe, and by the huge economic problems it had thrown into naked prominence, the women of the Suffrage movement had learnt that social regeneration is a long and mighty work.[19]

Many committed women who had placed the suffrage struggle first, now put party before feminist issues. In fact the 1920s saw much discussion about what exactly was a feminist issue. Was birth control a feminist issue? Was the question of family endowment a feminist issue? Interesting questions were raised but organised feminism dwindled. Feminism scattered into a number of pressure groups concentrating on one or more issues. There was no single large organisation or movement to which these pressure groups belonged. What is more, the women's movement failed to recruit sufficient numbers of younger women. A great age gap developed and feminism was made to look old fashioned. Many of the big names of feminism were very old. Every year the Women's Freedom League celebrated Mrs Despard's birthday; in 1930 she was eighty-six and wore a long dress and a Victorian-style bonnet. It may sound a trivial observation but to young women, in their short skirts and with their bobbed hair, Mrs Despard must have looked antediluvian. Young women had no time for feminism because they were told it was no longer necessary now that they had complete equality.[20]

In 1927 Vera Brittain said that the much maligned word feminism had come to stand for dowdiness and physical abnormality. Certainly it had many vocal new enemies. In 1923 Ludovici wrote his work of arch-antifeminism, *Woman: a Vindication*, in which he clearly stated: 'It is possible to say now quite positively that Feminism is stupid and wrong. It is possible to prophesy with complete certainty that Feminism will only aggravate the disasters already overtaking civilization'.[21]

Yet strangely Ludovici feared an enormous regeneration of feminism in the 1920s.[22] In Germany in the late 1920s and early 1930s fascism was raising its head. Hitler directed women back to the home and in Britain Oswald Mosley's fascist party agreed with him, as did many less extreme people. Translation of such German works as Adolf Heilborn's *The Opposite Sexes* were available in Britain. To Heilborn feminism was 'a product of a pan-European diseased mind'.[23] The times were not propitious and many women wanted, after the long suffrage struggle, to get on with other things. Lady Rhondda felt that after equal suffrage was attained she could feel free to 'drop the business'[24] and Winifred Holtby desired 'an end to the whole business, the demands for equality, the suggestions of sex warfare, the very name feminist'. She wanted to get on with things that interested her like race relations and writing novels, but she was prepared to be a feminist until all the inequality and injustice were done away with.[25] Feminism in fact turned out to be a life-long commitment in her case.

Feminism may have ceased to be a mass movement in the interwar years, but it would be very wrong to underplay its vigour, particularly in the 1920s. The activities and successes of women after the First World War are consistently played down, if not totally ignored, in traditional male revisions of history. This has made the women's movement look like a flash in the pan. On the other hand, women are depicted as having attained complete equality with men through legislative measures bestowed upon them by a benign, predominantly male, parliament. In one way developments in the post-war women's movement contributed to the fading prominence of the woman question. The WSPU and its headline-grabbing activities failed to survive the war. It was the much lower profile constitutional societies, the NUWSS and the WFL, which survived. As David Doughan has pointed out 'feminists from the 1920s onward, if not actually trying to live down the suffragette image, were certainly concerned to look as sober and responsible as they could'.[26] The constitutional feminists saw the way to further amelioration of women's position through parliamentary legislation and to that end they lobbied, wrote letters and held meetings. Once the straightforward demand for the vote had been granted there lay ahead a complex, often tedious and scarcely romantic (in the way fighting for the Cause had been!) programme of legislative work. It was 'boring, thankless, nit-picking work for the most part, entrusted to highly dedicated elite cadres'.[27]

The NUWSS adapted to the new circumstances of the post-war world. In 1919 it became the National Union of Societies for Equal Citizenship (NUSEC), a change of name which reflected the society's awareness of the need for broader aims now that the principle of women's suffrage had been conceded. Its new objective was 'To obtain all such reforms as are necessary to secure a real equality of liberties, status and opportunity between men and women'. NUSEC's programme was full and equal franchise on the same terms as men, together with an increase in the number of women MPs; equal rights of guardianship; opening the legal profession to women; pensions for widows; divorce law reform and reform of the laws on solicitation and prostitution; and equal pay.[28] NUSEC believed that this could be achieved through putting pressure on parliament and was remarkably successful in bringing much of this about, as the outline of 1920s legislation given above shows. But

NUSEC did not form a united front throughout the period. In 1919 Eleanor Rathbone, who had gained much insight into the plight of working-class wives in her native Liverpool, took over the presidency of NUSEC (from Millicent Garrett Fawcett). As early as 1918 Ray Strachey speaks of strong differences of opinion within the organisation with some people, notably Eleanor Rathbone, arguing that feminism should move in the direction of welfare for mothers and others arguing that it should adhere to the equal rights position.[29]

Rathbone's position, and that of others like her, was labelled 'New Feminism'. By fighting for the introduction of family allowances she thought that women would be free from financial dependence on their husbands and that wages in employment would be equal for women and men because they would be paid on a single person's rate without any talk of married men's extra needs. She argued that the nation could not overpay spinsters in the same way it overpaid bachelors. The only way forward was by paying family endowment to support dependent children.[30] As one good friend in NUSEC, but not a supporter of family endowment said to her, 'You are such a good fighter: *what* a pity you are such a bad feminist.'[31]

Rathbone insisted on the difference between men and women and did not want women to ape men: 'The more I see of some men, especially politicians, the less I want women to adopt their methods and standards of values'.[32] Eleanor Rathbone's views are clearly set out in *The Disinherited Family* (1924), but her shift in this direction perturbed many within NUSEC. Mrs Fawcett opposed the scheme because it took financial responsibility for children away from parents.[33] Other feminists, while believing social reform worthwhile, insisted on concentrating on attaining equal rights with men – especially in the professions. Winifred Holtby espoused Old Feminism with the motto 'Equality First'.[34] The division between new and old feminism roughly (but not entirely) corresponds to social class: working-class women and their sympathisers seemed to have more to gain from new feminism whilst middle-class women, who sought successful careers held on to old feminism. Protective legislation, which was another important issue for women in the mid 1920s, again showed this division: working-class women, trade unionists and women in the Labour party tended on the whole to support it but many middle-class old feminists had no time for any measure which they considered purely restrictive and kept women out of better paid jobs.

NUSEC never had the appeal to women of the old suffrage societies. Branches quickly collapsed. The Nelson, Lancashire, branch of NUSEC met once. In 1927 NUSEC split into two – the National Council for Equal Citizenship (NCEC), which continued the equal rights campaign, and the Townswomen's Guilds, which concentrated on bringing new women in, providing education for citizenship and a meeting place for women. By the early 1930s NCEC had dwindled but the guilds boomed. The guilds took up consumer, environmental and moral issues and they campaigned on one of the very big issues of the day, the need for women police. The guilds also operated as a training ground for women to enter local government.

The chief characteristic of inter-war feminism was its fragmentation. There were umbrella organisations, dating from the early 1920s. These did much the same work by much the same means and had broadly similar aims. The five main organisations were NUSEC, WFL, the Six Point Group, the National Council of Women and the London and National Society for Women's Service (later the Fawcett Society). Sadly the groups did not co-operate, and often, as David Doughan writes, barely acknowledged each other's existence.[35] There was weakness in disunity. Not only were there broad organisations which embraced many issues but there sprang up a series of single-interest specialist pressure groups – the Married Women's Association, the Association for Moral and Social Hygiene, the National Union of Women Teachers, the National Association of Women Civil Servants, the Open Door Council (which campaigned against restrictive legislation), the Housewives' League and others. Fragmentation meant that there was no clear feminist voice and no powerful united feminist lobby. This was clearly demonstrated when in the Second World War an Equal Citizenship (Blanket) Bill was proposed. It was a splendid rallying point which proposed total equality of the sexes in all legislation, including for example equal pay. It was a fine and worthy ideal but fragmentation had gone too far to regalvanise the women's movement.[36]

In short the inter-war feminist movement was characterised by a division between old and new feminists, by increasing fragmentation and by dwindling energies. In fact it is important to make a distinction between the 1920s and the 1930s – we can still talk of a fairly active feminist movement in the 1920s though not as dynamic as the pre-war mass movement. It was in the 1930s that the movement really began to dwindle. This may partly be explained by all the factors already stated but by the 1930s so pressing were major national and world problems that many women turned their energies to the struggle against unemployment at home and to the international fight against fascism and for peace. Before turning to these issues however it is necessary to examine women's role in parliament and in the political parties which many had joined.

The Eligibility of Women Act, which enabled women to stand

for and sit in parliament, had a surprisingly easy and swift passage through the Commons though a fairly slow one through the Lords. Ironically, women were allowed to stand for parliament from the age of 21, nine years before they could vote. The bill received the royal assent on 21 November 1918. It was just in time for the general election announced for 14 December. Seventeen women stood (one Conservative, four Labour, four Liberal and eight others). There were many well-known names in this first election at which women could stand.[37] The Labour candidates were Mary McArthur, the trade union leader, Mrs Emmeline Pethick Lawrence and Mrs Charlotte Despard (then aged seventy-four), both well-known suffrage leaders, and Mrs H.M. Mckenzie, professor of education at University College, Cardiff. Christabel Pankhurst stood as the Women's Party candidate. In this election the outgoing coalition government issued 'coupons' to candidates which it favoured and Christabel was the only woman to receive government backing.

The coalition government was returned with a resounding majority but only one woman won her seat. Constance Markievicz, who had been a leader of the Easter rising in 1916, stood as Sinn Fein candidate for Dublin St Patrick's. She, like the other Sinn Feiners, had no intention of taking her seat and was in fact in Holloway prison at the time. It was a galling twist of fate that the first elected woman was one who thought the election was 'like *Alice in Wonderland* or a Gilbert and Sullivan opera'.[38] A year later in 1919 the death of Viscount Astor caused a by-election in the Sutton division of Plymouth; his son, a successful and rising Conservative MP, was elevated to the Lords. On the new Lord Astor's suggestion, his wife Nancy was adopted as the Conservative candidate to fight the election and she won with a fairly large majority. American-born Nancy, Lady Astor – a dynamic quick-witted, elegant and rich woman – became the first woman to take her seat in parliament. She had not been a suffrage fighter and she can scarcely have been what many suffragists had had in mind as their first woman representative; they did not even know her. Lady Astor was a great and pleasant surprise. She wrote to the women's organisations offering her services: 'I trust that I may be of service both by asking questions and by affording an easier channel for making representations to the Government'.[39] She was determined to do her best for the causes and interests of women and she worked for equal franchise, pensions, better education and working conditions, reform of the property and marriage laws, and legislation to protect young children. She campaigned against brewers and gamblers. Though she had not been one of the suffrage campaigners, Lady Astor was quickly taken to their hearts. As the journal *Woman's*

Leader (NUSEC) put it in 1929, 'she was not only MP for Plymouth, she was MP for women from John O'Groats to Lands End'.[40] Suffragists admired her for her toughness, her espousal of their causes, her witty repartee and her white hot Puritanism. It was no easy task to be the only woman in the male stronghold of the House of Commons.

In 1921 Lady Astor was joined by the first Liberal woman MP, Mrs Wintringham, who was elected at a by-election at Louth caused by the death of her husband. Although there was a general election in 1922 and the number of women candidates almost doubled to thirty-three, no further women were elected. Lady Astor and Mrs Wintringham both retained their seats. In 1923 the revelation that the election agent of the MP for Berwick-upon-Tweed had engaged in fraudulent electoral practices led to the unseating of the member, Captain Hilton Philipson. He was debarred from standing but his wife stood in his place and was elected as a Conservative. She was well-known as a popular musical comedy star under the name of Mabel Russell and let it be known that she was keeping the seat warm for her husband. In short the first three women MPs to take their seats, excellent as both Lady Astor and Mrs Wintringham were, had all inherited their seats from their husbands. The general election of 1923 changed all that. The number of women MPs increased from three to eight: all the former sitting members were elected and they were joined by another Conservative member, Kitty, Duchess of Atholl, and another Liberal, Lady Terrington. But the importance of the 1923 election lies in the return of the first Labour women members. The three Labour women represented a new breed – they were all single and had all come up through the trade union movement. They were Susan Lawrence (East Ham North), Dorothy Jewson (Norwich), and Margaret Bondfield (Northampton). When the first Labour government took office in 1924 Margaret Bondfield became the first woman minister as Under Secretary of State to the Minister of Labour.

The fortunes of women MPs fluctuated throughout the remainder of the 1920s. The fall of the first Labour government meant a general election in October 1924, at which only four women were returned, three Conservatives and a new Labour member, Ellen Wilkinson. Several more women obtained seats at by-elections including Lawrence, Bondfield and in 1929 Jennie Lee, who was aged only twenty-four. The election of 1929 was a resounding success. The feminist societies played active roles. NUSEC supported Mrs Wintringham (Liberal), Lady Astor (Conservative), Susan Lawrence (Labour) and its president Eleanor Rathbone (Independent). Fourteen women were elected – nine Labour, three Conservatives, one Liberal and one Independent. The Liberal was Megan

Lloyd George and the Independent was Eleanor Rathbone. The new Labour government appointed Margaret Bondfield as the first woman Cabinet minister – Minister of Labour. Feminist journals revelled in the triumph but soon the picture changed. In 1931 fifteen women were elected. Megan Lloyd George remained as the only Liberal and Eleanor Rathbone as the only Independent; thirteen Conservative women were returned and no Labour women at all. The fortunes of the women MPs reflect the success or failure of particular parties. The interesting point about the Conservative women who entered the House in 1931 is that many of them represented a new type of woman MP who came up through public service and social work. In the final election of the inter-war years, that of 1935, the number of women returned dropped to nine, namely one Liberal, one Independent, one Labour (Ellen Wilkinson) and six Conservative (including Lady Astor).

Although women MPs made a significant breakthrough in the relatively short period since they had been allowed to stand, peeresses were forbidden to take their seats in the House of Lords. Lady Rhondda campaigned vigorously to take her seat and in 1922 it looked as though she had secured a legal victory. *Woman's Leader* was so confident that in March 1922 it stated, 'Whatever the future may hold for the Upper House, this inclusion of women is now secure and we congratulate Lady Rhondda'.[41] But this confidence was misplaced and the claim was turned down. Women were not allowed to sit in the Lords until 1958.

The relationship between feminism and party politics was very uneasy.[42] Feminist groups avoided associating themselves wholly with any one political party. Feminism transcended party and class issues. NUSEC called on women of all parties to unite in their loyalty to the cause of women.[43] This was just the sort of talk which disturbed the patriarchal political parties. The report of the National Executive Committee (NEC) of the Labour Party in 1923 expressed great pleasure in the phenomenal growth of women's membership of the party, in spite of the efforts by 'so called non-political' but 'anti-labour organizations (feminist groups) to recruit women to their ranks'.[44] Certain acts of feminist solidarity by women political candidates and MPs increased the unease. In 1922 Mrs Philip Snowden turned down the Labour party's invitation to stand in Plymouth against Lady Astor because, 'I am a Labour woman, but the work which Lady Astor is doing for women and children both in parliament and the country makes her services invaluable'. At the same election the Countess of Selborne refused to speak for the Independent Conservative candidate, to whose party she was affiliated, saying 'if I had a vote in that borough I should give it to Lady Astor'.[45] In 1928 Margaret Bondfield introduced a private member's bill to provide shoes and boots for children in the deprived areas. Every woman backbencher supported it though for many of them it meant voting against their party in office.[46] Women's groups supported individual women parliamentary candidates regardless of party, as the example of NUSEC demonstrates. But women politicians had to function within the confines of male constructed political parties, which were imbued with patriarchal values. Within these parties there were very clear clashes between women's issues and party politics. This was seen most clearly in the Labour party.

At the 1918 Labour party conference, Susan Lawrence, a member of the NEC and a feminist, stated 'women must combat the argument that women should organize themselves on sex lines'. She was supported in this by Dr Marion Phillips, whose feminism is more questionable. But despite these appeals, women found themselves in conflict with the policies of the Labour party. The issue of birth control shows both this conflict and the impotence of the women to get their views adopted as policy. The Women's Co-operative Guild had taken up the birth control question and its annual congress of 1923 passed a resolution calling on the Ministry of Health to alter its regulations prohibiting the dissemination of birth control information at the public clinics. Labour women attempted to pass a similar resolution at their conference in the same year but the question was deferred. Although many Labour women, led by Dora Russell (who was later to become a prominent member of the peace movement), urged this issue, the new Labour government of 1924 refused to take it up. The women's conference of that year (1924) passed the resolution by 1,000 votes to 8, and by 876 to 6 in 1925. The main party conference, however, long refused to consider the issue and when it did, in 1927, it voted overwhelmingly against the resolution. Labour women had to work for this issue outside the party. In 1930 Labour women and other groups were successful in obtaining a change of the Ministry of Health's regulations and public clinics were permitted to give out birth control information to certain groups of women as instructed by memorandum 153/MCW (see chapter 4).

The other issues which brought Labour women into conflict with the male-dominated party were family allowances, the right of married women to work and equal pay.[47] (On the other hand the issue of protective legislation for women workers was one which divided Labour women from many feminists, at least 'old feminists' of the equal rights brigade.) Although there were fundamental differences between the feminist agenda and party policy, the Labour party made great efforts to dissuade its women from feminism and to persuade them to concentrate on class difference, rather than on the common ground of sex issues. The result of this was, as Harold Smith writes, 'by the 1930s the concept of a united sisterhood fighting against common enemies had the same logical status as the *Adventures of Alice in Wonderland . . .* '[48]

Tory women appeared superficially to be more in step with their party but this was primarily because, as Beatrix Campbell has noted, 'Conservative women subsumed their concerns as women to an agenda determined not by them but by the paternalist leadership of the party'.[49] Conservative women were in fact confined to their own sphere; they were the protectors of tradition and Britishness (or more accurately Englishness), of the home and the Empire. On the whole Tory women toed the party line in the 1920s – except Lady Astor who was eccentric, anyway. Ironically, and in contrast to developments within the Labour party, they began to challenge it in the 1930s. Many were very unhappy about unemployment but it was the law and order issue which chipped away at their party loyalty. The actual sparking point of their new disloyalty was the Conservative government's intention to abolish flogging in 1939. This brought to the fore all the insecurity these women felt. They felt vulnerable on the streets of the cities and on the village green. Their efforts to keep flogging and capital punishment divided them from feminists on the left, but were not their attempts to prevent violence by men against women motivated by a feminist concern to protect women?

If women's issues tended to be swallowed up within the 'wider' policies of political parties, it must not be forgotten that women's groups, albeit more fragmented now, continued to fight for certain objectives. The achievements of the early 1920s have already been mentioned. The chief issues which exercised women over the succeeding years and which were to be found on the agenda of one or more groups, were birth control, legal abortion (supported by the Women's Co-operative Guild), family allowances, rights for unmarried mothers, equality of opportunity in education, equal pay, abolition of marriage bars and women police. Any gains made had to be fought for. There were campaigns too for unaccompanied women to be served in restaurants at night, for women-only railway compartments and to remove the word 'obey' from the marriage service. Feminist demands continued to be made throughout the whole of the inter-war period, whether from the relatively small but intellectual Six Point Group or the very large grassroots working-class Women's Co-operative Guild. It was however not the strong united voice which had called out for 'The Vote' in the old days.

It is important to remember too that women were involved in a whole range of issues which were not exclusively women's issues. Women took a stance on all the major domestic and international issues of the inter-war years. Women took part in the General Strike (on both sides) in 1926, though far more local research is needed to establish their roles. They participated in helping the miners and their families in the miners' lock-out of that year. Marion Phillips recorded how women organised a 'child adoption' scheme – whereby miners' children were taken into homes of sympathisers for a long break away from the hardship of home.[50] Women campaigned too against unemployment, the Means Test and the operation of the Unemployment Assistance Board (UAB). Maud Brown from Lancashire was a key organiser in the National Unemployed Workers Movement which organised, amongst other things, massive national hunger marches.

Ellen Wilkinson is justly famed for marching alongside the Jarrow marchers, but the contingents of women from Scotland, northern England and Wales who participated in hunger marches throughout the 1930s are often overlooked.[51] Dora Cox took part in a march from Tonypandy in South Wales, to London in early 1934. She told me,

> Once I was living in Wales and could see much more clearly the absolutely humiliating and devastating effect of unemployment on people particularly in the valleys, where all hope seemed to be gone . . . Well you couldn't *not* take part in any activity which would make people themselves feel that at least they were fighting back and also you felt it was absolutely essential to get other people to understand the enormity of the situation.[52]

In South Wales too women rose up against the Unemployment Assistance Board Act of 1934–5. The women of the Merthyr area, several hundred of them, marched through the snow in February 1935 behind Ceridwen Brown upon the UAB offices. They wrecked the offices and burned the records.[53] In fact during the 1930s so many pressing issues emerged, to which women responded, that it may be said such issues diverted them from purely women's questions. Chief amongst these was the issue of peace. To a generation which had seen the devastation and loss of the First World War this was understandably of paramount importance. The Women's International League for Peace and Freedom (WILPF) was formed in 1915 and worked consistently and with vigour to promote the international role of the League of Nations and to remove the causes of war. Its activities included organising the British Peace Pilgrimage of 1926, in which contingents of women set out from the north of Scotland to Land's End, holding meetings in towns and villages on the way, and culminating in a mass demonstration in Hyde Park.

In 1934 the British section of the WILPF was the most active of thirty-eight co-operating organisations in setting up a peace ballot.[54] It was mainly women who posted questionnaires through letter boxes and collected the eleven and a half million replies. The Women's Co-operative Guild too was firmly behind the peace movement. It supported the efforts of the League of Nations to settle international disputes, attempted to arouse public support for disarmament, lobbied local education authorities to abandon military training in schools and called upon the Co-operative Society to refrain from the manufacture of war-like toys. One of the most imaginative and successful propaganda initiatives in the Guild's peace campaign was the introduction of the white poppy – a pacifist emblem of remembrance for Armistice Day. Sales of white poppies for Armistice Day 1938 reached 85,000.[55] Then, as now, many women felt peace was the most important issue of the day. In the 1930s the rise of fascism made clear how frail a thing peace in Europe was. Many prominent women gave their energies to the anti-fascist cause – amongst them Winifred Holtby and Vera Brittain. Lady Rhondda wrote articles denouncing fascism not only *per se* but because it would mean for women the return to *Kinder, Kirche und Kuche*.

In 1934 the Women's World Committee Against War and Fascism (WWCAWAF) was established. Its British sponsors included many women from the Communist party, as well as Vera Brittain, Charlotte Despard, Sylvia Pankhurst, Storm Jameson, Ellen Wilkinson, Dame Evelyn Sharp and actress Sybil Thorndike. Selina Cooper, a former mill girl who had risen to become a magistrate in her native Nelson in Lancashire, travelled to Germany in 1934 on behalf of WWCAWAF to investigate conditions in Hitler's Germany. She too preached the message of Hitler's threat to women's hard-won rights.[56] When in 1936 the Spanish Civil war broke out and Franco and his fascists rose up against the elected Popular Front government, women in Britain made a positive contribution by helping Basque children. By mid May 1937 some 4,000 child refugees from fascism had been landed at Southampton and many were cared for in private homes.[57]

It is an impressive chronicle of activities. Of course the great majority of women did not get involved in anything – neither did the great majority of men. In the case of women this is not surprising, given the way in which girls were educated for domesticity and the barrage of policies and images which announced to women that their place was in the home. In the light of this, that so many women were involved in so many political or neo-political issues is indeed remarkable. It is important that we do not forget them.

NOTES

CHAPTER 1 DESIRABLE AND UNDESIRABLE IMAGES

1 For example J. King and M. Stott (eds), *Is This Your Life? Images of Women in the Media*, London, Routledge & Kegan Paul, 1977. See also A. Kuhn, *Women's Pictures: Feminism and Cinema*, London, Routledge & Kegan Paul, 1982; A. Kuhn, *The Power of the Image: Essays in Representation and Sexuality*, London, Routledge & Kegan Paul, 1985.

2 See D. Beddoe, *Discovering Women's History*, London, Pandora, 1983, pp. 20–40. This provides a survey of the changing images of women in Britain from the early nineteenth century to the Second World War.

3 C. Hall, 'The early formation of Victorian domestic ideology', in S. Burman (ed.), *Fit Work for Women*, London, Croom Helm, 1979.

4 *Punch* cartoons of the 1890s are an excellent source for this image.

5 See G. Braybon, *Women Workers in the First World War*, London, Croom Helm, 1981; A. Marwick, *Women at War 1914–1918*, London, Fontana, 1977.

6 See Braybon, op. cit., passim.

7 P. Ziegler, *Diana Cooper*, London, Hamish Hamilton, 1981, pp. 48–9.

8 J. Darracott and B. Loftus, *First World War Posters*, London, Imperial War Museum, 1972, p. 13.

9 H. Marwick, op. cit., back cover.

10 *Illustrated Sunday Herald*, 4 April 1916. Cited in Braybon, op. cit., p. 160.

11 *Daily Chronicle*, 16 August 1918. Cited in Braybon, op. cit., p. 159.

12 *Punch*, no. 149, 1915. Cited in Marwick, op. cit., p. 35.

13 R. Graves and A. Hodge, *The Long Weekend: A Social History of Great Britain, 1918–1939*, London, Faber & Faber, 1941, p. 40.

14 British Library, Colindale, *Everywoman's*, 25 January 1919.

15 Ibid., 1 February 1919.

16 Ibid., 8 February 1919.

17 Ibid., 15 February 1919.

18 Ibid., 8 March 1919.
19 Ibid., 22 March 1919.
20 Ibid., 5 April 1919.
21 Ibid., 26 April 1919.
22 Ibid., 19 April 1919.
23 Ibid., 8 February 1919.
24 R. Strachey, *The Cause: A Short History of The Women's Movement in Great Britain* (1928), London, Virago, 1984, p. 79.
25 F. W. Stella Browne, 'Women and birth control', in Paul and M. Eden (eds), *Population and Birth Control*, New York, 1917.
26 Graves and Hodge, op. cit., pp. 58–9.
27 Ibid., p. 303.
28 C. White, *Women's Magazines 1693–1968*, London, Michael Joseph, 1970.
29 British Library, Colindale, *Woman's Own*, 15 October 1932.
30 M. Grieve, *Millions Made My Story*, London, Gollancz, 1964, p. 89.
31 White, op. cit., p. 98.
32 These may be consulted at the Fawcett Library, City of London Polytechnic.
33 N. Beauman, *A Very Great Profession: The Woman's Novel 1914–39*, London, Virago, 1983.
34 For detailed histories of radio in this period see A. Briggs, *The Golden Age of Wireless. The History of Broadcasting in the United Kingdom*, vol. ii, Oxford University Press, 1965; M. Pegg, *Broadcasting and Society, 1918–1939*, London, Croom Helm, 1983.
35 *Woman's Own*, 24 December 1932, p. 373.
36 F. Inchfawn, *Homely Talks of a Homely Woman*, London, Ward Lock, undated.
37 *Woman's Own*, 21 October 1933, pp. 56–7.
38 Ibid., 12 November 1932, p. 167.
39 Ibid., 21 October 1933, p. 37.
40 A. M. Kaye, *A Student's Handbook of Housewifery*, London, Dent, 1940, p. 122.
41 *Woman's Own*, 15 October 1932, pp. 28–9.
42 Ibid., 22 October 1932, p. 65.
43 Ibid., 26 November, 1932, p. 121.
44 Ibid., 22 July 1933, p. 453.
45 See also the discussion on women's health in chapter 4.
46 PEP, *The Coming Fall in Population*, PEP Broadsheet, no. 75, 1936.
47 J. Struther, *Mrs Miniver*, London, Chatto & Windus, 1939, p. 221.

48 E. M. Delafield, *The Diary of a Provincial Lady* (1930), London, Virago, 1984, pp. 40–1.
49 For two fascinating surveys of the changing image of women in film see M. Haskell, *From Reverence to Rape*, New York, Penguin, 1974; M. Rosen, *Popcorn Venus*, New York, Avon, 1973.
50 Haskell, op. cit., p. 119.
51 *Peg's Paper*, 11 August 1927, p. 327.
52 *Woman's Own*, 29 October 1932, p. 89.
53 Ibid., 20 May 1933, pp. 176–7.
54 Graves and Hodge, op. cit., p. 43.
55 Rosen, op. cit., pp. 92–3.
56 *Peg's Paper*, 18 November 1930, p. 7.
57 Graves and Hodge, op. cit., p. 44.
58 Rosen, op. cit., p. 77.
59 Ibid., p. 79.
60 Graves and Hodge, op. cit., p. 44.
61 Rosen, op. cit., p. 87.
62 K. Anger, *Hollywood Babylon*, London, Arrow, 1986, pp. 137–42.
63 A. S. M. Hutchinson, *This Freedom*, London, Hodder & Stoughton, 1922.
64 J. Lewis, *Women in England 1870–1950, Sexual Divisions and Social Change*, Sussex, Wheatsheaf, 1984, pp. 4–5.
65 Cicely Hamilton, *The Englishwoman*, London, Longmans, 1940, p. 27.
66 See for example 'Surplus Women,' *Woman's Leader*, 5 August 1921.
67 A. M. Ludovici, *Woman: A Vindication*, London, Constable, 1923, p. 231.
68 Ibid., p. 232.
69 A. Bishop (ed.), *Chronicle of Friendship: Vera Brittain's Diary of the Thirties, 1932–1939*, London, Gollancz, 1986, p. 339.
70 On the use of this term see *The Vote*, 29 August 1930.
71 See L. Faderman, *Surpassing the Love of Men: Romantic Friendship and Love between Women from the Renaissance to the Present*, London, Junction Books, 1981; S. Jeffreys, *The Spinster and Her Enemies*, London, Pandora, 1985.
72 Havelock Ellis, *Sexual Inversion*, 1897, p. 250. Cited in Jeffreys, op. cit., p. 106.
73 R. Hall, *The Well of Loneliness* (1928), London, Virago, 1985, p. 70.
74 Ibid., p. 274.
75 See Faderman, op. cit., p. 322, for contemporary reactions.
76 Hall, op. cit., p. 386.

77 For a positive evaluation of *The Well*'s impact see A. Hennegan's introduction to the Virago reprint, op. cit., pp. vii–xvii.
78 *The Vote*, 1 January 1926.
79 Ibid., 22 January 1926.
80 Ibid., 19 March 1926.
81 Ibid., 27 March 1927.
82 Ibid., 8 March 1927.
83 Originally published in *Punch*, 27 June 1928.
84 *The Vote*, 14 February 1930.
85 W. Holtby, 'The wearer and the shoe' (*Manchester Guardian*, 31 January 1930), in P. Berry and A. Bishop (eds), *Testament of a Generation: The Journalism of Vera Brittain and Winifred Holtby*, London, Virago, 1985, p. 65.

CHAPTER 2 EDUCATION

1 G. A. N. Lowndes, *The Silent Social Revolution*, Oxford, Oxford University Press, 1969, p. 125.
2 Ibid., p. 137.
3 E. Roberts, *A Woman's Place: An Oral History of Working Class Women 1890–1940*, London, Blackwell, 1984, p. 29.
4 Oral Interview by Deirdre Beddoe with N. W.
5 W. Foley, *A Child in the Forest*, London, MacDonald, 1977, p. 50.
6 A. P. Jephcott, *Girls Growing Up*, London, Faber & Faber, 1942, pp. 47–8.
7 Birmingham Central Library, Aston Lane Board School, Punishment Book.
8 E. Manning, *Confessions and Impressions*, Harmondsworth, Penguin, 1936, p. 37.
9 See C. Dyhouse, 'Good wives and little mothers: social anxieties and the school girls' curriculum', *Oxford Review of Education*, vol. 5, no. 1, 1977.
10 See J. Lewis, *The Politics of Motherhood, Child and Maternal Welfare in England, 1900–1939*, London, Croom Helm, 1980, pp. 15–16.
11 Sir H. Llewelyn Smith, *The New Survey of London Life and Labour*, London, King, 1935, vol. 9, p. 328.
12 D. Scannell, *Mother Knew Best. An East End Childhood*, London, Macmillan, 1978, p. 136. Cited in Lewis, op. cit., p. 95.
13 Llewelyn Smith, op. cit., p. 328.
14 *The Times*, 1 December 1937.
15 Glamorgan Record Office, Bridgend Home Training Centre.

16 *The Times*, 25 September 1924.
17 Glamorgan Record Office, Albert Road Girls' School Log Book.
18 *Daily Herald*, 11 May 1939.
19 Glamorgan Record Office, Hannah Street Girls' School Log Book.
20 Public Record Office, ED 11/278, minute dated 18 June 1937, blamed the shortage of domestic servants on the education given to girls. Cited in Lewis op. cit., p. 110, no. 25.
21 Public Record Office, ED 11/278, letter of 14 July 1937.
22 Local authorities had already provided some secondary schools before the Act of 1902. By 1895 seventeen new secondary schools had been set up by county and county borough councils in England. In Wales fifteen such schools were provided by the Welsh Intermediate Education Act of 1889. Lowndes, op. cit., p. 83.
23 Ibid., p. 98.
24 J. Kamm, *Hope Deferred: Girls' Education in English History*, London, Methuen, 1965, p. 233.
25 *The Girls' School Year Book*, 1926, pp. 197–200.
26 Ibid., p. 233.
27 Ibid., p. 18.
28 Cited in F. Hunt, 'Divided aims: the educational implications of opposing ideologies in girls' secondary schooling, 1850–1940', in F. Hunt (ed.), *Lessons For Life: The Schooling of Girls and Women 1850–1950*, Oxford, Blackwell, 1987, p. 17.
29 *The Report of the Consultative Committee on the Differentiation of the Curriculum for Boys and Girls Respectively in Secondary Schools*, 1923, p. 130.
30 Ibid.
31 Ibid., p. 131.
32 Hunt, op. cit., pp. 19–20.
33 *Woman Teacher*, 1938.
34 P. Summerfield, 'Cultural reproduction in the education of girls: a study of girls' secondary schooling in two Lancashire towns, 1900–50', in Hunt, op. cit., p. 157.
35 F. W. Stella Browne, 'Sexual variety and variability among women', in S. Rowbotham, *A New World for Women: Stella Brown – Socialist Feminist*, London, Pluto, 1977, p. 95. I am grateful to Amanda Faraday for this reference.
36 A. Brazil, *The Luckiest Girl in the School*, London, Blackie, p. 137.
37 P. Tinkler, 'Learning through leisure: feminine ideology in girls' magazines 1920–50', in Hunt, op. cit., p. 62.
38 For an account of the working of one continuation school in Finsbury see *Woman's Leader*, 24 February 1922. See also B.

Simon, *The Politics of Educational Reform 1920–1940*, London, Lawrence & Wishart, 1974.

39 H. Forrester, *Liverpool Miss*, London, Fontana, 1974, p. 15.

40 M. J. Powell, *The History of Hillcroft College: The First Forty Years*, Hillcroft, 1964.

41 F. Widdowson, *Going Up Into The Next Class: Women and Elementary Teacher Training 1840–1914*, London, Hutchinson, 1983.

42 S. Fletcher, *Women First: The Female Tradition in English Physical Education, 1880–1980*, London, Athlone, 1984, p. 63.

43 Ibid., pp. 56–73.

44 F. A. Montgomery, *Edge Hill College: A History 1885–1985*, Edge Hill, 1985, p. 39.

45 Fletcher, op. cit., p. 66.

46 Cited in D. Spender, *Time and Tide Wait for No Man*, London, Pandora, 1984, p. 237.

47 V. Woolf, *A Room of One's Own* (1928), Harmondsworth, Penguin, 1970, pp. 13–20.

48 V. Brittain, *The Women at Oxford: A Fragment of History*, London, Harrap, 1960, p. 191.

49 B. Pym, *A Very Private Eye*, London, Macmillan, 1984, p. 17.

50 J. N. Harding, *Aberdare Hall*, Cardiff, Cardiff University Press, 1986.

CHAPTER 3 EMPLOYMENT

1 B. Drake, *Women in Trade Unions* (1920), London, Virago, 1984, table III.

2 J. Lewis, *Women in England 1870–1950*, Sussex, Wheatsheaf, 1984, p. 148.

3 Drake, op. cit., table III.

4 *New Witness*, 1 March 1918.

5 *Daily News Leader*, 28 February 1918.

6 *New Statesman*, 16 March 1918.

7 Ibid., 23 March 1918.

8 Drake, op. cit., p. 107.

9 Quoted in *The Vote*, 21 February 1919.

10 *Hansard*, 1920, vol. 129, 1900–1.

11 *The Vote*, 21 February 1919. Reprinted from the *Daily News*.

12 S. Lewenhak, *Women and Trade Unions*, London, Ernest Benn, 1977, p. 165.

13 J. D. Young, *Women and Popular Struggles: A History of Scottish and English Working Class Women*, Edinburgh, Mainstream, 1985, p. 147.

14 *Western Mail*, 17 February 1920.
15 *The Vote*, 7 May 1920.
16 Conference report in *The Vote*, 26 September 1919.
17 *Daily News*, 16 November 1918.
18 Ministry of Labour, 'Out of Work Donation: summary of scheme', November 1918.
19 *Daily Chronicle*, 7 December 1918.
20 *Daily Telegraph*, 30 December 1918.
21 *Daily Mail*, 23 May 1919.
22 *Reynolds News*, 30 March 1919.
23 *Portsmouth Evening News*, 13 February 1919.
24 Case cited by Madelaine Symons of the NFWW. *Daily Mail* 23 May 1919.
25 Umpires were granting nine out of ten appeals at this time. *The Times*, 15 December 1919.
26 *The Times*, 9 May 1919.
27 *Daily Chronicle*, 6 December 1918.
28 Ibid., 7 December 1918.
29 *The Vote*, 29 August 1919.
30 *Evening Standard*, 9 January 1919.
31 *Daily Telegraph*, 30 December 1919.
32 *Western Mail*, 20 January 1919.
33 *Glasgow Bulletin*, 19 December 1918.
34 *Aberdeen Free Press*, 4 February 1919.
35 *Western Mail*, 7 March 1919.
36 M. Zimmick, 'Strategies and stratagems for the employment of women in the British civil service, 1919–1939', *The Historical Journal*, vol. 27, no. 4, 1984, p. 910.
37 S. Glynn and G. Oxborrow, *Inter-war Britain: A Social and Economic History*, London, Allen & Unwin, 1976, p. 144.
38 Ibid., p. 148.
39 Ibid., pp. 14–22.
40 G. Alderman, *Modern Britain 1700–1983*, London, Croom Helm, 1986, p. 194.
41 In 1934 Northern England, West Cumberland and Tyne-side with most of Co Durham were designated as 'depressed'.
42 M. Glucksmann, Women and the 'New Industries': Changes in Class Relations in the 1930s, unpublished paper given to Economic and Social Research Council Symposium on Social Stratification and Gender, University of East Anglia, July 1984. See also M. Glucksmann, *Women Assemble: Women Workers in the New Industries of Inter-war Britain*, London, Routledge, 1989.
43 H. A. Marquand, *The Second Industrial Survey of South Wales*, HMSO, 1932, vol. 1, p. 21.
44 Ibid., vol. 1, p. 33.

45 Ibid., vol. 2, p. 80.

46 Pilgrim Trust, *Men Without Work*, Cambridge, Cambridge University Press, 1938, p. 231.

47 Ibid., p. 232.

48 For the years 1923–36 the figures are conveniently set out in the 18th–22nd *Abstract of Labour Gazette*. See otherwise *Ministry of Labour Gazette*. The figures are mostly readily available in B. R. Mitchell and P. Deane, *Abstracts of British Historical Statistics*, Cambridge, Cambridge University Press, 1971.

49 G. Darcy, Changes and Problems in Women's Work in England and Wales 1918–1939, unpublished Ph.D, University of London, 1984, p. 43.

50 C. Hakim, *Occupational Segregation*, Research Paper no. 9, table 8, London, Department of Employment, 1979, p. 12.

51 Lewis, op. cit., pp. 150–1.

52 Darcy, op. cit., p. 48.

53 J. Blainey, *The Woman Worker and Protective Legislation*, London, Arrowsmith, 1928. See also W. Holtby, *Women and Changing Civilization*, London, Bodley Head, 1934, pp. 76–82.

54 *Woman's Leader*, 1 April 1920.

55 Ibid.

56 J. Beauchamp, *Women Who Work*, London, Lawrence & Wishart, 1937, p. 74.

57 Ibid.

58 Interview by Anne Jones with Mrs E.

59 M. Powell, *Below Stairs*, London, Pan, 1970, p. 58.

60 Interview by Anne Jones with Miss D.

61 Lewis, op. cit., pp. 190–1.

62 *Reports of the Ministry of Labour for 1923–4*, Cmd. 2481, HMSO, 1925, pp. 222–3.

63 Public Records Office, Ministry of Labour, Lab 2/1219/20 ETJ 1178, 1932.

64 Ibid., Lab 2/1365.

65 Fawcett Society Library, Records of the National Vigilance Association, Welsh Box/C.

66 Trades Union Congress Library, HD 6072 (1934).

67 Beauchamp, op. cit., p. 14. Source 1931 Census of Population. See also Darcy, op. cit., p. 49.

68 J. Norris, Gender and Class in Industry and the Home: Women Silk Workers in Macclesfield, unpublished MA thesis, University of Keele, p. 22.

69 Beauchamp, op. cit., p. 14.

70 Ibid.

71 Ibid., p. 15.

72 Ibid., p. 16.

73 Lewenhak, op. cit., p. 201.
74 Darcy, op. cit., p. 142.
75 E. Roberts, 'Working wives and their families', in T. Barker and M. Drake (eds), *Population and Society in Britain 1850–1980*, London, 1982, p. 143.
76 E. Roberts, *A Woman's Place: An Oral History of Working Class Women 1890–1940*, London, Blackwell, 1984, p. 102.
77 Cited in Norris, op. cit., p. 83.
78 Ibid., p. 81.
79 Beauchamp, op. cit., p. 79.
80 'Mass Observation' was begun in 1937 by Tom Harrison, Charles Madge and Humphrey Jennings with the object of carrying out an anthropological study of contemporary British life. University of Sussex, Mass Observation Archive, Worktown, Box 33, File G; report by Penelope Barlow.
81 G. Orwell, *The Road to Wigan Pier* (1935), Harmondsworth, Penguin, 1969, p. 5.
82 Glucksmann, 1984, op. cit., p. 11.
83 Ibid., pp. 15, 18.
84 Ibid., p. 18.
85 Ibid., p. 20.
86 J. Gollan, *Youth in British Industry: A Survey of Labour Conditions Today*, London, Lawrence & Wishart, 1937, p. 76.
87 Ibid., pp. 74–5.
88 Interview with J. E. conducted by Miriam Glucksmann.
89 Beauchamp, op. cit., p. 42. Almost certainly Cadbury's.
90 Gollan, op. cit., p. 107.
91 Ibid., p. 108.
92 Interview with D. H. conducted by Miriam Glucksmann.
93 Interview with J. E. conducted by Miriam Glucksmann.
94 Beauchamp, op. cit., p. 29.
95 Ibid., p. 29.
96 Ibid., p. 30.
97 Darcy, op. cit., p. 187.
98 Ibid.
99 Television broadcast, *All Our Working Lives: Counter Revolution*. 1987.
100 M. Gardiner, *The Other Side of The Counter: The Life of a Shop Girl 1925–45*, Queenspark Book, no. 17, p. 18.
101 Beauchamp, op. cit., p. 47.
102 Ibid.
103 Cited in Darcy, op. cit., pp. 207–9.
104 Gollan, op. cit., p. 135.
105 Beauchamp, op. cit., p. 47.
106 Gardiner, op. cit., p. 14.

107 Beauchamp, op. cit., p. 50.

108 For an account of the pre-First World War system, see Margaret Bondfield, *A Life's Work*, London, Hutchinson, 1949.

109 G. Orwell, *Keep the Aspidistra Flying* (1936), Harmondsworth, Penguin, 1975, p. 50.

110 Beauchamp, op. cit., p. 50.

111 Interview with D. S.

112 Beauchamp, op. cit., p. 50.

113 T. Davy, ' "A cissy job for men: a nice job for girls": women shorthand typists in London 1900–1939', in L. Davidoff and B. Westover, *Our Work, Our Lives, Our Words*, London, Macmillan, 1986, p. 130.

114 See table 4.

115 T. Davy, Female Shorthand Typists and Typists 1900–1939: The Years of Transition, unpublished MA Diss., University of Essex, 1980, p. 90.

116 F. Donaldson, *Child of the Twenties*, London, Weidenfeld & Nicolson, 1986.

117 Ibid., p. 139.

118 H. Forrester, *Liverpool Miss*, London, Fontana, 1974, p. 161.

119 See chapter 5, note 31.

120 Beauchamp, op. cit., p. 57.

121 R. Strachey (ed.), *Our Freedom*, London, Hogarth Press, 1936, p. 124.

122 D. Spender (ed.), *Time and Tide Wait for No Man*, London, Pandora, 1984, p. 131.

123 See chapter 1.

124 Winifred Holtby, 'A generation of women's progress', reprinted in P. Berry and A. Bishop, *Testament of a Generation: The Journalism of Vera Brittain and Winifred Holtby*, London, Virago, 1985, p. 95.

125 C. Haldane, *Motherhood and Its Enemies*, New York, 1928, p. 197.

126 Strachey, op. cit., p. 134.

127 V. Brittain, *Women's Work in Modern England*, London, Noel Douglas, 1928, p. 75.

128 *The Vote*, 19 March 1926.

129 For a full account of women in the medical profession see E. Moberly Bell, *Storming the Citadel: The Rise of the Woman Doctor*, London, Constable, 1953.

130 For a brief discussion of the setbacks suffered by women doctors in the 1920s see Spender (ed.), op. cit., pp. 242–55.

131 *Woman's Leader*, March 1928.

132 Brittain, op. cit., p. 81.

133 Cited in R. Adam, *A Woman's Place*, London, Chatto & Windus, 1975, p. 102.
134 Beauchamp, op. cit., p. 69.
135 Ibid., p. 70.
136 F. Widdowson, ' "Educating teacher": women and elementary teaching in London, 1900–1914', in Davidoff and Westover, op. cit., p. 112. See also Adam, op. cit., p. 103.
137 Ibid., p. 101.
138 Lewis, op. cit., p. 198.
139 Brittain, op. cit., p. 59.
140 Beauchamp, op. cit., p. 64.
141 S. J. Curtis, *History of Education in Great Britain*, London, University Tutorial Press, 1968, p. 408.
142 *The Vote*, 2 April 1920.
143 *The Vote*, 25 March 1921.
144 Spender (ed.), op. cit., p. 193.
145 Lewis, op. cit., p. 199.
146 A. Oram, ' "Serving two masters?" The introduction of a marriage bar in teaching in the 1920s', in London Feminist History Group, *The Sexual Dynamics of History*, London, Pluto, 1983, p. 47.
147 Zimmick, op. cit., p. 147.
148 *The Vote*, 27 June 1919.
149 Strachey (1984), op. cit., p. 376.
150 Zimmick, op. cit.
151 Ibid., p. 902.
152 Ibid., p. 923.
153 Ibid., p. 907.
154 *Western Mail*, 17 February 1920.
155 Holtby (1934), op. cit., p. 113.
156 Gollan, op. cit., p. 108.
157 Beauchamp, op. cit., p. 27.
158 J. Hurstfield, 'Women's unemployment in the 1930s: some comparisons with the 1980s', in S. Allen *et al.*, *The Experience of Unemployment*, London, Macmillan/BSA, 1986.
159 *Decisions Given by the Umpire Respecting Claims to Benefit*, vol. 1, 1921, case no. 716.
160 A. Deacon, 'Concession and coercion: the politics of unemployment insurance in the twenties', in J. Saville and A. Briggs (eds), *Essays in Labour History*, vol. 3, London, Croom Helm, 1977, p. 16.
161 Ibid., p. 16.
162 *The Vote*, 25 May 1923.
163 Deacon, loc. cit., p. 27.

164 D. Caradog Jones (ed.), *The Social Survey of Merseyside*, Liverpool, Liverpool University Press, 1934, p. 384.
165 See M. Thibert, 'The economic depression and the employment of women: I', *International Labour Review*, vol. XXVII, no. 4, April 1933, pp. 443–70.
166 Priestley, op. cit., p. 186.
167 Holtby, op. cit., p. 72.
168 Pilgrim Trust, op. cit., p. 239.

CHAPTER 4 HOME AND HEALTH

1 M. Pember Reeves, *Round About A Pound A Week* (1913), London, Virago, 1979, p. 3.
2 Ibid., p. 41.
3 M. Spring Rice, *Working Class Wives* (1939), London, Virago, 1981.
4 *The Vote*, 2 May 1919.
5 Ibid., 18 April 1924.
6 Ibid., 2 May 1919.
7 M.L. Eyles, *The Woman in the Little House*, London, Grant Richards, 1922, p. 23.
8 *Woman's Leader*, 15 July 1921.
9 N. Branson and M. Heinemann, *Britain in the Nineteen Thirties*, London, Weidenfeld & Nicolson, 1971, p. 180.
10 Ibid., p. 183.
11 Spring Rice, op.cit., p. 138.
12 Ibid.
13 Ibid., p. 139.
14 Pember Reeves, op.cit., p. 23.
15 George Orwell, *The Road to Wigan Pier* (1937), Harmondsworth, Penguin, 1969, p. 83.
16 Eyles, op.cit., pp. 35–7.
17 Branson and Heinemann, op.cit., p. 180.
18 See E. Hopkins, *A Social History of the English Working Class*, London, Edward Arnold, 1979, pp. 237–8.
19 Branson and Heinemann, op.cit., p. 184.
20 I have taken the information on council housing in Bristol from a very useful essay: M. Dresser, 'People's housing in Bristol 1870–1939', in *Bristol's Other History*, Bristol Broadsides, 1983.
21 For an interesting and readable account of this committee's activities see B. McFarlane, 'Homes fit for heroines: housing in the twenties', in Matrix, *Making Space: Women and the Manmade Environment*, London, Pluto, 1984, pp. 26–37.
22 Dresser, loc.cit., p. 153.

23 *Woman's Leader*, 5 January 1923.
24 Spring Rice, op.cit., pp. 132–3.
25 Mass Observation Archive, Worktown, Box 39A E/89.
26 Dresser, loc.cit., p. 155.
27 Ibid.
28 Mass Observation Archive, Worktown, Box 39A E/89.
29 Ibid., E/91.
30 Branson and Heinemann, op.cit., p.186.
31 Ibid., p. 187.
32 G. Orwell, *Coming up for Air* (1939), Harmondsworth, Penguin, 1983, p. 14.
33 Ibid., p. 16.
34 See A. Quiney, *House and Home: A History of the Small English House*, London, British Broadcasting Corporation, 1986, chapter 7.
35 Ibid., p. 164.
36 *Woman's Leader*, 16 June 1922.
37 *The Vote*, 14 March 1924.
38 Lewis, op.cit., p. 10.
39 *Woman's Own*, 4 February 1933.
40 Lewis, op.cit., p. 66.
41 E. Roberts, *A Woman's Place: An Oral History of Working Class Women, 1890–1940*, London, Blackwell, 1984, p. 136.
42 Spring Rice, op.cit., p. 155.
43 Ibid., p. 157.
44 Ibid., p. 180.
45 Ibid., p. 179.
46 Orwell (1937), op.cit., pp. 84–5.
47 Roberts, op.cit., p. 142.
48 Ibid., p. 179.
49 *The Vote*, 22 August 1924.
50 Lewis, op.cit., p. 53.
51 B. Braithwaite, N. Walsh and G. Davies, *Ragtime to Wartime: The Best of Good Housekeeping 1922–1937*, London, Ebury, 1986, pp. 123–4.
52 Ibid., p. 11.
53 Lewis, op.cit., p. 116.
54 See chapter 1.
55 Ibid.
56 D. Gittins, *Fair Sex: Family Size and Structure 1900–39*, London, Hutchinson, 1982, p. 33.
57 Ibid., pp. 62–3.
58 R. Hall (ed.), *Dear Dr Stopes: Sex in the 1920s*, Harmondsworth, Penguin, 1981, p. 14.
59 Eyles, op.cit., p. 129.

60 *The New Generation*, January 1924.
61 Lewis, op.cit., p. 16.
62 Gittins, op.cit., p. 157.
63 Lewis, op.cit., p. 18.
64 Roberts, op.cit., p. 102.
65 J. Weeks, *Sex, Politics and Society: The Regulation of Sexuality since 1800*, London, Longman, 1981, p. 188.
66 P. Fryer, *The Birth Controllers*, London, Corgi, 1967, p. 252.
67 A. Leathard, *The Fight for Family Planning*, London, Macmillan, 1980, p. 15.
68 See chapter 6.
69 See Beddoe (1983) op.cit., chapter 6.
70 Leathard, op.cit., p. 66.
71 Roberts, op.cit., p. 85.
72 Lewis, op.cit., p. 17.
73 Ibid., p. 18.
74 Cited in Gittins, op.cit., pp. 163–4.
75 *Daily Herald*, 21 April 1932.
76 Cited in Roberts, op.cit., p. 97.
77 Leathard, op.cit., p. 37.
78 Ibid., pp. 63–4.
79 Branson and Heinemann, op.cit., p. 222.
80 Ibid., p. 204.
81 Ibid.
82 Ibid., pp. 201–20.
83 Spring Rice, op.cit., pp. 57–61.
84 Ibid., p. 59.
85 Quoted in *The Vote*, 11 April 1930.
86 Spring Rice, op.cit., p. 69.
87 *Woman's Own*, 31 December 1932.
88 C. Kenner, *No Time for Women*, London, Pandora, 1985, p. 40.
89 For information on the treatment of ill health among women see Spring Rice, op.cit., chapter 3.

CHAPTER 5 LEISURE

1 R. Graves and A. Hodge, *The Long Weekend: A Social History of Great Britain, 1918–1939*, London, Faber & Faber, 1941, p. 45.
2 F. Donaldson, *Child of the Twenties*, London, Weidenfeld & Nicolson, 1986, p. 132.
3 Ibid., p. 133.

4　M. Haig Mackworth, Viscountess Rhondda, *Leisured Women*, London, Hogarth, 1928, p. 26.

5　Ibid., pp. 29–30.

6　M. Haig Mackworth, letter in *Woman's Leader*, 29 June 1928.

7　M. Spring Rice, *Working Class Wives* (1939), London, Virago, 1981, p. 110.

8　J. Richards, *The Age of the Dream Palace: Cinema and Society in Britain 1930–1939*, London, Routledge & Kegan Paul, 1984, p. 11. This book is a mine of information on British cinema in the 1930s.

9　Ibid., p. 12.

10　D. Caradog Jones (ed.), *The Social Survey of Merseyside*, Liverpool, Liverpool University Press, 1934, p. 279.

11　B. Seebohm Rowntree, *Poverty and Progress*, London, 1946, pp. 412–13.

12　Cited in Richards, op.cit., p. 13.

13　J.P. Mayer, *British Cinemas and Their Audiences*, London, Dennis Dobson, 1948, p. 225.

14　A.P. Jephcott, *Girls Growing Up*, London, Faber & Faber, 1942, p. 116.

15　G. Meara, *Juvenile Unemployment in South Wales*, Cardiff, University of Wales Press, 1936, p. 98.

16　A.J. Jenkinson, *What do Boys and Girls Read?* London, Methuen, 1940, p. 237.

17　Mass Observation Archive, University of Sussex, Worktown, 29/A.

18　Mass Observation Archive, 29/A.

19　Ibid.

20　Ibid.

21　Ibid.

22　See chapter 1.

23　*Peg's Paper*, no. 93, 15 February 1921.

24　S.G. Jones, *Workers at Play: A Social and Economic History of Leisure 1918–1939*, London, Routledge & Kegan Paul, 1986, p. 44.

25　Jephcott, op.cit., p. 115.

26　Ibid.

27　For example, *Peg's Paper*, no. 113, 1921.

28　Marion Marian, 'When the moment came', *Peg's Paper*, no. 297, 1925, pp. 5–6.

29　W. Holtby, 'Ladies in restaurants', in P. Berry and A. Bishop, *Testament of a Generation: The Journalism of Vera Brittain and Winifred Holtby*, London, Virago, 1985, pp. 67–70.

30　British Broadcasting Corporation Report, 'What Time do People Have Their Meals?' 1938. Cited in A. Marwick, *Class:*

Image and Reality in Britain, France and the USA Since 1930, London, Fontana, 1981, p. 165.

31 Ethel Manning, *All Experience*, London, Jarrolds, 1932, pp. 64–5.

32 Mass Observation Archive, Worktown, Box 1, file C.

33 Cited in J.F.C. Harrison, *The Common People: A History from the Norman Conquest to the Present Day*, London, Flamingo, 1984, p. 327.

34 J. Stevenson, *Social Conditions in Britain between the Wars*, Harmondsworth, Penguin, 1977, p. 44.

35 Cicely Hamilton, *The Englishwoman*, London, British Council, 1940, p. 33.

36 'The needs of village women', *Manchester Guardian*, 24 May 1922.

37 M. Stott, *Organization Woman, The Story of the National Union of Townswomen's Guilds*, London, Heinemann, 1978.

38 J. Gaffin and D. Thomas, *Caring and Sharing: The Centenary History of the Co-operative Women's Guild*, Manchester, Co-operative Union, 1983, pp. 95–6.

39 Jones, op.cit., pp. 68–9.

40 M. Rooff, *Youth and Leisure: A Survey of Girls' Organizations in England and Wales*, Edinburgh, Carnegie UK Trust, 1935, p. 235.

41 Jephcott, op.cit., pp. 141–5.

42 'Women and aviation', *The Vote*, 22 January 1926.

43 J.S. Fry Archive, Somerdale, Work's magazine, vol. 1, 1921–2.

44 Mass Observation Archive, Worktown, Box 2/E.

45 M. Howard, 'Fashions for winter sports and southern', in B. Braithwaite, N. Walsh, G. Davies, *Ragtime to Wartime: The Best of Good Housekeeping*, London, Ebury, 1986, pp. 92–3.

46 E.M. Delafield, *Diary of a Provincial Lady* (1930), London, Virago, 1984, pp. 88–94.

47 C. Hall, *The Twenties in Vogue*, London, Octopus, 1983, p. 20.

48 Ibid., pp. 130–1.

49 Manning, op.cit., pp. 29–30.

50 Jones, op.cit., pp. 19–20.

51 Mass Observation Archive, Worktown, Box 54.

52 Jones, op.cit., p. 28.

53 Mass Observation Archive, Worktown, Box 54.

54 J.B. Priestley, *English Journey* (1934), Harmondsworth, Penguin, 1981, pp. 250–55.

55 Mass Observation Archive, Worktown, Box 55/E.

56 H. Forrester, *Liverpool Miss*, London, Fontana, 1974.

57 Mass Observation Archive, Worktown, Box 55/D.

58 Ibid., 54/A.

59 Ibid.
60 A. Calder and D. Sheridan, *Speak for Yourself: A Mass Observation Anthology 1937–1949*, Oxford, Oxford University Press, 1985, p. 51.
61 Hall, op.cit., p. 136.
62 B. Braithwaite, N. Walsh and G. Davies, *Ragtime to Wartime: The Best of Good Housekeeping 1922–1937*, London, Ebury, 1986, p. 72.
63 M. Dickens, *An Open Book*, London, Book Club Associates, 1978, p. 4.
64 R. Macaulay, *Crewe Train* (1926), Harmondsworth, Penguin, 1939, pp. 247–8.
65 N. Beauman, *A Very Great Profession: The Woman's Novel 1914–39*, London, Virago, 1983, p. 10.
66 Mass Observation Archive, Worktown, Box 33/G.
67 A.J. Jenkinson, *What do Boys and Girls Read?* London, Methuen, 1940, p. 215 and Jephcott, op.cit., p. 215.
68 G. Orwell, *Coming up for Air* (1939), Harmondsworth, Penguin, 1983, p. 52.
69 Ibid., pp. 53–4.
70 Orwell, op.cit., (1937) p. 104.
71 L. Eyles, *The Woman in the Little House*, London, Grant Richards, 1922, p. 96.
72 J. Lewis, *Women in England, 1870–1950*, Sussex, Wheatsheaf, 1984, p. 116.
73 Hall, op.cit., p. 130.
74 Ibid.
75 M. Pegg, *Broadcasting and Society 1918–1939*, London, Croom Helm, 1983, p. 45.
76 Ibid., p. 47.
77 Ibid., p. 16.
78 H. Jennings and W. Gill, *Broadcasting in Everyday Life: A Survey of the Social Effects of the Coming of Broadcasting*, London, British Broadcasting Corporation, 1939.
79 Ibid., p. 24.
80 Ibid., p. 18.
81 Ibid., p. 13.
82 Ibid., p. 13.
83 Ibid., p. 24.
84 Pegg, op.cit., p. 5.
85 Mass Observation Archive, Worktown, Box 2/F.
86 Ibid.

CHAPTER 6 POLITICS AND ISSUES

1 R. Strachey, *The Cause: A Short History of the Women's Movement in Great Britain* (1928), London, Virago, 1984, p. 336.
2 Ibid., p. 338.
3 Ibid., p. 348.
4 Ibid., p. 361.
5 Ibid., p. 366.
6 S. Pankhurst, *The Suffragette Movement* (1931), London, Virago, 1977, p. 607.
7 R.J. Evans, *The Feminists*, London, Croom Helm, 1979, pp. 222–3.
8 *The Vote*, 3 January 1919.
9 Ibid., 5 February 1926.
10 Ibid., 20 May 1927.
11 Ibid.
12 Ibid., 11 November 1927.
13 O. Banks, *Faces of Feminism*, Oxford, Martin Robertson, 1981, p. 149.
14 S. Rowbotham, *Hidden from History*, London, Pluto, 1973, p. 162.
15 Banks, op.cit., p. 150.
16 W. Holtby, 'Feminism divided', in P. Berry and A. Bishop, *Testament of a Generation: The Journalism of Vera Brittain and Winifred Holtby*, London, Virago, 1985, p. 47.
17 W. Holtby, *Women and a Changing Civilization*, London, John Lane, 1934, p. 115.
18 D. Spender, *There's Always been a Woman's Movement This Century*, London, Pandora, 1983.
19 Pankhurst, op.cit., p. 608.
20 V. Brittain, 'Why feminism lives' (1927), in Berry and Bishop, op.cit., p. 97.
21 A.M. Ludovici, *Woman: A Vindication*, London, Constable, 1923, p. 362.
22 Ibid., p. 364.
23 A. Heilborn, *The Opposite Sexes*, London, Methuen, 1927, p. 152.
24 Viscountess Rhondda, *This Was My World*, London, Macmillan, 1933, p. 299.
25 W. Holtby, 'Feminism divided' (1926), in Berry and Bishop, op.cit., p. 48.
26 D. Doughan, *Lobbying for Liberation, British Feminism 1918–1968*, London, City of London Polytechnic, 1980, p. 4.
27 Ibid.

28 See J. Lewis, 'Beyond suffrage: English feminism in the 1920s', *The Maryland Historian*, VI, 1975, pp. 1–17.
29 For an account of Eleanor Rathbone's life see M. Stocks, *Eleanor Rathbone*, London, Gollancz, 1949. For a shorter account of her campaign for family allowances see J. Lewis, 'The English movement for family allowances', *Histoire Sociale*, 11, 1978, pp. 441–59.
30 *Woman's Leader*, 4 March 1921.
31 Ibid., 9 March 1923.
32 Ibid.
33 Ibid., 30 January 1925.
34 W. Holtby, 'Feminism divided', in Berry and Bishop, op.cit., p. 48.
35 See Doughan, op.cit.
36 Ibid., pp. 7–8.
37 For a very useful survey of women in parliament see P. Brookes, *Women at Westminster*, London, Peter Davies, 1967.
38 Ibid., p. 13.
39 *Woman's Leader*, 19 December 1919.
40 Ibid., 19 April 1929.
41 Ibid., 10 March 1922.
42 A great deal more work is necessary on the relationship between feminism and the various political parties. The same is true of women's role in local government in these years.
43 *Woman's Leader*, 2 March 1923.
44 Cited in H. Smith, 'Sex vs class: British feminists and the Labour movement 1919–1929', *The Historian*, 47, 1984, p. 23, from *Report of the 23rd Annual Conference of the Labour Party*, London, 1923, p. 60.
45 Brookes, op.cit., p. 34.
46 Ibid., p. 64.
47 See Smith, loc.cit.
48 Ibid., p. 37.
49 Beatrix Campbell, *The Iron Ladies: Why Do Women Vote Tory?* London, Virago, 1987, p. 67. This provides an interesting account of the main concerns of Conservative women.
50 Marion Phillips, *The Miners' Lock-Out*, London, Labour Publishing Company, 1927.
51 P. Kingsford, *The Hunger Marchers in Britain 1920–40*, London, Lawrence & Wishart, 1982.
52 Interview by Deirdre Beddoe. This can be seen in the film *I'll Be Here for All Time*, Wales, Boadicea Films, 1985, available from Circles, Film Distribution, 113 Roman Road, London, E2 OHU.

53 See G.A. Williams, *When Was Wales?* Harmondsworth, Penguin, 1985, pp. 262–3.

54 See G. Bussey and M. Timms, *Pioneers for Peace: Women's International League for Peace and Freedom 1915–1965*, London, Women's International League for Peace and Freedom, 1980.

55 J. Gaffin and D. Thoms, *Caring and Sharing: The Centenary History of the Co-operative Women's Guild*, Manchester, Co-operative Union, 1983, pp. 109–13.

56 J. Liddington, *The Life and Times of a Respectable Rebel, Selina Cooper, 1864–1946*, London, Virago, 1984, pp. 410–18.

57 See C. Salt, P. Schweitzer and M. Wilson (eds), *Of Whole Heart Cometh Hope: Centenary Memories of the Co-operative Women's Guild*, London, Age Exchange Theatre, 1984; H. Francis, *Miners Against Fascism*, London, Lawrence & Wishart, 1984.

BIBLIOGRAPHY

(i) BOOKS AND JOURNALS

Adam, R., *A Woman's Place*, London, Chatto & Windus, 1975.

Alderman, G., *Modern Britain 1700–1983*, London, Croom Helm, 1986.

Banks, O., *Faces of Feminism*, Oxford, Martin Robertson, 1981.

Beauchamp, J., *Women Who Work*, London, Lawrence & Wishart, 1937.

Beauman, N., *A Very Great Profession: The Woman's Novel 1914–39*, London, Virago, 1983.

Beddoe, D., *Discovering Women's History*, London, Pandora, 1983.

Beddoe, D., 'Hindrances and helpmeets: women in the writings of George Orwell', in C. Norris (ed.), *Inside the Myth. Orwell: Views from the Left*, London, Lawrence & Wishart, 1984.

Beddoe, D., 'Women between the wars', in G. Jones and T. Herbert, *Wales between the Wars*, Open University/University of Wales Press, 1988.

Bell, E. Moberley, *Storming the Citadel: The Rise of the Woman Doctor*, London, Constable, 1953.

Berry, P. and Bishop A., *Testament of a Generation: The Journalism of Vera Brittain and Winifred Holtby*, London, Virago, 1985.

Bishop, A. (ed.), *Chronicle of Friendship: Vera Brittain's Diary of the Thirties, 1932–1939*, London, Gollancz, 1986.

Blainey, J., *The Woman Worker and Protective Legislation*, London, Arrowsmith, 1928.

Blumer, H., *Movies and Conduct*, New York, Macmillan, 1933.

Blumer, H. and Hauser, P.M., *Movies, Delinquency and Crime*, New York, Macmillan, 1933.

Bondfield, M., *A Life's Work*, London, Hutchinson, 1949.

Braithwaite, B., Walsh, N. and Davies, G., *Ragtime to Wartime: The Best of Good Housekeeping 1922–1937*, London, Ebury, 1986.

Branson, N. and Heinemann, M., *Britain in the Nineteen Thirties*, London, Weidenfeld & Nicolson, 1971.

Broadbrook, M.C., *That Infidel Place: A Short History of Girton College 1869–1969*, London, Chatto & Windus, 1969.

Braybon, G., *Women Workers in the First World War*, London, Croom Helm, 1981.

Briggs, A., *The Golden Age of Wireless. The History of Broadcasting in the United Kingdom*, Oxford, Oxford University Press, 1965.

Brittain, V., *Women's Work in Modern England*, London, Noel Douglas, 1928.

Brittain, V., *The Women at Oxford, A Fragment of History*, London, Harrap, 1960.

Brookes, P., *Women At Westminster*, London, Peter Davies, 1967.

Browne, F.W.S., 'The sexual variety and variability among women' (1917), in S. Rowbotham, *A New World for Women: Stella Browne – Socialist Feminist*, London, Pluto, 1977.

Bussey, G. and Timms, M., *Pioneers for Peace: Women's International League for Peace and Freedom*, London, Women's International League for Peace and Freedom, 1980.

Calder, A. and Sheridan, D., *Speak for Yourself: A Mass Observation Anthology 1937–1949*, Oxford, Oxford University Press, 1985.

Campbell, B., *The Iron Ladies: Why Do Women Vote Tory?* London, Virago, 1987.

Curtis, S.J., *History of Education in Great Britain*, London, University Tutorial Press, 1968.

Davey, T., ' "A cissy job for men: a nice job for girls": women shorthand typists in London 1900–1939', in L. Davidoff and B. Westover, *Our Work, Our Lives, Our Words*, London, Macmillan, 1986.

Deacon, A., 'Concession and coercion: the politics of unemployment insurance in the twenties', in J. Saville and A. Briggs, *Essays in Labour History*, vol. 3, London, Croom Helm, 1977.

Delafield, E.M., *Diary of a Provincial Lady* (1930), London, Virago, 1984.

Dickens, M., *An Open Book*, London, Book Club Associates, 1978.

Donaldson, F., *Child of the Twenties*, London, Weidenfeld & Nicolson, 1986.

Doughan, D., *Lobbying for Liberation, British Feminism 1918–1968*, London, City of London Polytechnic, 1980.

Drake, B., *Women in Trade Unions* (1920), London, Virago, 1984.

Dresser, M., 'People's housing in Bristol 1870–1939', *Bristol's Other History*, Bristol, Bristol Broadsides, 1983.

Dyhouse, C., 'Good wives and little mothers: social anxieties and the schoolgirls' curriculum', *Oxford Review of Education*, vol. 5, no. 1, 1977.

Evans, R.J., *The Feminists*, London, Croom Helm, 1979.

Eyles, M.L., *The Woman in the Little House*, London, Grant Richards, 1922.

Faderman, L., *Surpassing the Love of Men: Romantic Friendship and Love between Women from the Renaissance to the Present*, London, Junction, 1981.

Fletcher, S., *Women First: The Female Tradition in English Physical Education 1880–1980*, London, Athlone, 1984.

Foley, W., *A Child in the Forest*, London, MacDonald, 1977.

Forman, H.J., *Our Movie Made Children*, New York, Macmillan, 1935.

Forrester, H., *Liverpool Miss*, London, Fontana, 1974.

Francis, H., *Miners Against Fascism*, London, Lawrence & Wishart, 1984.

Fryer, P., *The Birth Controllers*, London, Corgi, 1967.

Gaffin, J. and Thomas, D., *Caring and Sharing: The Centenary History of the Co-operative Women's Guild*, Manchester, Co-operative Union, 1983.

Gardiner, M., *The Other Side of The Counter: The Life of a Shop Girl 1925–45*, Queenspark Book, no. 17.

Gittins, D., *Fair Sex: Family Size and Structure 1900–39*, London, Hutchinson, 1982.

Glucksmann, M., 'In a class of their own? Women workers in the new industries in inter-war Britain', *Feminist Review*, no. 24, October 1986, pp. 7–37.

Glucksmann, M., *Women Assemble: Women Workers in the New Industries of Inter-War Britain*, London, Routledge, 1989.

Glynn, S. and Oxborrow, G., *Inter-war Britain: A Social and Economic History*, London, Allen & Unwin, 1976.

Gollan, J., *Youth in British Industry: A Survey of Labour Conditions Today*, London, Lawrence & Wishart, 1937.

Graves, R. and Hodge, A., *The Long Weekend: A Social History of Great Britain 1918–1939*, London, Faber & Faber, 1941.

Grieve, M., *Millions Made My Story*, London, Gollancz, 1964.

Hakim, C., *Occupational Segregation*, London, Department of Employment, 1979.

Haldane, C., *Motherhood and Its Enemies*, New York, 1928.

Hall, C., 'The early formation of Victorian domestic ideology', in S. Burman (ed.), *Fit Work For Women*, London, Croom Helm, 1979.

Hall, C., *The Twenties in Vogue*, London, Octopus, 1983.

Hall, R., *Dear Dr. Stopes: Sex in the 1920s*, Harmondsworth, Penguin, 1981.

Hall, R., *The Unlit Lamp* (1924), London, Virago, 1981.

Hall, R., *The Well of Loneliness* (1928), London, Virago, 1985.

Hamilton, C., *The Englishwoman*, London, British Council, 1940.

Harding, J.N., *Aberdare Hall*, Cardiff, Cardiff University Press, 1986.

Harrison, J.F.C., *The Common People: A History from the Norman Conquest to the Present Day*, London, Flamingo, 1984.

Haskell, M., *From Reverence to Rape*, New York, Penguin, 1974.

Heilborn, A., *The Opposite Sexes*, London, Methuen, 1927.

Holtby, W., *Women and a Changing Civilization*, London, John Lane, 1934.

Holtby, W., *Poor Caroline* (1931), London, Virago, 1985.

Hopkins, E., *A Social History of the English Working Class*, London, Edward Arnold, 1979.

Hunt, F., 'Divided aims – the educational implications of opposing ideologies in girls' secondary schooling, 1850–1940', in F. Hunt (ed.), *Lessons for Life: The Schooling of Girls and Women 1850–1950*, London, Blackwell, 1987.

Hurstfield, J., 'Women's unemployment in the 1930s: some comparison with the 1980s', in S. Allen *et al.*, *The Experience of Unemployment*, London, Macmillan/British Sociological Association, 1986.

Hutchinson, A.S.M., *This Freedom*, London, Hodder & Stoughton, 1922.

Jeffreys, S., *The Spinster and Her Enemies*, London, Pandora, 1985.

Jenkinson, A.J., *What do Boys and Girls Read?* London, Methuen, 1940.

Jennings, H., *Broadcasting in Everyday Life: A Survey of the Social Effects of the Coming of Broadcasting*, London, British Broadcasting Corporation, 1939.

Jephcott, A.P., *Girls Growing Up*, London, Faber & Faber, 1942.

Jones, D. Caradog, *The Social Survey of Merseyside*, Liverpool, Liverpool University Press, 1934.

Jones, S.G., *Workers at Play: A Social and Economic History of Leisure 1918–1939*, London, Routledge & Kegan Paul, 1986.

Kamm, J., *Hope Deferred: Girls' Education in English History*, London, Methuen, 1965.

Kaye, K.M., *A Student's Handbook of Housewifery*, London, Dent, 1940.

Kenner, C., *No Time for Women*, London, Pandora, 1985.

King, J., *Is This Your Life? Images of Women in the Media*, London, Routledge & Kegan Paul, 1977.

Kingsford, P., *The Hunger Marches in Britain 1920–1940*, London, Lawrence & Wishart, 1982.

Kuhn, A., *Women's Pictures: Feminism and Cinema*, London, Routledge & Kegan Paul, 1982.

Kuhn, A., *The Power of the Image: Essays in Representation and Sexuality*, London, Routledge & Kegan Paul, 1985.

Leathard, A., *The Fight for Family Planning*, London, Macmillan, 1980.

Lehmann, R., *Dusty Answer* (1927), Harmondsworth, Penguin, 1983.

Lewenhak, S., *Women and Trade Unions*, London, Ernest Benn, 1977.

Lewis, J., 'Beyond suffrage: English feminism in the 1920s', *The Maryland Historian*, vi, 1975, pp. 1–17.

Lewis, J., 'The English movement for family allowances', *Histoire Sociale*, 11, 1978, pp. 441–59.

Lewis, J., *Women in England, 1870–1950: Sexual Divisions and Social Change*, Sussex, Wheatsheaf, 1984.

Liddington, J., *The Life and Times of a Respectable Rebel, Selina Cooper, 1864–1946*, London, Virago, 1984.

Ludovici, A.M., *Woman: A Vindication*, London, Constable, 1923.

Macaulay, R., *Crewe Train* (1926), Harmondsworth, Penguin, 1939.

McFarlane, B., 'Homes fit for heroines: housing in the twenties', in Matrix, *Making Space: Women and the Man-made Environment*, London, Pluto, 1984.

Manning, E., *All Experience*, London, Jarrolds, 1932.

Manning, E., *Confessions and Impressions*, Harmondsworth, Penguin, 1936.

Marquand, H.A., *The Second Industrial Survey of South Wales*, London, Her Majesty's Stationery Office, 1932.

Marwick, A., *Class: Image and Reality in Britain, France and the USA since 1930*, London, Fontana, 1981.

Mayer, J.P., *Sociology of Film*, London, Faber & Faber, 1946.

Mayer, J.P., *British Cinemas and their Audiences*, London, Dennis Dobson, 1948.

Mayor, F.M., *The Rector's Daughter* (1924), Harmondsworth, Penguin, 1982.

Meara, G., *Juvenile Unemployment in South Wales*, Cardiff, University of Wales Press, 1936.

Meyers, J., 'Dyke goes to the movies', *Dyke*, Spring, 1976, New York.

Mitchell, B.R., *Abstracts of British Historical Statistics*, Cambridge, Cambridge University Press, 1971.

Montgomery, F.A., *Edge Hill College: A History 1885–1985*, Edge Hill, 1985.

Orwell, G., *A Clergyman's Daughter* (1935), Harmondsworth, Penguin, 1982.

Orwell, G., *Keep the Aspidistra Flying* (1936), Harmondsworth, Penguin, 1975.

Orwell, G., *The Road to Wigan Pier* (1937), Harmondsworth, Penguin, 1969.

Orwell, G., *Coming up for Air* (1939), Harmondsworth, Penguin, 1983.

Orwell, G., *Inside the Whale and Other Essays* (1957), Harmondsworth, Penguin, 1957.

Pegg, M., *Broadcasting and Society 1918–1939*, London, Croom Helm, 1983.

Phillips, M., *The Miners' Lock-Out*, London, Labour Publishing Company, 1927.

Pilgrim Trust, *Men Without Work*, Cambridge, Cambridge University Press, 1938.

Powell, M., *Below Stairs*, London, Pan, 1970.

Powell, M.J., *The History of Hillcroft College: The First Forty Years*, Hillcroft, 1964.

Priestley, J.B., *English Journey* (1934), Harmondsworth, Penguin, 1981.

Pym, B., *A Very Private Eye*, London, Macmillan, 1984.

Quiney, A., *House and Home: A History of the Small English House*, London, British Broadcasting Corporation, 1986.

Rhondda, Viscountess (Mackworth M. Haig), *Leisured Women*, London, Hogarth, 1928.

Rhondda, Viscountess (Mackworth M. Haig), *This Was My World*, London, Macmillan, 1933.

Rice, M. Spring, *Working Class Wives* (1939), London, Virago, 1981.

Richards, J., *The Age of the Dream Palace: Cinema and Society in Britain 1930–1939*, London, Routledge & Kegan Paul, 1984.

Roberts, E., 'Working wives and their families', in T. Barker and M. Drake (eds), *Population and Society in Britain, 1850–1980*, London, 1982.

Roberts, E., *A Woman's Place: An Oral History of Working Class Women 1890–1940*, London, Blackwell, 1984.

Rooff, M., *Youth and Leisure: A Survey of Girls' Organizations in England and Wales*, Edinburgh, Carnegie United Kingdom Trust, 1935.

Rosen, M., *Popcorn Venus*, New York, Avon, 1973.

Rowbotham, S., *Hidden From History*, London, Pluto, 1973.

Rowntree, B. Seebohm, *Poverty and Progress: A Second Social Survey of York*, London, Longmans, 1941.

Salt, C., Schweitzer, P. and Wilson, M., *Of Whole Heart Cometh Hope: Centenary Memories of the Co-operative Women's Guild*, London, Age Exchange Theatre, 1984.

Scannell, D., *Mother Knew Best: An East End Childhood*, London, Macmillan, 1978.

Shelton, C., 'Lesbians and film', in R. Dyer (ed.), *Gays and Film*, London, British Film Institute, 1977.

Simon, B., *The Politics of Educational Reform 1920–1940*, London, Lawrence & Wishart, 1974.

Smith, H., 'Sex vs class: British feminists and the labour movement', *The Historian*, 47, November 1984, pp. 19–37.

Smith, H. Llewelyn, *The New Survey of London Life and Labour*, London, King, 1935.

Spender, D., *There's Always Been A Woman's Movement This Century*, London, Pandora, 1983.

Spender, D. (ed.), *Time and Tide Wait for No Man*, London, Pandora, 1984.

Stevenson, J., *Social Conditions in Britain Between the Wars*, Harmondsworth, Penguin, 1977.

Stocks, M., *Eleanor Rathbone*, London, Gollancz, 1949.

Strachey, R., *Our Freedom*, London, Hogarth Press, 1936.

Strachey, R., *The Cause: A Short History of the Women's Movement in Great Britain* (1928), London, Virago, 1984.

Struther, I., *Mrs. Miniver*, London, Chatto & Windus, 1939.

Summerfield, P., 'Cultural reproduction in the education of girls: a study of girls' secondary schooling in two Lancashire towns, 1900–1950', in F. Hunt (ed.), *Lessons for Life: The Schooling of Girls and Women 1900–1950*, London, Blackwell, 1987.

Thibert, M., 'The economic depression and the employment of women: I', *International Labour Review*, vol. xxvii, no. 4, pp. 443–70, 1933.

Tinker, P., 'Learning through leisure: feminine ideology in girls' magazines 1920–1950', in F. Hunt (ed.), *Lessons for Life: The Schooling of Girls and Women 1900–1950*, London, Blackwell, 1987.

Weeks, J., *Sex, Politics and Society: The Regulation of Sexuality since 1800*, London, Longmans, 1981.

White, C., *Women's Magazines 1693–1968*, London, Michael Joseph, 1970.

Widdowson, F., *Going Up Into the Next Class: Women and Elementary Teacher Training, 1840–1914*, London, Hutchinson, 1983.

Williams, G.A., *When Was Wales?* Harmondsworth, Penguin, 1985.

Woolf, V., *A Room of One's Own* (1928), Harmondsworth, Penguin, 1970.

Young, J.D., *Women and Popular Struggles: A History of Scottish and English Working Class Women*, Edinburgh, Mainstream, 1985.

Ziegler, P., *Diana Cooper*, London, Hamish Hamilton, 1981.

Zimmick, M., 'Strategies and stratagems for the employment of women in the British civil service, 1919–1939', *The Historical Journal*, vol. 27, no. 4, pp. 901–23, 1984.

(ii) OTHER SOURCES

Magazines:

Everywoman's
Good Housekeeping

Lady's Companion
New Statesman
New Witness
Oracle
Peg's Paper
Vogue
The Vote
Woman
Woman's Leader
Woman's Own
Woman Teacher

Newspapers:

Aberdeen Free Press
Daily Chronicle
Daily Express
Daily Herald
Daily Mail
Daily News
Daily Telegraph
Evening Standard
Glasgow Bulletin
Manchester Guardian
Portsmouth Evening News
Western Mail
Reynolds News
The Times

Archive Collections:

Birmingham Central Library
Fawcett Society Library, London Guildhall University
Glamorgan County Record Office
Mass Observation Archive, University of Sussex
Public Record Office, Kew
Trades Union Congress Library

INDEX

Note: WWI in this index stands for World War I

abortion, 6, 108–9
advertisements, 12–13, 16
age: and employment, 57, 58
Astor, Nancy, Lady, 141–2, 143, 145
aviatrixes, 32

Bailey, Lady, 32
birth control, 5–6, 104–9, 144
Blackpool, 124–5
Bloom, Ursula: 'Houseproud', 19
Bolton: housing, 94, 95; leisure, 116,
    117, 120, 124, 125, 127
Bondfield, Margaret, 142, 143–4
Boots Library, 126
Bow, Clara, 24–5
Bowen, Elizabeth, 16, 116
Brazil, Angela, 43–4
Bristol, 49; housing, 93, 94–5
Brittain, Vera, 27, 79, 116, 137, 147
Browne, Stella, 14, 43, 105, 109
budgets, 99–102

Cardiff: women workers in, 49
career women, 9, 10, 25–6
cars, 123
Caston Senior Girls School, 39
Cavell, Edith, 133
Central Committee for Women's
    Employment, 63
child welfare and childcare, 38, 39,
    65–6, 103–4, 112; family allowance,
    136, 139; legislation, 134
childbirth, 5, 109
church, 120
cinemas, 115–17; *see also* films
civil service, 49, 53, 75, 82–3, 84
class, social, 5, 34, 114–19
clubs, 120–1
Conservative Party, 134, 141, 142, 143,
    145
conveyor belts, 68–9
Cooper, Lady Diana, 10–11
Cooper, Selina, 147
Courier, The, 66
Cox, Dora, 146

Daily Chronicle, 11, 52
dancing, 117–19
Delafield, E. M., 16: *Consequence*, 27;
    The Diary of a Provincial Lady, 21,
    61, 122
Depression, inter-war, 54–9
Despard, Charlotte, 136, 137, 141, 147
diet, 100–1, 102, 110
Dietrich, Marlene, 21–2, 25, 31
doctors: payment, 112; women as, 76,
    78–9
domestic service, 5, 51–3, 60;
    conditions, 61–3, 64; training, 63–4
domestic subjects teaching, 37–9, 41
Donaldson, Frances, 73–4, 114
Duke, Ivy, 117

earnings: electrical engineering, 68;
    kitchen and waitresses, 72; office, 74;
    shops, 71; teaching, 80–1; unequal,
    84; weavers, 65
eating out, 119–20
education, 33, 34–47; elementary, 34,
    35–40; secondary, 34, 40–4;
    continuation, 44; evening classes,
    44–5; colleges, 45; teacher training
    colleges, 35, 45–6; universities, 46–7;
    co-education, 43; domestic subjects,
    37–9; punishment, 37
elementary schools, 34, 35–40
Eligibility of Women Act, 50, 134,
    140–1
employment, women's, 4–5, 48–88; in
    WWI, 10–14, 48; at end WWI, 3–4,
    48–54; censuses, 56; and age, 57, 58;
    and marriage, 57–9, 87; occupation,
    59–60; opposition, 60; legislation,
    60, 139; *see also* unemployment *and*
    types
Equal Franchise Bill, 134–5
equal pay, 81
equality, 138–40
Evening Standard, 52–3
Eyles, Leonora: *The Woman in the Little
    House*, 91, 92, 105, 128

factory work, 64–9
family allowance, 136, 139
family budgets, 99–102
family size, 100–1, 103, 104–8
fascism, 137, 147
Fawcett, Millicent Garrett, 132, 135, 139
feminism: pre-WWI, 135–6; heroines, 31–2; inter-war, 6, 136–40; 1920s, 6, 135–40; fragmentation, 6, 136–7, 140–5; 'New', 6, 136–7, 139–40; and politics, 142–5
films: development, 17; popularity, 116–17; women portrayed in, 21, 24–6, 30–1
flappers, 22–4
Foley, Winifred, 37
food, 5; on holiday, 124–5; home entertaining, 126; nutrition, 100–1, 102, 110
football pools, 130–1
franchise, 6, 50, 132–5, 138

Garbo, Greta, 25, 31
General Strike, 1926, 146
Germany, 87, 137, 147
Girl Guides, 121
girls' clubs, 121
Glamorgan, 55, 104; education, 39, 46
Glasgow, 49; housing, 91
Good Housekeeping, 5, 14, 102, 103, 122, 126, 128
Grieve, Mary, 15

Hall, Radclyffe: *The Unlit Lamp*, 27, 28; *The Well of Loneliness*, 29–30
Harlow, Jean, 25
health, 5–6, 89, 100–13; of army recruits, 38, 90; treatment, 112–13
Hillcroft College, 45
hire purchase, 103
holidays, 122–6; pay, 124
Holtby, Winifred, 16, 32–3, 47, 75–6, 87, 119, 136, 137–8, 139; *The Crowded Street*, 28; *Poor Caroline*, 27; *South Riding*, 27
home, 89, 99; entertainment, 126
House of Lords, 133, 134–5, 143
housewives, 99–122; education, preparatory, 39; image, 8, 9–10, 17–22, 99
housework, 4, 102–3, 115
housing, 89–99, 111; council houses, 93–5; legislation, 93; ownership, 95–8; single women, 98–9

hunger marches, 146
Hutchinson, A.S.M.: *This Freedom*, 26

images, media, 4, 8–33
income, family, 99–102
industry, 64–9

Johnson, Amy, 32

kitchen workers, 72

labour exchanges, postwar I, 50–4, 60, 63; 'out-of-work donation', 50–4
Labour Party, 6–7, 142–3, 144–5
Lawrence, Susan, 142, 144
lawyers, 77–8
legislation, postwar, 50, 133–4; housing, 93; protective 60, 139
leisure, 5, 114–31
lesbians, 4, 28–31
Lewis, Jane, 63, 99, 103, 106
Liverpool, 139; housing, 91; leisure, 115; poverty, 101; unemployment, 55
Lloyd George, Megan, 142–3
Lords, House of, 133, 134–5, 143
Lucas: strikes, 69
Ludovici, Anthony, 4, 27, 137

Macaulay, Rose, 16, 117, 126
Macclesfield, 66
Madchen in Uniform (film), 31
magazines, 14–16, 17–20, 22–3; feminist, 9, 16, 31–2; film, 117; girls', 44; readers, 15–16, 126, 127; WWI, 11
Manning, Ethel, 119–20, 123–4
Markievicz, Constance, 141
marriage: and employment, 57–9, 87, 99; legislation, 134; status, 99
marriage bars, 5, 85; to civil service, 83; teaching, 42, 82
Men Without Work (Pilgrim Trust), 55, 88
Mitford, Nancy, 123, 128–9
money lenders, 101

National Federation of Women Workers, 48–9, 51, 52
National Union of Societies for Equal Citizenship, 138–40, 142
National Union of Women's Suffrage Societies, 16, 135, 138
'New Woman', 9, 10

newspapers, 11, 14, 126, 127; *see also titles*
North London Collegiate School, 40–1
novels, 16–17; reading, 126; women portrayed in, 20–1, 26, 27–30, 126
nurses, 79–80

office work, 72–4, 84
organisations, women's: housing campaigns, 90; social, 120–1; *see also names*
Orwell, George: *A Clergyman's Daughter*, 27; *Coming Up For Air*, 96, 127; *Keep the Aspidistra Flying*, 72; *The Road to Wigan Pier*, 66, 92, 101, 128
Oxford University, 46–7

Pankhurst, Christabel, 135, 136, 141
Pankhurst, Emmeline, 134, 135
Pankhurst, Sylvia, 133, 136–7, 147
parliament, membership, 6, 140–4
peace work, 146–7
Peg's Paper, 15–16, 22, 23, 117, 127
Pember Reeves, Maud, 89, 90, 91
'Perfect Lady', 9–10
politics, 6–7, 132–47
poverty, 89, 101, 110–11
Powell, Margaret, 62
pressure groups, 140
Priestley, J. B., 87, 124
professions, 75–83
Punch, 11, 24, 32
Pym, Barbara, 116

radio, 17, 129–30
Rathbone, Eleanor, 136, 139, 142–3
reading, 126–7
rent, 92, 94, 98
Representation of the People Act, 50, 132, 134
Restoration of Pre-War Practices Act, 48
Rhondda, Lady, 136, 137, 147; seat in House of Lords, 143; *Leisured Women*, 114–15; letter to *Daily News*, 49
Rhondda Valley, Mid-Glam, 55, 104
Russell, Mabel, 142
Russia, 133

Scotland: birth control, 108
servants, *see* domestic service
sewing, 128–9

Sex Disqualification (Removal) Act, 50, 75, 134
sex symbols, 24–5
shop assistants, 69–72
Spanish Civil War, 147
spinsters: housing, 98–9; image, 26–7; teachers, 42
sport, 121–2, 123
Spring Rice, Margery: *Working Class Wives*, 91–2, 100, 104, 110
Stopes, Marie, 105, 106–7, 108
Stott, Mary, 136
Strachey, Ray, 13, 75, 77, 83, 133
strikes, 69
suffrage, 6, 50, 132–5; societies, 16, 135, 138

teacher training, 35, 45–6
teaching, 80–2
television, 130
textile industry, 64–6
Townswomen's Guild, 120–1, 140
training, 63–4
travel, 122–3, 124

unemployment, 2, 54–6, 84–8; of women, 49, 54, 56, 85–8; women campaign against, 146
Unemployment Assistance Board: attacked, 146
unemployment benefit, 5, 50–4, 60–1, 86; married women, 60–1; rates, 100
universities, 46–7

Victoria the Great (film), 22, 117
Vogue, 15, 16, 122, 126, 128–9
vote, parliamentary, 6, 50, 132–5, 138
Vote, The, 16, 31–2, 52, 90, 134

waitresses, 72
Wales: depression, 55; education, 39, 40, 46; employment, 53, 56; servants from, 64; unemployment, 146
war work, 10–14, 48
weavers, 64–5
Webb, Sydney, 86–7
West, Mae, 25
Western Mail, 53, 84
Wilkinson, Ellen, 142, 146, 147
Wintringham, Mrs, MP, 142
Woman, 14, 15
Woman's Leader, 16, 31, 61, 117, 141–2, 143
Woman's Own, 14–15, 17–18, 20, 22, 111

Women's Co-operative Guild, 90, 105,
121, 144, 145; peace movement, 147;
social activities, 121
Women's Freedom League, 16, 136,
137, 138, 140
Women's Health Enquiry, 6, 89, 94,
100, 102, 110, 111, 112
Women's Housing Sub-Committee,
93–4

Women's Institute, 120
Women's International League for
Peace and Freedom, 146–7
'Women's Right to Work' conference, 50
Women's Social and Political Union,
135, 138
Woolf, Virginia, 16, 46–7
work, *see* employment
World War I, 10–14, 48; end, 3–4, 48

DATE DUE

2/3			

#47-0108 Peel Off Pressure Sensitive